FISCAL YEAR 2019

**EFFICIENT, EFFECTIVE, ACCOUNTABLE**

# AN
# AMERICAN
# BUDGET

## BUDGET OF THE U.S. GOVERNMENT

OFFICE OF MANAGEMENT AND BUDGET | OMB.GOV

*Budget of the United States Government, Fiscal Year 2019* contains the Budget Message of the President, information on the President's priorities, and summary tables.

*Analytical Perspectives, Budget of the United States Government, Fiscal Year 2019* contains analyses that are designed to highlight specified subject areas or provide other significant presentations of budget data that place the budget in perspective. This volume includes economic and accounting analyses; information on Federal receipts and collections; analyses of Federal spending; information on Federal borrowing and debt; baseline or current services estimates; and other technical presentations.

The *Analytical Perspectives* volume also has supplemental materials that are available on the internet at *www.whitehouse.gov/omb/analytical-perspectives/* and on the Budget CD-ROM. These supplemental materials include tables showing the budget by agency and account and by function, subfunction, and program.

*Appendix, Budget of the United States Government, Fiscal Year 2019* contains detailed information on the various appropriations and funds that constitute the budget and is designed primarily for the use of the Appropriations Committees. The *Appendix* contains more detailed financial information on individual programs and appropriation accounts than any of the other budget documents. It includes for each agency: the proposed text of appropriations language; budget schedules for each account; legislative proposals; narrative explanations of each budget account; and proposed general provisions applicable to the appropriations of entire agencies or group of agencies.

Information is also provided on certain activities whose transactions are not part of the budget totals.

## ELECTRONIC SOURCES OF BUDGET INFORMATION

The information contained in these documents is available in electronic format from the following sources:

*Internet.* All budget documents, including documents that are released at a future date, spreadsheets of many of the budget tables, and a public use budget database are available for downloading in several formats from the internet at *www.whitehouse.gov/omb/budget/*. Links to documents and materials from budgets of prior years are also provided.

*Budget CD-ROM.* The CD-ROM contains all of the printed budget documents in fully indexed PDF format along with the software required for viewing the documents.

The Internet and CD-ROM also include many of the budget tables in spreadsheet format, and supplemental materials that are part of the *Analytical Perspectives* volume. It also includes *Historical Tables* that provide data on budget receipts, outlays, surpluses or deficits, Federal debt, and Federal employment over an extended time period, generally from 1940 or earlier to 2019 or 2023.

For more information on access to electronic versions of the budget documents (except CD-ROMs), call (202) 512-1530 in the D.C. area or toll-free (888) 293-6498. To purchase the Budget CD-ROM or printed documents call (202) 512-1800.

---

### GENERAL NOTES

1. All years referenced for budget data are fiscal years unless otherwise noted. All years referenced for economic data are calendar years unless otherwise noted.

2. At the time of this writing, none of the full-year appropriations bills for 2018 have been enacted, therefore, the programs and activities normally provided for in the full-year appropriations bills were operating under a continuing resolution (Public Law 115-56, division D, as amended). In addition, the Additional Supplemental Appropriations for Disaster Relief Requirements Act, 2017 (Public Law 115-72, division A) provided additional appropriations for 2018 for certain accounts within the Departments of Agriculture, Homeland Security, and the Interior. The Department of Defense Missile Defeat and Defense Enhancements Appropriations Act, 2018 (Public Law 115-96, division B) also provided additional appropriations for 2018 for certain accounts within the Department of Defense. Accordingly, references to 2018 spending in the text and tables reflect the levels provided by the continuing resolution and, if applicable, Public Laws 115-72 (division A) and 115-96 (division B).

3. The Budget does not incorporate the effects of Public Law 115-120, including the reauthorization of the Children's Health Insurance Program and amendments to the tax code in that law.

4. Detail in this document may not add to the totals due to rounding.

---

The Office of Management and Budget (OMB) has prepared an addendum to the Fiscal year 2019 President's Budget to account for changes to discretionary spending limits pursuant to the recently enacted Bipartisan budget Act of 208. To view this addendum, please visit: http://www.whithouse.gov/omb/budget.

ISBN: 978-164143-293-1

# Table of Contents

# THE BUDGET MESSAGE OF THE PRESIDENT

To the Congress of the United States:

In one year of working together, we have laid the foundation for a new era of American Greatness. We have boosted economic growth, created more than two million jobs, and added nearly $5 trillion in new wealth to the stock market. Unemployment is at a 17-year low, wages are rising, and jobs are returning to America. Starting this month, hardworking Americans are going to see increased take home pay because of the massive tax cuts and tax reform legislation we enacted at the end of last year.

America is back to winning again. A great spirit of optimism continues to sweep across our Nation. Americans can once again be truly confident that our brightest days are ahead of us.

This year's Budget builds upon our incredible successes over the past year and rests on the following pillars of reform:

**Ending Wasteful Spending.** The United States is laboring under the highest level of debt held by the public since shortly after the Second World War. The current fiscal path is unsustainable, and future generations deserve better. The Budget makes the hard choices needed to stop wasteful spending, lower the national debt, and focus Government on what matters most—protecting the Nation.

**Expanding Economic Growth and Opportunity.** The Budget continues our efforts to grow the economy, create millions of new jobs, and raise wages. To accompany our efforts to cut spending and implement massive tax cuts and reforms for American families, workers, and businesses, we will continue to relentlessly target unnecessary regulations for elimination. We will also continue driving America toward energy dominance and making the United States a net energy exporter by 2026.

The Budget also redefines what is possible, by putting the American economy on a path to sustainable 3-percent long-term economic growth. Over the next decade, a steady rate of 3-percent economic growth will infuse trillions of additional dollars into our economy, fueling the dreams of the American people and sustaining a new era of American Greatness.

**Preserving Peace Through Strength.** The Budget recognizes that we confront political, economic, and military adversaries and competitors that have required us to adjust our national security strategy. Foremost, the Budget rebuilds and modernizes the military—to fulfill a core constitutional responsibility of the Federal Government. The Budget provides resources to enhance missile defense and to build the planes, tanks, warships, and cyber tools that the brave men and women who defend us need to deter aggression and, when necessary, to fight and win. Most importantly, the Budget provides funds to increase the size of our Armed Forces and to give our men and women in uniform a well-earned pay raise. The Budget recognizes that we must deftly employ all of our tools of statecraft—diplomatic, intelligence-related, military, and economic—to compete and

1

advance American influence. A world that supports American interests and reflects our values makes America more secure and prosperous.

**Building the Wall, Dismantling Transnational Criminal Organizations, and Enforcing Our Immigration Laws.** The Budget reflects my Administration's serious and ongoing commitment to fully secure our border, take the fight to criminal gangs like MS-13, and make our immigration system work for Americans. The Budget provides funding for a wall on our Southwest border and additional resources for law enforcement at the Departments of Homeland Security and Justice. The Budget also funds an increase in the number of Immigration and Customs Enforcement officers, Border Patrol agents, and immigration judges to improve enforcement at the border and within the United States.

**Rebuilding our Infrastructure.** World-class infrastructure is possible for the American people. Together we will build stunning new bridges, railways, waterways, tunnels, water treatment facilities, and highways. The Budget reflects a new vision for American infrastructure that would generate $1 trillion in infrastructure investment and speed its delivery to the American people.

**Supporting American Working Families.** Due to changes in family structures, labor force composition, and participation rates, the demands on American families have never been more complex or expensive to address. In addition to the middle income tax relief achieved with the passage of tax reform, the Budget reflects the importance of investing in American working families by making paid family leave available to new parents, investing in effective approaches to skills training like formal apprenticeships, and maintaining Federal funding and leveraging additional State dollars for programs that help America's working families access and afford child care. With these strategic investments, the Budget empowers Americans to thrive in our modern economy.

**Protecting Our Veterans.** The Budget fulfills our promise and obligation to care for our veterans and their families—men and women who answered our Nation's call for help and sacrificed so much to defend us. Our veterans have earned nothing less than the absolute best care and benefits after their service has ended, and the Budget provides the funding necessary to treat them with the honor and respect they deserve. It is our Nation's duty to ensure veterans have access to the medical treatment they need, when they need it—and that they have a choice when it comes to their care. The Budget also ensures that veterans receive training and support to re-enter the workforce and find well-paying jobs.

**Combatting Opioid Addiction.** More Americans died from drug overdoses in 2016 than those who lost their lives in the Vietnam War. Opioids caused the overwhelming majority of these deaths, which is why my Administration has declared a nationwide Public Health Emergency with respect to opioids. The Budget reflects a solemn and unshakable commitment to liberate communities from the scourge of opioids and drug addiction.

**Fighting High Medical Drug Prices.** Many patients face illness that could be cured or managed with the right medical drugs. But the prices for the drugs they need are often exorbitant. Unnecessarily high drug prices force many patients to choose between going without the medicines they need or making tremendous financial sacrifices. In addition, taxpayers all too often are left to pay inflated prices for drugs for patients who obtain them through Government programs. The Budget proposes new strategies to address high drug prices and increase access to drugs by addressing perverse payment incentives and exposing drug companies to more aggressive competition, all while continuing to promote innovation and extend American dominance in the pharmaceutical field.

**Moving from Welfare to Work.** Millions of our fellow Americans have been robbed of the dignity and independence that comes through the opportunity to work. Despite significant economic improvements and a strong recovery in the job market, enrollment in welfare programs remains stubbornly high in many places around the Nation. Millions of Americans are in a tragic state of dependency on a welfare system that does not reward work, and in many cases, pays people not to work. These programs, expanded during the previous administration, must now be reformed. While moving able-bodied Americans back into the workforce, welfare reform must also protect public resources for the truly needy, especially the low-income elderly, children, and Americans with disabilities. The Budget includes sensible reforms to problems in our current welfare system, and aims to end debilitating dependency while ensuring that our safety net is reserved for those Americans who truly need help.

**More Pathways to Affordable Education and Well-Paying Jobs.** The Budget takes important steps to expand opportunities for Americans to access affordable, employment-relevant education that puts them on the path to a well-paying job and, ultimately, a fulfilling career. The Budget promotes formal apprenticeships, an evidence-based system that allows individuals to "earn-while they learn." The Budget also makes important investments in science, technology, engineering, and mathematics (STEM) education in K-12 schools, and supports career and technical education in high schools and postsecondary institutions.

**Promoting School Choice.** So many of America's poorest children—especially African-American and Hispanic children—attend failing public schools that afford them little hope of fulfilling their great potential. That is why families should be free to choose the public, private, charter, magnet, religious, or home school option that is right for them. The Budget empowers parents, especially of our disadvantaged youth, to choose the very best school for their children.

\* \* \* \* \*

The Budget reflects our commitment to the safety, prosperity, and security of the American people. The more room our economy has to grow, and the more American companies are freed from constricting over-regulation, the stronger and safer we become as a Nation.

It is now up to the Congress to act. I pledge my full cooperation in unleashing the incredible and unparalleled potential of the American people. There is no limit to the promise of America when we keep our commitments to our fellow Americans and continue to put their interests first. Working together, we will do just that.

DONALD J. TRUMP

THE WHITE HOUSE,
    FEBRUARY 2018

# AN AMERICAN BUDGET

The President has placed America on a new course, one that promises an era of a prouder, stronger, and more prosperous Nation. This new course has unleashed liberty and opportunity. It also makes the tough choices to produce a more efficient, effective, and accountable Government.

The engines of America are indeed running again. In his inaugural address, the President envisioned a Nation where "prosperity and strength" would return again. He laid out, in his first words as President, a simple but familiar American strategy: "winning again, winning like never before." Most importantly, the President insisted on a simple, but forgotten principle—America First.

The President's first Budget was built on the principle that Government is a steward of taxpayer dollars, not an owner. That means fiscal responsibility and prioritizing the most effective programs.

To date, the Administration's focus on the economic health of the Nation has resulted in the elimination of 22 costly regulations for every new one created. This represents an important first step in cutting red tape, and getting the Federal Government out of the way of the private enterprise system that has made America the greatest force for prosperity in the world.

Under the leadership of the President, the first major re-write of the tax code in more than three decades has been delivered to the American people. The new tax code is designed to restore a healthy American economy—by putting American taxpayers before the Government.

Tax cuts and deregulation will allow us to unleash the American economy. However, economic growth must be met with spending restraint to ensure long-term fiscal health. The Budget takes a critical step toward balance, and bringing greater security for America's fiscal future.

Washington has a spending problem. Debt and deficits are not only a problem in and of themselves, but they are also the symptoms of something much larger—little appetite in the Congress to restrain spending.

The Budget creates a steady vision inspired by the hardworking spirit of the Nation that will lead us toward prudent spending choices that will promote a safer, more prosperous, and secure America. Economic growth coupled with fiscal restraint is not just the end goal, it is the means by which a vision for a New America can be realized. The pillars of this vision, and thus the Budget, are:

- the safety and security of the American people;

- a stronger, healthier American economy;

- an enhanced quality of life for hardworking Americans; and

- a commitment to a better future.

***The safety and security of the American people*** is the foundation on which the Administration built the Budget. First and foremost, the Federal Government must protect its citizens. This is not just a priority, it is a promise. The Budget makes significant investments in border security, specifically in the Southwest border wall and robust immigration enforcement.

It is imperative to keep those who seek to harm us out of the United States, and the Budget ensures that America can quickly and decisively respond to any threat to U.S. safety, security, and sovereignty.

Furthermore, the Budget rebuilds the military with significant investments dedicated to enhancing the capacity and lethality of America's Armed Forces, missile defense, troop readiness, counterterrorism, and counter proliferation. The Budget strengthens America's capabilities, including nuclear, in space, and cyberspace.

*A stronger, healthier American economy* promotes opportunity and benefits American families, workers, and companies. When major tax relief and reform are coupled with the elimination of excessive and unnecessary regulations, consumer and business confidence increases and economic prospects rise. The Budget supports important activities aimed at reducing the maze of Federal regulations that often serve as an obstacle to Americans seeking to grow their businesses. When taxpayers are allowed to keep their own money, it not only promotes economic growth, it also rewards the dignity of work. To further support this, the Budget also makes strategic investments in Federal programs that support American workers. For example, the Budget bolsters the workforce by investing in apprenticeships which are a proven strategy for preparing workers to fill high-growth jobs.

*An enhanced quality of life for hardworking Americans* reassures both those who have worked throughout their lifetime and those who are still working now that prosperity is possible. The Budget protects programs that retirees rely upon by negotiating better deals and leveraging the U.S. Government's buying power. The Budget also avoids more intrusive, crushing Government growth that would result in further crippling debt leaving less for seniors and future generations.

*A commitment to a better future* is what the Budget provides for all Americans. When this President was elected, bloated budgets and stagnant economic growth painted a grim picture of a bleak future. If the Federal deficit continued to rise without restraint, the future would indeed be desolate and prompt future calls for tax increases. The Budget shines a light through that darkness. The Budget is a plan that secures generations of Americans through efficient, effective, and accountable Government.

# MODERNIZING GOVERNMENT FOR THE 21ST CENTURY

## WHERE WE ARE: FEDERAL CONTEXT

When America's Founders established the Constitution, they laid out a clear mission for the Federal Government, from providing for the common defense to securing the blessings of liberty. To this day, the business of Government remains to serve the American people by meeting their expectations in these foundational mission areas.

Nearly two decades into the 21st Century, the public still believes that the Federal Government serves critical roles and, in some areas, does them well.[1] Yet public trust in the Federal Government continues to decline, sitting at near-historic lows.[2] The Nation faces a significant national debt and annual deficits that require Government to change how it operates.

## HOW WE GOT HERE: ROOT CAUSE CHALLENGES AND EFFECTS

Many of the Federal Government's challenges and shortcomings arise from practices designed in the past and trends that can no longer be sustained. Major root cause challenges facing the Federal Government include:

**Accumulated Regulatory Burden.** Over many decades, Federal agencies have imposed countless regulatory requirements on individuals, businesses, landowners, and State and local governments. Some of these regulations serve important public purposes. Many regulations, however, are outdated, duplicative, or unnecessary, yet continue to impose costly burdens.

Careful reconsideration of the regulatory burden is necessary to promote economic growth and individual freedom.

**Structural Issues.** Silos across Federal agencies and offices can stymie collaboration, resulting in fragmented services and piecemeal efforts. Greater coordination is needed among and within agencies and also with the Congress to improve management of the Federal Government and to remove outdated regulations and other obstacles to change.

**Decision-Making and Processes.** The public lacks sufficient opportunities to give feedback on Federal programs and services, making it harder to identify weaknesses and make improvements. Smarter use of data and evidence is needed to orient decisions and accountability around service and results.

**Leadership and Culture.** Achieving beneficial outcomes that serve the public should be the Federal Government's primary focus. Yet service delivery sometimes suffers due to checking unnecessary bureaucratic boxes. Managers need greater discretion to execute programs effectively, foster the highest-performing workforce, and solve real-time problems.

**Capabilities and Competencies.** Antiquated, unsecure technology risks can leave the public frustrated and vulnerable. Too many Federal employees perform outdated duties that rely on outdated skillsets, and Government too often struggles to award effective, timely contracts. A more nimble and effective approach is needed to keep technologies and workforce skills current and to ensure that the Federal workforce can meet future needs.

---

[1] Pew Research Center, December 2017, "Government Gets Lower Ratings for Handling Health Care, Environment, Disaster Response."

[2] Pew Research Center, May 2017, "Public Trust in Government Remains Near Historic Lows as Partisan Attitudes Shift."

## WHERE WE ARE HEADED: A MULTI-GENERATIONAL VISION FOR REFORM

The vision for reform must be multi-generational, enabling the Federal Government to continue adapting to changing needs over time. The Administration cannot pursue short-term fixes only to see Government quickly become outdated once again. Deep-seated transformation takes time and will not happen in one or two years.

In March, the Administration will announce the President's Management Agenda, which will set forth a long-term vision for an effective Government that works on behalf of the American people and is focused on the following:

**Mission:** The American people count on the Federal Government every day, from national security to infrastructure to food and water safety. Public servants must be accountable for mission-driven results and have the necessary tools to deliver.

**Service:** Federal customers range from small businesses seeking loans, to families receiving disaster support, to veterans owed proper benefits and medical care. They deserve a customer experience that compares to—or exceeds—that of leading private organizations.

**Stewardship:** Effective stewardship of taxpayer funds is a crucial responsibility, from preventing fraud to maximizing impact. Taxpayer dollars must go to effective programs that efficiently produce results. The Budget conservatively projects that $139 billion in savings can be achieved over the next decade through the prevention of improper payments alone.

## HOW WE WILL GET THERE: KEY DRIVERS OF REFORM

The Federal Government's challenges have not arisen in isolation, and cannot be solved through isolated efforts. The Administration will drive Government modernization by working at the junctions where these drivers intersect, rather than working in silos. Over time, it will target broad impacts on underlying issues, including legislative changes.

While challenges are complex, a few key drivers will determine the Administration's success at reform. Modernizing and strengthening these drivers will bolster results throughout Federal agencies and mission areas.

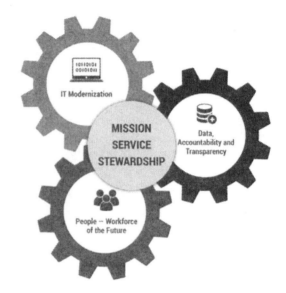

**Modern information technology** will function as the backbone of how Government serves the public in ways that meet their expectations and keep sensitive data and systems secure.

**Data, accountability, and transparency** will provide the tools to deliver visibly better results to the public and hold agencies accountable to taxpayers.

**A modern workforce** will enable senior leaders and front line managers to align staff skills with evolving mission needs. This will require more nimble and agile management of the workforce, including reskilling and redeploying existing workers to keep pace with an environment of change.

## FROM VISION TO ACTION: COMMITMENTS

The Administration will make aggressive down payments on this vision, paving the way for sustained improvement over time that is efficient, effective, and accountable. The Administration will carry out this important work through multiple channels that, together, will yield tangible improvements for the Nation, its people, and the economy.

**The President's Management Agenda.** In March, the Administration will announce specific efforts to advance the vision and improve the three drivers of reform. The Administration will name senior accountable officials and establish concrete goals and trackable metrics to ensure public accountability. This agenda will address critical challenges where Government as a whole still operates in the past. Specific goal areas will include:

- **Modernizing Information Technology (IT) to Increase Productivity and Security.** Although the Federal Government spends roughly $90 billion annually on IT, these systems remain outdated and poorly protected. The Administration will increase the use of modern technologies, retire highly insecure and outdated systems, and direct modernization cost savings to mission-driven outcomes. The Administration will improve its ability to identify and combat cybersecurity risks to agencies' data, systems, and networks.

- **Creating a 21st Century Framework for Data that Drives Efficiency, Accountability, and Transparency.** The Federal Government needs a robust, integrated approach to using data to deliver on mission, serve customers, and steward resources. The Administration will better manage and leverage data as an asset to better grow the economy, increase the effectiveness of Government, facilitate oversight, and promote transparency.

- **Developing a Workforce for the 21st Century.** Outdated rules and technology have often left the Federal Government struggling to attract the best talent, to hire quickly, or to hold workers and leaders accountable. The Administration will modernize processes and practices to bring out the best in employees and enable the Federal workforce to more effectively deliver mission results.

- **Improving the Customer Experience with Federal Services.** The American people expect high-quality customer service from Federal programs. The Administration will ensure that Government no longer lags behind the private sector in customer experience.[3]

- **Shifting from Low-Value to High-Value Work.** Hundreds of burdensome rules and requirements built up over decades force Federal agencies to devote their resources toward meaningless compliance. These resources can be better spent serving citizen needs. The Administration will clear out low-value, unnecessary, and obsolete policies and requirements to shift resources toward high-value work. The Administration has already begun this process by eliminating outdated plans and reports that burden Federal employees with unnecessary hours of paperwork. With the Budget, Federal agencies are also proposing that the Congress eliminate or modify approximately 400 plans and reports because they are outdated or duplicative (a list of these proposals is available on *www.performance.gov*).

- **Improving the Efficiency and Effectiveness of Administrative Services across Government.** Agency missions are imperiled and taxpayer dollars are squandered when administrative functions across agencies—such as IT, human resources, and contracting—are inefficient or fail to take advantage of economies of scale. Half of Federal agencies report low satisfaction with such administrative functions. The Administration will improve the quality and efficiency of administrative services, freeing resources to improve outcomes and accountability for the American people.

To drive these long-term Presidential priorities, the Administration will leverage cross-agency priority (CAP) goals to coordinate and

---

[3] American Customer Satisfaction Index. *National, Sector, and Industry Results.* December 2017.

publicly track implementation across agencies. CAP goals will also strengthen Federal Government management in other priority areas, such as improving management of major acquisitions, reducing improper payments, increasing transparency of IT costs, enhancing accountability for grant spending, and improving purchasing across Government as an enterprise. CAP goal teams will lead the execution of related Administration priorities, such as implementing the recommendations of the *Report to the President on Federal IT Modernization* focused on Network Modernization, Cybersecurity, and Shared Services. The Administration will establish Centers of Excellence inside the General Services Administration to focus on critical priorities such as cloud migration, data center consolidation, and modernizing call centers to better serve citizens. The Administration will work to strengthen fundamental capabilities, such as the ability to manage data comprehensively and to use data routinely to improve operations, which are the backbone of how business is accomplished in the modern era. In addition to cross-agency efforts, each major Federal agency is publishing an updated strategic plan with the Budget, establishing strategic objectives for the Administration's first term and committing to agency priority goals for the next two years. A full list of agency performance plans is available at *www.performance.gov*.

**Reorganization and Reform.** Last March, the President sent out a call for change in Executive Order 13781, "Comprehensive Plan for Reorganizing the Executive Branch," where he tasked the Office of Management and Budget (OMB) Director with providing a plan to reorganize the Executive Branch. The Budget is a first step in presenting this plan to the American people. This plan includes changes that can be accomplished with existing authorities as well as others that would require new funding and authorities. These changes also include reforms identified by individual Federal employees, who answered the Administration's request for their best ideas to improve public services or better use taxpayer dollars.

These reforms include, for example: eliminating unnecessary political positions; using shared services to improve IT services and reduce costs through economies of scale; realigning offices and personnel; and revamping regional offices. For instance, in order to improve customer service, the Department of the Interior has already begun to shift employees away from Washington, District of Columbia, closer to the citizens the Agency serves. The Department of Energy is also planning to review its existing laboratory network and identify potential efficiencies.

As part of this plan, the Administration is also planning to review how it can restructure functions across Federal agencies. For instance, it is planning a review of how it can streamline Federal statistical functions across multiple Federal agencies. The Administration is also reviewing Federal development finance activities—currently spread across the Overseas Private Investment Corporation and multiple offices at the United States Agency for International Development and other Federal agencies—to identify ways to reduce duplication and better achieve national security and international development outcomes while supporting U.S. business and jobs. The Budget proposes to consolidate these functions into a new Development Finance Institution, including reforms that protect taxpayer dollars.

In the months ahead, the Administration plans to unveil additional reorganization proposals designed to refocus programs around current and future needs.

**Getting Government Out of the Way.** Within 10 days of taking office, the President issued Executive Order 13771, "Reducing Regulation and Controlling Regulatory Costs," which directs agencies to reduce regulatory burdens by eliminating two existing regulations for each new one issued and impose no net regulatory burden in 2017.

The Administration recognizes that excessive and unnecessary Federal regulations limit individual freedom and suppress the innovation and entrepreneurship that make America great. Starting with confidence in private markets and individual choices, this Administration is reassessing existing regulatory burdens. Agencies have identified regulatory actions ripe for reform and are working to eliminate or modify those requirements. The Administration also approaches the imposition of new regulatory requirements with caution to ensure that regulations are consistent with law, necessary to correct a substantial market failure, and net beneficial to the public.

The Administration's regulatory philosophy and approach emphasize the connection between limited Government intervention and individual liberty. Regulatory policy should serve the American people by staying within legal limits and administering the law with respect for due process and fair notice.

In December 2017, OMB released its *Regulatory Reform Status Report: Two-for-One and Regulatory Cost Maps*, which assessed agency performance under Executive Order 13771 during 2017. At the same time, OMB released the *Unified Agenda of Regulatory and Deregulatory Actions and the Regulatory Plan*, which set forth the Administration's roadmap for a more limited, effective, and accountable regulatory policy in 2018 and beyond.

- **Regulatory Reform in 2017.** In just its first eight months, the Administration eliminated 67 regulations and adopted only three significant new regulations. This 22-to-one ratio far exceeds the President's "two-for-one" requirement. It also generated $8.1 billion in net regulatory cost savings (present value), far surpassing the President's requirement to hold net costs to zero. The Administration took further action to withdraw or delay more than 1,500 regulations in the pipeline, and has been transparent about these planned regulatory actions. This pace and scope of deregulation is unprecedented.

- **Regulatory Reform in 2018 and Beyond.** The Administration's *Unified Agenda* currently projects the elimination of approximately 448 regulations and the addition of only 131 new regulations. In 2018, Federal agencies are committed to cutting more than $9.8 billion in lifetime regulatory costs. Across the Government, this Agenda will drive substantial reductions in regulatory costs beyond what has already been accomplished. For additional information, please visit *www.reginfo.gov*.

At its core, regulatory reform not only promotes individual liberty and a flourishing economy, but also supports America's constitutional democracy. OMB's regulatory review process ensures that agencies stay within the legal authority given by the Congress. Where the law leaves discretion, however, the Administration will work with agencies to ensure that regulatory policy reflects Presidential priorities. This executive direction grounds the rulemaking process in democratic accountability.

By starting from a foundation of confidence in markets, individual choice, and the hardworking men and women of America, the Administration has already achieved—and will continue to achieve—dramatic reductions in the regulatory burden on the American economy and individual freedom. The agenda for the coming year promises a regulatory policy that works for the American people.

**A Clear Roadmap Ahead.** The Federal Government cannot be fully equipped to meet modern management challenges without support from the Congress. In some cases, real change will demand different agency structures. In other cases, the Administration may need to update rigid requirements from the past that hold back Government.

Government must recognize that it can no longer meet modern needs with the same approaches, technology, and skillsets from centuries past. By acknowledging shortcomings, setting a modern vision, and delivering on concrete goals, the Administration can adapt Federal programs, capabilities, and the Federal workforce to more efficiently, effectively and accountably meet mission demands and public expectations.

# A NEW FEDERAL BUDGET THAT WORKS FOR THE AMERICAN PEOPLE

The President's first Budget laid the foundation for an era of American greatness. The Budget enshrined fiscal responsibility and fiscal restraint while prioritizing spending to programs Americans need most. The Budget rights the wrongs of previous administrations by reprioritizing spending to protect the American citizen and the homeland, bringing dignity back to the American worker, and strengthening national defense. By building on policies laid out in the President's first Budget, the 2019 Budget provides the gateway to America's future.

## KEEPING AMERICA SECURE

As described in the National Security Strategy, the Government's fundamental responsibility is to protect the American people, the homeland, and American way of life. The National Security Strategy recognizes that an America that is strong and prosperous at home is an America capable of defending its interests and advancing its influence abroad. By leading abroad in concert with allies and partners, the United States can help create a world that is aligned with America's interests and values. Such a world makes us more secure and prosperous here at home. While America possesses enduring national strengths, the Nation now faces an era of increased strategic competition, global disorder, and erosion of the U.S. comparative military advantage. To effectively compete, deter, and win in this challenging new era, the United States must continue to invest in and adapt U.S. national security programs.

The Budget invests in protecting America and the homeland, including through a layered missile defense system to defend the homeland against missile attacks. The Budget also requests funds to pursue threats to their sources, so that jihadist terrorists and transnational criminals are stopped before they ever reach the Nation's borders. The Budget supports: efforts by the Department of State, Department of Energy, and Department of Defense (DOD) to strengthen international partnerships to stop the proliferation of the materials, technologies, weapons, and delivery systems necessary to build and deploy weapons of mass destruction; DOD capabilities to disrupt efforts to produce weapons of mass destruction; efforts by the Departments of State of the Treasury to hold accountable those that engage in proliferation activities or support these illicit programs; Department of Homeland Security (DHS) initiatives to identify weapons of mass destruction and their components before they reach the U.S. homeland or can be used on U.S. soil; and Federal Bureau of Investigation and DOD capabilities to thwart terrorists that attempt to use weapons of mass destruction.

The Budget advances the goal of preserving peace through strength by rebuilding the U.S. military so that it remains preeminent, deters adversaries, and if necessary, is able to fight and win. By investing in the capacity, capabilities, and modernization of America's Armed Forces, the Budget would continue to strengthen America's full spectrum of military capabilities and associated personnel—including in space and cyberspace.

To maintain the advantages America's Armed Forces enjoy and build upon its strengths, the Budget requests $716 billion for national defense. These investments fund a military that protects America's vital national interests in an increasingly competitive world. However, America and its allies cannot be defended if the Nation is not both strong and solvent. Recognizing the importance of solvency, the Budget proposes to pay for increases for the military with $65 billion in reductions from the non-Defense discretionary caps in 2019 under current law. DOD will also pursue an aggressive reform agenda to achieve savings that it will reinvest in higher priority needs.

The U.S. military cannot expect success fighting tomorrow's conflicts with yesterday's weapons or equipment. Rather, it will shift to a more lethal, resilient, and agile force able to take on and prevail against any foe, even in the face of aggressive military modernization campaigns on the part of potential adversaries.

To that end, the Budget makes significant investments in the capability of the joint force, and especially in its lethality, resilience, and agility to better deter and, if necessary, fight and prevail against any opponent. In particular, the Budget focuses on improving the joint force's capability to take on potential great power adversaries. At the same time, the Budget invests to recover full-spectrum readiness while acquiring new and improved capabilities, enabling the United States to meet security challenges now and into the future. The Budget ensures U.S. forces are ready to fight by providing critical funding for training, munitions, logistics, and maintenance while also enabling America's forces to recover readiness against high-end adversaries. The Budget also requests funds to selectively increase the size of the Army, Air Force, Navy, and Marine Corps and requests funds for the modernization of equipment, including armored vehicles, artillery, new warships, stealthy fighter aircraft, and the next generation of bombers. These investments would strengthen deterrence by ensuring the military is ready to confront even the most capable adversaries. Deterring adversaries from choosing a military option would support a peaceful and open international order that underpins the prosperity of the United States and its allies.

Although the U.S. military will remain second to none, adversaries and competitors are increasingly challenging the United States across the political, economic, and military arenas. To that end, the Budget supports the missions of the Department of State, U.S. Agency for International Development, and other international programs to help America compete against hostile actors and ideologies and advance American interests. The Budget builds upon key reforms begun in last year's Budget to prioritize civilian activities that support more resilient, democratic, and prosperous societies, leading to a more secure and peaceful world. The Budget prioritizes efforts to ensure that the burden of responding to global crises is borne globally, rather than disproportionately by the people and economy of the United States. By focusing on programs and policies that catalyze other countries' economic and political development, America can help aspiring partners become economic and security partners, shield them from competitors, and promote a stable world reflecting these principles.

In recognition of the dedication and sacrifice of the men and women who have served in the Armed Forces, and those who continue to serve today, the Budget also reflects a renewed commitment to honor the service of veterans. The Budget supports veterans spanning multiple generations including during periods of conflict and peace. Specifically, the Budget would build upon the Veteran's Choice program to improve healthcare and implement a modernized appeals system to provide veterans with better medical options. The Budget would also provide enhanced access to education benefits through the Forever GI Bill signed into law by the President in August 2017. In addition, the Budget funds long-term efforts to improve infrastructure and modernize the Department of Veterans Affairs (VA) to ensure it is positioned to support future generations of veterans.

## HELPING AMERICANS MOVE FROM WELFARE TO WORK

More than 20 years have passed since the Congress implemented significant reforms to America's safety net. In 1996, the Congress passed the Personal Responsibility and Work Opportunity Reconciliation Act (PRWORA), and transformed the way Government provided support to low-income families. Recognizing the value of State innovation, and promoting work as the best pathway out of poverty, PRWORA ushered in an era where success was no longer measured by how many people received welfare assistance but instead by how well Government helped families progress toward self-sufficiency. Building off of this framework, the Budget empowers States to develop innovative strategies to help welfare recipients achieve economic independence through work, while preserving the basic safety net necessary to help those most in need.

### *Promoting the Value of Work*

Work is a fundamental element in moving welfare recipients toward self-sufficiency and economic security. This plan proposes to reinforce one of the original principles of welfare reform—able-bodied people should be required to work or prepare for work in order to receive Government assistance. The Budget, therefore, requires States to ensure that work-capable individuals are on a pathway to work. In addition, an abrupt end to welfare assistance is often an impediment to sustained employment, creating churn on the welfare rolls. To further increase employment outcomes, the Budget also encourages States to provide the support necessary to ease this transition.

### *Improving Food Assistance*

The Budget proposes a bold new approach to administering the Supplemental Nutrition Assistance Program (SNAP) that combines traditional SNAP benefits with 100-percent American grown foods provided directly to households and focuses administrative reforms on outcome-based employment strategies. The Budget expands on previous SNAP proposals to strengthen expectations for work among able-bodied adults, preserves benefits for those most in need, promotes efficiency in State operations, and improves program integrity. Combined, these reforms would maintain the commitment to ensure Americans in need of assistance have access to a nutritious diet while significantly reducing the cost to taxpayers.

### *Encouraging State Innovation*

Today, there are still more than 80 single-purpose welfare programs that comprise a Federal safety net intended to help those living in poverty. This complex and bureaucratic system has proven to be ineffective. The Budget proposes to streamline, simplify, and improve the efficiency of the welfare system by proposing a new approach to assisting low-income Americans rise to their potential.

The Administration recognizes that States and local communities best understand the conditions and circumstances of their economically vulnerable citizens. Therefore, the Budget offers States the opportunity to propose Welfare to Work Projects that streamline funding from multiple welfare programs, and provide services that are tailored to their constituents' specific needs, helping them progress from welfare to work. Reducing burdens and inefficiencies in overlapping—or at times competing—program requirements would remove barriers to employment and self-sufficiency for families dependent on welfare programs.

This new opportunity would be accompanied by a strong accountability framework. Specifically, plans to combine safety net programs would be subject to rigorous, random-assignment evaluations, measuring achievement in targeted outcomes that focus on fostering employment, reducing welfare dependency, and promoting child and family well-being. These projects would serve to build the evidence base of best practices to help low-income individuals and families achieve self-sufficiency, and would inform the design of more comprehensive welfare reform efforts in the future.

Altogether, the Budget offers a bold new vision for America's safety net, and reinforces this Administration's commitment to helping all Americans achieve their full potential.

## PROTECTING AMERICANS WHILE ENHANCING LEGAL IMMIGRATION

Since taking office, the President has made clear that he would restore order and integrity to the U.S. immigration system. There are three primary efforts underlying this goal: strengthening border security; ensuring enforcement of immigration laws; and reforming the legal immigration system, while recognizing that legal immigration is an important driver of a thriving economy. The Budget requests more than $28.2 billion for the agencies that have primary responsibility for carrying out immigration programs at DHS and the Department of Justice (DOJ). This includes funding for U.S. Customs and Border Protection (CBP), U.S. Immigration and Customs Enforcement (ICE), and U.S. Citizenship and Immigration Services within DHS, and the Executive Office for Immigration Review (EOIR) within DOJ.

Within the Administration's proposal for $18 billion to fund the border wall, the Budget invests $1.6 billion to support CBP efforts to gain operational control of the Southwest border. Until the porous borders are closed to the criminals, terrorists, and gang members that exploit it, America remains at risk. Furthermore, since most of the illegal drugs that enter the United States come through the Southwest border, a border wall is critical to combating the scourge of drug addiction that leads to thousands of unnecessary deaths. The border wall would stop smugglers in their tracks and help make America safe.

The Budget also requests $211 million for 750 additional Border Patrol agents in 2019, continuing the President's commitment to increase the ranks of the Border Patrol by 5,000 new agents. Funding would be used to recruit, hire, and train new agents, and for staff to support the men and women on the front line of America's border defenses. These new personnel would supplement investments in the border wall by guarding the border and apprehending and swiftly removing illegal aliens at the border.

The Budget furthers investment in CBP technology and targeting systems such as the National Targeting Center (NTC) and the Biometric Entry-Exit System. The Budget requests a total of $253 million for NTC, an increase of $79 million, for its overall mission, including the background vetting of individuals seeking to enter the United States before they arrive. These programs would enable the Government to better identify terrorists and other criminals and prevent their entry into the United States. Completion of the long-required Biometric Entry-Exit System would increase law enforcement's ability to identify and remove those who overstay their visas. Future investments in enhanced vetting and targeting programs would further the Administration's goal of shifting such costs to visa and immigration applicants while continuing to facilitate legitimate travel to the United States.

The Budget makes major investments in immigration law enforcement in the interior of the Nation, focusing on efforts to identify, arrest, prosecute, and remove illegal aliens. Within ICE, the Budget proposes $571 million to hire and support 2,000 new officers and agents, which directly supports the President's order for ICE to arrest all illegal aliens it encounters. Since the President's inauguration, ICE arrests have increased by 42 percent and the Agency has increased requests to local law enforcement to transfer custody of illegal aliens to ICE by 81 percent during the same time period in the previous fiscal year.

As ICE increases its arrests and deportations of illegal aliens, it also requires additional detention and removal capacity. The Budget requests more than $2.5 billion for these critical law enforcement functions, funding an average daily detention capacity of 47,000 illegal aliens in facilities across the United States. To ensure immigration cases are heard expeditiously, the Budget also requests an increase of $40 million for 75 new immigration judge teams at EOIR and nearly $40 million for 338 new prosecuting attorneys at ICE. These investments are critical to the prompt resolution of newly-brought immigration charges and to reduce the 650,000 backlog of cases currently pending in the immigration courts.

The Budget requests $208 million in new funding for 300 additional ICE Special Agents, support staff, and other activities for the Agency's Homeland Security Investigations' (HSI) mission. HSI staff lead efforts to ensure only those with legal permission to work in the United States are employed here, investigate and disrupt transnational criminal organizations (TCOs) that perpetuate human smuggling and trafficking, and stop immigration fraud, which directly facilitates illegal immigration. Because these investigations protect the integrity of the legal immigration system, the Budget proposes collecting the $208 million for these purposes from the immigration applicants who want to come to the United States and benefit from the Nation's opportunities.

The integrity of the immigration system relies upon everyone in the United States doing their part to follow the law. The Budget invests $23 million to expand the E-Verify Program for mandatory nationwide use, ensuring that businesses employ only those authorized to work in the United States. Further, the Budget proposes to amend the Illegal Immigration Reform and Immigrant Responsibility Act to condition DHS and DOJ grants and cooperative agreements on States and local governments agreeing to cooperate with immigration enforcement activities. This proposal takes important steps to mitigate the risk that sanctuary cities pose to public safety and ensures appropriate alignment between State and Federal immigration enforcement.

The Budget supports efforts to reform the legal immigration system by ending family chain migration and the diversity visa lottery and replacing them with a merit-based regime that selects immigrants based on their skills, likelihood to assimilate, and ability to contribute to the economy. This is similar to the approach used by Canada and Australia and would reduce overall immigration while limiting low-skilled and unskilled labor entering the United States. The Budget requests the resources needed to adjudicate immigration and visa applications and identify and counter fraud in the immigration process, ensuring that businesses and individuals petitioning for foreign workers and relatives do so in a manner consistent with the Nation's immigration laws, while ensuring that the American economy continues to access the labor force critically needed for growth.

## REBUILDING AMERICA THROUGH THE INFRASTRUCTURE INITIATIVE

America's infrastructure is a key component to its historic success. With the world's most efficient rail and interstate highway systems, America was a fierce global competitor. Local roads and water systems provided a clean and safe environment for communities and families.

In recent decades, however, we have chronically under-invested in public infrastructure, leading to the frustration of long commutes and the loss of life when a lack of maintenance creates safety hazards. The challenge of restoring this infrastructure is complicated by the fact that virtually all public infrastructure is owned by State and local governments, not the Federal Government. Interstate highways, drinking and waste water systems, commuter railroads, airports, power lines, telecommunications, and ports are all non-Federal. While the Federal Government has co-invested in State and local infrastructure, using Federal dollars to pay for non-Federal infrastructure projects has created an unhealthy dynamic in which State and local governments delay projects in the hope of receiving Federal funds.

The Administration's infrastructure initiative would address the imbalances between infrastructure investment, ownership, and responsibility and generate $1 trillion in total infrastructure investment through a combination of direct Federal funding and incentivized non-Federal funding. The Budget requests $200 billion dedicated to this effort, as follows:

- **Incentive Grants**—$100 billion is requested to encourage increased State, local, and private infrastructure investment by awarding incentives to project sponsors for demonstrating innovative approaches that would generate new revenue streams, prioritize maintenance, modernize procurement practices, and generate a social and economic return on investment. Incentives would be provided in the form of competitive grants.

- **Rural Formula Funds**—$50 billion is requested for this program, which would address the significant need for investment in rural infrastructure, including broadband internet service. Federal funding would be made available to States via formula distribution, along with a bonus competition based on State performance in achieving goals outlined in State-developed rural infrastructure plans. Within this amount, funding is set aside for federally recognized Tribes and U.S. Territories.

- **Transformative Projects**—$20 billion is requested to support bold, innovative, and transformative infrastructure projects that can significantly improve existing infrastructure conditions and services. Funding would be awarded on a competitive basis for commercially viable projects that are capable of generating revenue, provide net public benefits, and would have a significant positive impact on the Nation, a region, State, or metropolitan area.

- **Existing Credit Programs**—$14 billion is requested in additional subsidy funding for the key Federal credit programs providing financing to infrastructure projects. This funding would significantly increase Federal credit assistance to infrastructure via the Department of Transportation's Transportation Infrastructure Finance and Innovation Act (TIFIA) and Railroad Rehabilitation and Improvement Financing programs, the Environmental Protection Agency's Water Infrastructure Finance and Innovation Act program, and

the Department of Agriculture's Rural Utilities Service program. For example, historically the TIFIA program has leveraged about $40 in transportation infrastructure improvement for each $1 of TIFIA assistance provided. The initiative would also expand eligibility for these credit programs to include other governmental infrastructure such as airports and ports.

- **Federal Capital Revolving Fund**—$10 billion is requested to establish a mandatory revolving fund to finance purchases, construction, or renovation of federally owned civilian real property. The Federal Government is currently utilizing inefficient leases to access necessary property. Leases are being used due to the unavailability of the large upfront capital needed to acquire real property projects. Upon approval in annual appropriations acts, the revolving fund would transfer money to agencies to finance large-dollar real property projects. Purchasing agencies would then be required to repay the Fund using discretionary appropriations.

- **Private Activity Bonds (PABs)**—the initiative would expand flexibility and broaden eligibility for PABs, which play an important part in delivering many large, regionally- and nationally-significant projects. PABs provided for this broadened definition of "core public infrastructure projects" would not be subject to volume caps, but would require the projects to be available to the public and either Government-owned or privately-owned but subject to Government regulatory or contractual control and approval. The Budget requests $6 billion related to this expansion.

- **Real Property Reforms**—the Budget supports several proposals to streamline and improve the Federal real property disposal processes, Government-wide, including the retention of sales proceeds.

These proposals would increase the opportunities to sell off real property no longer needed by the Federal Government, thereby generating revenue to improve other mission critical Federal facilities. Disposal of unneeded Federal facilities would also allow the disposed buildings to be returned to private use, potentially spurring local economic development. The Budget also supports flexibilities for VA to leverage existing assets to continue its efforts to reduce the number of vacant buildings in its inventory, leverage VA assets for the construction of needed new facilities to serve veterans, and align the VA lease prospectus threshold with the General Services Administration threshold.

- **Reduce Deferred Maintenance on Public Lands**—the Budget also proposes a new Public Lands Infrastructure Fund for the Department of the Interior to support infrastructure investments in national parks, refuges, and Bureau of Indian Education schools. The Fund would be supported by half of the incremental receipts from expanded energy development that exceed previous projections and are not allocated for other purposes.

- **Streamline Permits**—in addition, the infrastructure initiative includes several proposals to streamline permitting decisions to accelerate project delivery while maintaining environmental safeguards. For example, the initiative proposes creating a new "One Federal Decision" structure that includes firm deadlines for completing environmental reviews, eliminating redundant agency reviews, delegating responsibilities to States where appropriate, and pilot programs to experiment with innovative approaches to environmental reviews.

## COMBATTING THE DRUG ABUSE AND OPIOID OVERDOSE EPIDEMIC

The drug abuse and overdose epidemic, particularly related to opioids, is tearing apart America's families and devastating communities. Last year, more people died from drug overdoses than traffic accidents. The two million people who are addicted to opioids, a class of drugs that includes both legal and illicit drugs such as certain prescription painkillers, heroin, and synthetic opioids such as fentanyl, are especially at risk. In 2016, approximately 64,000 people died from drug overdoses, 174 lives per day.

In 2017, the President said: "I made a promise to the American people to take action to keep drugs from pouring into our country and to help those who have been so badly affected by them." The Administration has taken a number of significant actions to address the crisis. The President created the Commission on Combating Drug Addiction and the Opioid Crisis and the Administration declared the opioid epidemic a nationwide public health emergency. The Administration provided nearly $500 million in new resources to States to prevent and treat opioid abuse and addiction in 2017, in addition to last year's Budget that requested another $500 million.

As the President noted: "Ending the epidemic will require mobilization of Government, local communities, and private organizations. It will require the resolve of our entire country." The Budget requests more than $30 billion in drug control funding in 2019, of which the Office of National Drug Control Policy estimates that more than $7 billion combats the opioid crisis, with efforts spanning prevention, treatment, interdiction, international operations, and law enforcement across 14 Executive Branch Departments, the Federal Judiciary, and the District of Columbia.

The Budget requests $5 billion in new resources for the Department of Health and Human Services (HHS) over the next five years, including $1 billion in 2019, to combat the opioid epidemic by preventing opioid abuse and helping those who are addicted get access to overdose reversal drugs, treatment, and recovery support services. The Budget request includes: $50 million for a media campaign; $625 million for States to respond to the crisis; $50 million to improve first responder access to overdose-reversal drugs; $100 million for surveillance and opioid abuse prevention activities, including improving State-based Prescription Drug Monitoring Programs (PDMPs); $20 million for drug courts; $10 million for pregnant and post-partum women treatment programs; $10 million for the Food and Drug Administration's (FDA) regulatory science activities to develop tools to stem the misuse and abuse of opioids; $65 million to support multi-sector, county-level teams in high-risk rural communities to improve access to care, and expand treatment and recovery services; $45 million for supplemental grants for opioid abuse prevention, treatment, and recovery services in American Indian and Alaska Native communities; and $25 million to evaluate the impact of medication assisted treatment on reducing overdose deaths.

In addition to the requested $5 billion, the Budget also continues and expands existing activities in HHS that specifically address key strategies to combat the opioid crisis. The Budget requests $100 million for the National Institutes of Health to support a public-private partnership with the pharmaceutical industry to develop prevention and treatments for addiction, overdose-reversal, and non-addictive therapies for pain. The Budget requests $123 million in the Substance Abuse and Mental Health Services Administration for opioid abuse prevention, treatment, recovery support, and overdose reversal. The Budget also requests $126 million in the Centers for Disease Control and Prevention to support opioid abuse prevention and surveillance activities, including support to States to improve the capabilities and use of State-based PDMPs.

Further, the Administration supports more rigorous research to better understand how existing programs or policies might be contributing to or mitigating the opioid epidemic.

For Medicaid, the Budget calls for expanding coverage of comprehensive and evidence-based medication assisted treatment options, previews forthcoming guidance from the Centers for Medicare and Medicaid Services that would set minimum standards for State Drug Utilization Reviews to reduce clinical abuse, and requires States to track and act on prescribers that do not adopt best practices.

For Medicare, the Budget proposes to test and expand nationwide a bundled payment for community-based medication assisted treatment, including Medicare reimbursement for methadone treatment for the first time. The Budget also proposes to prevent prescription drug abuse in Medicare Part D and protect beneficiaries from potentially harmful drugs by requiring plan participation in a program to prevent prescription drug abuse. In addition, the Budget proposes to authorize the Secretary of HHS to work with the Drug Enforcement Administration (DEA) to revoke a provider's certificate (which allows a provider to prescribe controlled substances) when that provider is barred from billing Medicare based on a pattern of abusive prescribing. Cutting off Medicare funding for abusive prescription practices not only helps bring premiums down for seniors, it promotes sound public health policy.

The President also recognizes that combatting the opioid crisis means not only helping those suffering from drug addiction but also dismantling drug trafficking organizations profiting from this deadly scourge. The Budget requests $2.2 billion for the DEA, including an additional $41 million to enhance efforts to target the illicit drug traffickers that prey on communities. In addition, the Budget requests $103 million within DOJ for opioid-related State and local assistance including: $20 million for the Comprehensive Opioid Abuse Program to support a variety of activities such as treatment and recovery support services, diversion, and alternative to incarceration programs; $59 million for Drug Courts, Mental Health Courts, and Veterans Treatment Courts; $12 million for Residential Substance Abuse Treatment; and $12 million to support PDMPs, in tandem with HHS efforts.

The Budget also requests a range of investments that would strengthen efforts at DHS to identify, screen, and interdict drug shipments coming into the United States, and to investigate those responsible for bringing illegal drugs into the United States. The Budget request increases funding for CBP's NTC by $79 million, for a total of $253 million, which would also allow the Agency to better target its efforts to stop illicit goods, including illicit drugs, from entering the United States. The Budget also requests a $44 million investment in new Non-Intrusive Inspection technology at Ports of Entry, which is used to examine cargo and conveyances for contraband and weapons of mass effect. The Budget requests an increase of $42 million, funded by both fees and discretionary appropriations, to enable CBP to screen inbound packages at express consignment carrier facilities such as FedEx, UPS, and DHL. The Budget continues investments in presumptive testing devices to improve customs officers' capability to detect and interdict fentanyl and other opioids, and requests an additional $1.2 million, for a total of $46 million, for scientific support to CBP officers for rapid identification of suspected illicit materials, in particular suspected opioids. In addition, the Budget fully supports all 57 ICE Border Enforcement Security Task Force units around the United States, which are the Agency's primary platform to investigate opioid smuggling, and continues support for DHS's Joint Task Force—Investigations, which works to identify, disrupt, and dismantle TCOs that seek to import opioids and other drugs into the United States.

## RETHINKING DRUG PRICING TO PUT AMERICAN PATIENTS FIRST

Many drugs are too expensive for Americans and too many patients continue to be priced out of the medicines they need. Lowering prescription drug prices is one of the most important issues facing the Nation. Recent well-publicized instances of price manipulation and the disparity between U.S. drug prices and prices overseas also add to the growing frustration Americans feel. While American innovators bring life-saving pharmaceutical products to the world, drugs are purchased through an inefficient, opaque maze of segmented channels and a poorly understood network of pricing schemes. Complex regulations and barriers to entry for suppliers drive up drug costs for Americans. Americans unfairly shoulder a disproportionate amount of burden for research and development, allowing foreign governments to achieve better deals for their citizens at the expense of the American people. The goal of the Administration's comprehensive strategy is to address the problem of high drug prices, provide greater access to lifesaving medical products, and to ensure that the United States remains the leader in biomedical innovation.

The Administration has already taken a number of significant administrative steps to reduce drug costs. For example, in 2017, FDA approved the highest annual total number of generic drugs (1,027) in the Agency's history.

FDA is also increasing competition in the market for prescription drugs, and facilitating entry of lower-cost alternatives, by providing greater transparency and expediting the review of generic drug applications for products with limited competition. CMS modified payment policies for biosimilars to encourage innovation and a robust market, which should encourage competition and innovation and help lower prices in the long run. The Administration also took steps to lower the costs seniors pay for certain drugs in the hospital outpatient setting, so that patients could benefit from the discounts hospitals receive under the 340B Program. This action is expected to save seniors an estimated $320 million on drug copayments in calendar year 2018 alone. In addition, the Budget once again proposes reforms to improve 340B Program integrity to ensure that the benefits derived from participation in the program are used to benefit patients, especially low-income and uninsured populations, and to require entities to report on use of 340B Program savings.

The Budget proposes new strategies to address high drug prices and increase access to lifesaving medicines by: rationalizing the current incentive structure; fostering greater competition; and extending American leadership in innovation to put American patients first.

The Budget calls for new Medicaid demonstration authority for up to five States to test drug coverage and financing reforms that build on private sector best practices. Participating States would determine their own drug formularies, coupled with an appeals process to protect beneficiary access to non-covered drugs based on medical need, and negotiate drug prices directly with manufacturers.

Within the Medicare program, the Budget modernizes the Part D drug benefit, based upon 12 years of program experience, to improve plans' ability to deliver affordable drug coverage for seniors and reduce their costs at the pharmacy counter. Seniors would benefit from the Budget's proposals, which are designed to better protect beneficiaries from high drug prices, give plans more tools to manage spending, and address the misaligned incentives of the Part D drug benefit structure. The proposed changes enhance Part D plans' negotiation power with manufacturers, encourage utilization of higher value drugs, discourage drug manufacturers' price and rebate strategies that increase spending for both beneficiaries and the Government, and provide beneficiaries with more predictable annual drug expenses through the creation of a new out-of-pocket spending cap. The Budget also modifies payment for Part B drugs to discourage manufacturers from increasing prices faster than inflation and improves payment accuracy. In addition, the Budget also modifies hospitals' payment for drugs acquired through the 340B drug discount program by rewarding hospitals that provide charity care and reducing payments to hospitals that provide little to no charity care.

The Budget also proposes to give FDA greater ability to bring generics to the market faster by incentivizing more competition among generic manufacturers. The Budget proposes to ensure that first-to-file generic applicants who have been awarded a 180-day exclusivity period do not unreasonably and indefinitely block subsequent generics from entering the market beyond the exclusivity period.

The Administration is updating a study from 2004 to analyze drug prices paid in countries that are a part of the Organization for Economic Cooperation and Development. HHS, working in conjunction with the Department of Commerce and the U.S. Trade Representative, will develop the knowledge base to understand the unfair disparity between the drug prices in America and other developed countries. The Administration is committed to making the regulatory changes and seeking legislative solutions to put American patients first.

# DEPARTMENT OF AGRICULTURE

---

**Highlights:**

- The U.S. Department of Agriculture (USDA) provides leadership on issues related to food, agriculture, and natural resources based on sound public policy, the best available science, and efficient management.

- The Budget focuses on core mission-critical activities such as expansion of agricultural production jobs and research, while also supporting the Secretary's Department-wide reorganization efforts. Demonstrating fiscal constraint and responsible use of taxpayer resources, the Budget eliminates funding for unnecessary or lower priority activities and those that are duplicative of private sector efforts.

- The Budget requests $19 billion for USDA (excluding changes in mandatory programs), a $3.7 billion or 16-percent decrease from the 2017 enacted level.

---

**The President's 2019 Budget:**

USDA works to expand agriculture productivity and rural prosperity through the development of innovative practices and research, by improving access to technology and by providing financing needed to help grow job prospects, raise income levels and improve housing, utilities, and community infrastructure in rural America. The Department also works to promote sustainable agricultural production to protect natural resources and the long-term availability of safe and affordable food. USDA programs safeguard and protect America's food supply by reducing the incidence of food-borne hazards from farm to table.

The Department's programs also improve nutrition and health through food assistance and nutrition education. USDA works to increase foreign market access for U.S. agricultural products and provides data and analysis of foreign market conditions. This helps U.S. agricultural producers make informed decisions on international trade opportunities, and supports the U.S. economy through increased exports. In addition, USDA manages and protects America's public and private lands by working cooperatively across the Government and the private sector to preserve and conserve the Nation's natural resources through restored forests, improved watersheds, and healthy private working lands. The Budget continues some of the reforms outlined in the 2018 Budget while also streamlining programs to focus on core mission areas.

**Safeguards the Nation's Food Supply.** The Budget fully funds the costs necessary to support about 8,100 personnel located at more than 6,400 processing and slaughter establishments for meat, poultry, and egg products in the United States. These personnel act as front line inspectors and investigators; they provide surveillance to protect the Nation's food supply and further the mission of the Food Safety and Inspection Service.

**Protects Health Outcomes for Pregnant Women, Infants, and Young Children.** The Budget requests $5.8 billion to serve all projected participants in the Special Supplemental Nutrition Program for Women, Infants, and Children (WIC). This program provides nutritious supplemental food packages, nutrition education and counseling, and health and immunization referrals to low-income and nutritionally at-risk pregnant and postpartum women, infants, and children.

> *"Our farmers deserve a Government that serves their interest and empowers them to do the hard work that they love to do so much."*
>
> President Donald J. Trump
> January 8, 2018

**Reforms the Food Safety Net While Promoting Work.** The Budget proposes a bold new approach to nutrition assistance that combines traditional Supplemental Nutrition Assistance Program (SNAP) benefits with 100-percent American grown foods provided directly to households and focuses administrative reforms on outcome-based employment strategies. In addition, the Budget expands on previous proposals to strengthen expectations for work among able-bodied adults, preserve benefits for those most in need, promote efficiency in State operations, and improve program integrity. Combined, these reforms maintain the Administration's commitment to ensuring Americans in need of assistance have access to a nutritious diet while significantly reducing the cost to taxpayers.

**Reorganizes the Department.** The Budget supports the Secretary's efforts to reorganize Agency functions to improve the customer and consumer experience. Under the new structure, the Farm Service Agency, Risk Management Agency, and the Natural Resources Conservation Service would be merged under the Under Secretary for Farm Production and Conservation. In addition, the Secretary has established an Under Secretary of Trade and Foreign Agricultural Affairs to sharpen USDA's focus on increasing agriculture exports to foreign markets. The Budget also supports consolidating fair practices, standards work, and commodity procurement within the Agricultural Marketing Service. These, and other related reorganizations, are expected to improve the way USDA delivers its services. In addition, the Budget supports the creation of a business innovation center in each mission area that would handle support activities in order to avoid duplicative functions and maximize collaboration between agencies.

**Improves Customer Service.** Modernizing program delivery and improving customer service at USDA is an important focus of the Administration. USDA is partnering with the White House Office of American Innovation to modernize its systems undertaking four key strategies: strengthening strategic IT governance; consolidating end-user services and data centers; enabling a strategic approach to data management and introducing data-driven capabilities; and improving the USDA customer experience. The Budget supports these efforts to improve service delivery by requesting funds to develop a centralized customer service portal for customers served by the Department's three service center agencies. This single, integrated, producer-centric web portal would provide expanded and more effective and efficient access to useful online USDA services to meet the needs of agricultural producers. By optimizing service delivery, USDA can support agricultural producers to reach their productive potential and advance the U.S. economy.

**Prioritizes Agricultural Research.** USDA research plays a key role in fostering innovation and advancing technologies that increase the efficiency, sustainability, and profitability of American agriculture. As such, the Budget prioritizes the USDA research portfolio by funding competitive research through the Department's flagship competitive research grant program, the Agriculture and Food Research Initiative (AFRI). The Budget requests $375 million for AFRI, consistent with the 2017 enacted level. The Budget also requests formula funding for research and extension activities at land-grant universities at the 2017 enacted level. The Budget proposes more than $1 billion for the Agriculture Research Service, which conducts in-house basic and applied research. Funding is targeted to achieve the President and Secretary's vision of advancing the competitiveness of American agriculture and nutritional security. This funding level would enable USDA to focus on priority research areas in the Farm Bill such as plant and animal health and production. The Budget also proposes to transfer operational responsibility for the National Bio and Agro-Defense Facility (NBAF) from the Department of Homeland Security to USDA and requests $42 million for operations costs in 2019. Once construction is complete, USDA would operate the NBAF and use the facility to study diseases that threaten the animal agricultural industry and public health.

**Streamlines and Refocuses USDA Statistical Activities to Core Mission Responsibilities.** The Budget proposes to streamline the research efforts of the Economic Research Service by eliminating low priority research that is being conducted within the private sector and by non-profits and focusing on core data analyses in line with priority research areas. The Budget fully funds the anticipated needs for the release of the Census of Agriculture and provides a framework to better streamline the Department's statistical functions, leverage administrative efficiencies, and focus on core data products similar to other statistical agencies elsewhere within the Government.

**Educates America's Next Generation of Farmers.** The Budget requests $50 million to increase agriculture science literacy programs and other community based efforts, such as 4H Clubs. These programs are a key component in exposing students to agriculture, developing necessary skillsets, and providing an awareness of the vast career opportunities in the agriculture sector. Developing a future agriculture workforce is not only critical to the Nation's food security, but also vital in promoting rural prosperity and improving quality of life.

**Supports Trade and U.S. Agriculture Abroad.** USDA's Foreign Agricultural Service works to improve foreign market access for U.S. agricultural products, build new markets, improve the competitive position of U.S. agriculture in the global marketplace, and provide technical assistance to foreign countries. The Budget requests funding to support trade policy, trade promotion activities, and capacity building abroad. In addition, the Animal and Plant Health Inspection Service also helps facilitate trade by keeping agricultural industries free from pests and diseases, and certifying that agriculture and food products meet importing countries' entry requirements.

**Proposes a Comprehensive Solution to Wildfire Suppression Funding.** The Forest Service routinely exceeds the funds appropriated to fight wildfire, covering these

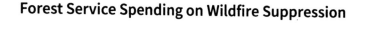

### Forest Service Spending on Wildfire Suppression

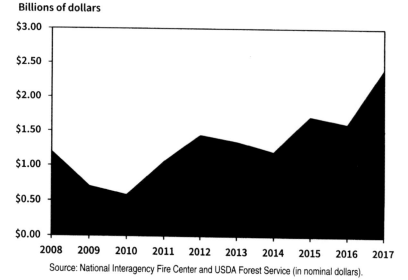

Billions of dollars

Source: National Interagency Fire Center and USDA Forest Service (in nominal dollars).

costs through transfers from other land management programs. For example, in 2017, Forest Service wildfire suppression spending reached a record $2.4 billion as a result of increasing frequency and severity of wildfires, necessitating transfers of $527 million from other programs. Historically, these transfers have been repaid in subsequent appropriations; however, "fire borrowing" impedes the missions of land management agencies to reduce the risk of catastrophic fire and restore and maintain healthy functioning ecosystems. To resolve concerns about the sufficiency of land management and funding wildfire suppression, the Budget responsibly funds 100 percent of the rolling 10-year average cost for wildfire suppression in the Departments of Agriculture and the Interior within discretionary budget caps. Similar to how unanticipated funding needs for other natural disasters are addressed, the Budget proposes a separate fund that would include an annual cap adjustment appropriation for wildfire suppression operations in order to ensure that adequate resources are available to fight wildland fires, protect communities, and safeguard human life during the most severe wildland fire seasons. In addition, the Administration believes that meaningful forest management reforms to strengthen our ability to restore the Nation's forests and improve their resilience to destructive wildfires should be a part of any permanent solution.

**Modernizes Inspection Activities.** Currently, the cost to support programs under the Federal Grain Inspection Service is funded with taxpayer dollars. The Budget proposes to offset this cost by assessing a fee to the companies that benefit directly from these programs. Similarly, the Budget proposes a user fee to cover the cost of providing Agricultural Quarantine and Inspections (AQI) within the United States, which is consistent with how AQI activities are funded for passengers and cargo originating outside of the United States.

**Supports Farmers and Rural Communities through Lending.** USDA invests in rural infrastructure to lift up low-income rural communities through its community facilities and water and wastewater direct loan programs. Through the Secretary's leadership of the Task Force on Agriculture and Rural Prosperity (Task Force), the Department has identified actions to improve the quality of life and expand economic development in rural communities. Many of these actions are supported through investments made in USDA lending activities to rural utilities and communities, and those that strengthen investments in housing programs. The Budget supports a $3.5 billion loan level for community facility direct loans, which provide assistance to rural communities to develop or improve essential public services and facilities across rural America, such as health clinics or fire and rescue stations. The Budget also requests $1.2 billion in direct loans for rural communities unable to get financing elsewhere to build and rehabilitate water and wastewater treatment facilities. USDA assists approved lenders in providing low- to moderate-income households the opportunity to own their primary residence through the single family housing guaranteed loan program. This program works through the private credit market and provides guarantees that collateralize private sector lending. The Budget supports a robust guaranteed single family housing loan level of $24 billion.

In addition, the Budget requests a loan level of $8 billion to support farm lending, providing crucial operating

### Promoting Prosperity in Rural America

In April 2017, the President issued Executive Order 13790, "Promoting Agriculture and Rural Prosperity in America," which established an inter-Departmental Task Force.

This Task Force, chaired by the Secretary of Agriculture, has identified barriers to economic prosperity in rural America and made recommendations on how innovation, infrastructure, and technology can assist agriculture and help rural communities thrive.

Supporting this effort, the Budget takes action to address problems by promoting electronic connectivity through broadband grants and loans for rural communities, and reducing regulatory burden for farmers.

capital through the Department's suite of farm loan programs, including loans that aid farmers in owning and operating their farms.

**Promotes E-connectivity in Rural Areas.** Electronic connectivity is fundamental for economic development, innovation, advancements in technology, workforce readiness, and an improved quality of life—reasons why such access was identified as a critical component by the Task Force. Unfortunately, access to affordable high-speed internet in rural and tribal areas still lags behind that of urban areas. Tremendous opportunities are unlocked when next generation networks connect rural communities, allowing doctors to reach patients, students to access knowledge, and small businesses to expand with access to online marketing, credit card processing, and online banking. To provide rural communities with modern information access, the Budget proposes $30 million to fund broadband grants, $23 million in broadband loans, and $24 million to fund distance learning and telemedicine grants.

**Supports Comprehensive Farm Safety Net Reforms and Reduces Waste.** The Budget proposes to optimize and improve crop insurance and commodity programs in a way that maintains a strong safety net. The Budget does this while also achieving savings, eliminating subsidies to higher income farmers, and reducing overly generous crop insurance premium subsidies to farmers and payments made to private sector insurance companies. The Budget includes a bold set of proposals, including those that would reduce the average premium subsidy for crop insurance from 62 percent to 48 percent and limit commodity, conservation, and crop insurance subsidies to those producers that have an Adjusted Gross Income of $500,000 or less.

In addition, the Budget proposes reductions to overly generous subsidies provided to participating insurance companies by capping underwriting gains at 12 percent, which would ensure that the companies receive a reasonable rate of return given the risks associated with their participation in the crop insurance program. The Budget proposes to eliminate an unnecessary and separate payment limit for peanut producers and limit eligibility for commodity subsidies to one manager per farm.

The Budget also includes proposals to streamline Federal conservation efforts to focus on programs that protect environmentally sensitive land and increase conservation practice implementation.

# DEPARTMENT OF COMMERCE

---

**Highlights:**

- The Department of Commerce (DOC) promotes job creation and economic growth by ensuring fair and secure trade, providing the data necessary to support commerce, securing America's national security and technological leadership through export controls and an effective patent system, and fostering innovation by setting standards and conducting foundational research and development.

- The Budget request for DOC prioritizes and protects investments in core Government functions such as preparing for the 2020 Decennial Census, providing the observational infrastructure and personnel to produce timely and accurate weather forecasts, and enforcing laws that promote fair and secure trade.

- The Budget requests $9.8 billion for DOC (including changes in mandatory programs), a $546 million or a 6-percent increase from the 2017 enacted level.

---

## The President's 2019 Budget:

DOC contributes to U.S. economic growth and prosperity through a broad portfolio of business, data, and science-driven programs that are used by American companies, Government officials, and citizens for decision-making every day. The Budget focuses on supporting these core missions in ways that enhance economic security, national security, and technological leadership, and protect the taxpayer through streamlined and effective implementation.

Accordingly, the Budget provides strong support for high priority, mission-critical programs such as the 2020 Decennial Census, trade enforcement, intellectual property, weather and Earth observations, and spectrum management. In order to adequately fund these priorities, the Budget reduces funding for extramural grants, eliminates duplicative or unnecessary programs, and consolidates others. These choices support American prosperity, the national economy, and the interests of all taxpayers.

**Supports a Fair, Modern, and Accurate 2020 Decennial Census.** The Decennial Census is a constitutional requirement and DOC's highest priority in 2019. The Budget provides $3.8 billion, an increase of more than $2.3 billion, for the U.S. Census Bureau. This additional funding prioritizes fundamental investments in information technology and field infrastructure, which would allow the Bureau to continue preparations to conduct a modern, efficient, and accurate 2020 Decennial

Census. An accurate Decennial Census is imperative because of the important role this data plays in shaping the political landscape and informing the policy making process. Most importantly, the Decennial Census governs the apportionment of seats in the House of Representatives allocated to the States. In addition, Census data is used by governmental entities at the State and local levels for defining the representative boundaries for congressional districts, State legislative districts, school districts, and voting precincts. Further, Census data informs the allocation of slightly more than $675 billion annually in Federal funds to local communities, supporting a wide range of Federal and non-Federal policies, such as homeland security, education, and infrastructure. The Budget's substantial investment in the 2020 Decennial recognizes the importance of this program.

**Promotes Free and Fair Trade.** The Budget includes an additional $3 million for the Department's International Trade Administration (ITA) to expand and enhance the Department's efforts to level the global playing field for U.S. businesses, and provides slightly more than $90 million total for ITA's Enforcement and Compliance unit. This would allow ITA to conduct robust investigations into alleged trade violations, aggressively advocate for U.S. businesses facing tariff and non-tariff barriers abroad, and increase the capacity to closely review proposed foreign investments in U.S. businesses.

## Increasing Trade Enforcement

**The Administration has taken strong action to support its commitment to free and fair trade.**

| Trade Enforcement Activity | 2016 | 2017 |
|---|---|---|
| Anti-Dumping/ Countervailing Duty Investigations Initiated | 52 | 82 |
| Trade Agreement Compliance Cases Resolved Successfully | 39 | 47 |
| Trade Barriers Reduced, Removed or Prevented | 79 | 92 |

Source: DOC

In the first year of the Administration, the Department has already initiated almost 60 percent more anti-dumping and countervailing duty investigations than in the previous year. These investigations are key to stemming the surge of unfairly traded imports from entering the United States. The Department has also increased the number of successfully resolved trade agreement compliance cases by 21 percent and the number of trade barriers reduced, removed, or prevented by 16 percent compared to the previous year, demonstrating a commitment to holding trading partners accountable for their free trade commitments. The additional resources requested in the Budget would continue to support the Administration's aggressive approach to a global market that allows U.S. businesses to compete fairly.

**Protects Lives and Property.** Advance notice provided by weather forecasts enables the Nation's leaders, decision makers, and media to provide better warnings and advisories to first responders, the public, and businesses. Getting this right reduces the catastrophic loss of human life and property and the damaging effects on the national economy. Polar-orbiting satellites are critical to this mission, providing space-based observations that improve the accuracy of weather predictions. In recognition of the value these satellites provide, the Budget includes $878 million for the National Oceanic and Atmospheric Administration's (NOAA) polar weather satellites. These funds would allow NOAA to operate satellites currently in orbit and continue the development of its future polar orbiting satellites, reducing the risk of a devastating gap in coverage.

**Advances the Development of Next Generation Communications Technologies.** The Budget continues to support the National Telecommunications and Information Administration (NTIA) in representing the U.S. interest at multi-stakeholder forums on internet governance and digital commerce. The Budget supports the commercial sector's development of next generation wireless services, including 5G and the Internet of Things, by funding NTIA's mission of evaluating and ensuring the most efficient use of spectrum resources by Government users. Ensuring adequate access to scarce spectrum resources by both the commercial and Government sectors is a crucial factor for economic growth and national security.

**Modernizes Support for Minority Owned Businesses.** Minority owned businesses face unique challenges in obtaining the capital and support necessary to start and operate businesses. The Minority Business Development Agency (MBDA) within the Department of Commerce is solely dedicated to addressing these challenges and helping minority businesses thrive. To further this mission, the Budget proposes to reform the operations of MBDA to expand its reach and better help it meet its programmatic objectives. These reforms would eliminate the business outreach centers operated by MBDA, which are duplicative of programs operated by other Federal agencies, but would establish MBDA as a policy office that is positioned to advocate for minority businesses across all Federal programs.

**Eliminates Duplicative and Unnecessary Programs.** American prosperity depends on fiscal restraint to direct funding to the highest priorities. The Budget eliminates the Economic Development Administration, which provides small grants with limited measurable impacts and duplicates other Federal programs, such as Rural Utilities Service grants at the U.S. Department of Agriculture and formula grants to States from the Department of Transportation. By eliminating this Agency, the Budget reduces waste and saves approximately $300 million from the 2017 enacted level.

The Budget also eliminates Federal funding for the Manufacturing Extension Partnership (MEP) program, which subsidizes up to half the cost of State centers that provide consulting services to small- and medium-sized manufacturers. This proposal saves $125 million, and directs MEP centers to transition solely to non-Federal revenue sources as originally intended when the program was established.

# DEPARTMENT OF DEFENSE

---

**Highlights:**

- The Department of Defense (DOD) provides the military forces needed to deter war and to protect the security of the United States.

- Aligned with the new National Security and National Defense Strategies, the Budget expands the military's competitive space, builds a more lethal force, achieves greater performance at affordability and speed, and enhances posture for a more capable alliance and partnership network. The Budget is critical for protecting the homeland, promoting American prosperity, preserving peace through strength, and advancing American influence.

- The Budget requests $686 billion for DOD, an $80 billion or 13-percent increase from the 2017 enacted level. This includes $597 billion for the base budget, and $89 billion for Overseas Contingency Operations.

---

**The President's 2019 Budget:**

## *Preserves Peace through Strength*

The Budget requests the resources DOD needs to defend the homeland, remain the predominant military power in the world, maintain a world order that reflects America's values, support America's allies and partners, promote America's prosperity, and advance America's security interests. The United States faces an increasingly competitive and dangerous international security environment, characterized by the reemergence of great power competition with China and Russia, dangerous new technologies, empowered non-state actors, and the proliferation of weapons of mass destruction. The Budget requests resources needed to compete with great powers and others, deter conflict, and win the Nation's wars. The Budget builds a more lethal, ready, and larger joint force that, combined with a robust system of allies and partners, would sustain American influence and preserve stable regional balances of power that have proven conducive to peace and prosperity.

The Budget supports the Department's pursuit of innovation and reform, while making disciplined increases to sustain America's military advantage and to account for the long-term costs of contingencies. Over the 10-year budget window, funding for DOD is $1 trillion above projections from the previous administration, dramatically improving the warfighting ability of the joint force. Failure to provide adequate funding to meet these defense objectives would embolden America's enemies, thereby increasing the risk of armed conflict, and result in decreased U.S. influence which would erode alliances and partnerships, and reduced access to markets which would contribute to a decline in prosperity and standard of living.

**Compete—Deter—Win.** The surest way to prevent war is to be prepared to win one. The Budget promotes peace through strength, and continues multiyear investments to develop a lethal, agile, and resilient force. Long-term strategic competitions with China and Russia are the principal priorities for the Department. These competitions require both increased and sustained investment, reflected in the Budget request, because of the magnitude of the threats they pose to U.S. security and prosperity today, and the potential for those threats to increase in the future. Concurrently, the Budget requests funding for sustained DOD efforts to deter and counter rogue regimes such as North Korea and Iran, defeat terrorist threats to the United States, and consolidate gains in Iraq and Afghanistan while ensuring these approaches are resource-sustainable. The Budget ensures the United States can maintain a joint force that possesses decisive advantages for any likely conflict, while remaining proficient across the entire spectrum of conflict.

The Budget ensures that DOD has the right force posture and capabilities to account for the uncertainty that exists in the changing global strategic environment. Modern adversaries have built sophisticated anti-access and area-denial networks that require U.S. forces to rely on resiliency, lethality, speed, and surprise to win. The Budget prioritizes maintaining ready forces for major combat, while providing options for proactive and scalable employment of the joint force no matter what mission it is asked to undertake.

In addition, the Budget continues investments to increase U.S. defense posture and presence in the Indo-Pacific Region. The Budget supports the Department's long-term strategy of deterring Chinese military coercion and aggression in the Indo-Pacific region through strengthened forward presence. The Budget request provides the Department with the necessary armament, infrastructure, and logistics to address threats from North Korea, including missile defenses for America's homeland. In addition, the Budget strengthens relationships with allies and partners in the region through continued military exercises and security cooperation.

The Budget also requests the necessary resources to maintain the U.S.'s unwavering commitment to peace and security in Europe. The Budget requests more than $6.3 billion for DOD's European Deterrence Initiative (EDI), a multiyear program that is rebuilding a U.S. combat-credible forward military presence in Europe and building partner capacity in order to better counter Russian coercion and deter Russian aggression in the region. The EDI request maintains a robust heel-to-toe schedule for U.S. forces to train with and advise North Atlantic Treaty Organization (NATO) allies and partners, especially in Eastern Europe, and sustains the United States as a framework nation in NATO's Enhanced Forward Presence mission by maintaining a U.S. battalion in Poland. EDI would also increase prepositioned U.S. stocks, modernize Army equipment in Europe, enhance the Air Force's ability to rapidly scale operations in contested environments, harden communications and logistical infrastructure, catalyze front line allies' and partners' efforts to defend themselves, and provide $250 million to help Ukraine protect its territorial sovereignty.

The Budget supports a U.S. military presence in the Middle East necessary to protect the United States and its allies from terrorist attacks and preserve a favorable regional balance of power. The Budget would enable DOD to assist regional partners in strengthening their institutions and capabilities to conduct counterterrorism and counterinsurgency efforts, procure interoperable missile defense and other capabilities to better defend against active missile threats, and neutralize Iran's malign activities in the region.

**Builds a More Lethal, Resilient, and Agile Force for Great Power Competition.** The Budget begins what would be a sustained multiyear effort to transition the joint force from its post-Cold War mindset and posture toward a new paradigm of thinking about and preparing for the possibility of major war. History has taught us—from the Civil War through the World Wars of the 20th Century— that wars fought during periods of rapid technological change tend to be deadly and destructive in ways that had previously seemed unimaginable. The Budget begins the process of averting such a catastrophe by preparing the joint force to exploit new technologies and concepts to become more lethal, resilient, and agile.

- Lethality—the Budget invests in a variety of new weapons systems capable of delivering lethal fires in contested domains, while simultaneously developing leap-ahead systems that would enable the joint force to operate in new ways to defeat aggression in the future.

- Resilience—a powerful punch is meaningless if married to a glass jaw. The Budget therefore makes investments to ensure that the joint force can operate effectively while under attack in all domains. This includes investments to: harden and disperse forward bases and posture; make command and control, intelligence, surveillance, reconnaissance, position, navigation, and timing capabilities more resilient to attacks; improve countermeasures; and build up stockpiles of key munitions and materiel.

- Agility—as a global superpower with myriad responsibilities, the United States does not have the luxury of focusing on one problem at a time. The United States must be able to respond to a variety of contingencies simultaneously. While this poses a difficult challenge for the joint force, America's global posture, logistics and sustainment capabilities, and constellation of allies and partners gives the United States a unique advantage that no competitor or adversary can match. The Budget makes investments in logistics, sustainment, forces, and posture that would enable the joint force to operate with agility globally.

**Ensures the Readiness of U.S. Armed Forces.** The Budget provides the resources necessary to continue rebuilding military readiness, which has been degraded by budget reductions imposed by the Budget Control Act and more than 16 years of warfighting. Increased funding for the U.S. Army would modernize existing forces, provide additional training for U.S. soldiers, and establish new security assistance brigades to support counterterrorism efforts abroad. The Budget funds continuing efforts to improve Navy and Marine Corps aviation readiness, with increases for maintenance, spare parts, and flying hours. In response to recent Navy surface fleet incidents, the Budget requests more than $70 million in additional resources to enhance surface fleet equipment and training. The Budget also fully funds Air Force flight training, provides resources to alleviate pilot shortages, and invests in training for high-end combat to ensure the United States can effectively confront its most technologically advanced adversaries.

**Sustains the Defense Industrial Base.** At the direction of the President, DOD is undertaking a whole-of-Government assessment of the health and strength of America's manufacturing and defense industrial base and identifying any potential gaps in its capabilities. As part of this broad assessment, the Budget proposes to ensure sustained investment in the defense industrial base as a key component of economic and national security, recognizing that critical facilities, workforce skills, and the long-term health of the defense industrial base are fundamental to economic and national security.

**Modernizes the Nuclear Deterrent.** A tailored and flexible American nuclear deterrent is key to protecting national security and future prosperity for both the homeland and America's allies and partners. In line with the Nuclear Posture Review, the Budget supports a nuclear enterprise that is appropriately tailored to deter 21st Century threats. To that end, the Budget requests $24 billion to modernize and sustain the three legs of the nuclear triad—land, sea, and air—as well as nuclear command, control, and communications systems.

**Invests in Military Hardware to Meet the Challenges of Tomorrow.** The Budget makes significant investments in new, improved hardware to ensure that the Army, Air Force, Navy, and Marine Corps remain lethal and resilient even against technologically advanced adversaries. This includes funding to harden equipment against cyber-attacks. These investments include:

- Funding Cost-Effective Capabilities for Irregular Warfare and Counterterrorism—recognizing the enduring nature of irregular warfare and counterterrorism, the Budget requests funding to develop more cost-effective means of conducting these missions—including Army Security Force Assistance Brigades and Air Force affordable light-attack aircraft. The Budget also prioritizes efforts to ensure that the burden of responding to global crises is borne globally, rather than disproportionately by the people and the economy of the United States.

- Investing in Ground Combat Capabilities—the Budget funds critical ground combat capabilities including new investments in armored vehicles, long-range artillery, amphibious vehicles, rotorcraft, and munitions. The Budget accelerates the modernization of the Army's armored brigades to four over the five-year window and adds a 16th heavy combat team. The Budget also supports the Marine Corps' 24 active infantry battalions and 18 active MV-22 Osprey squadrons.

- Maintaining Control of the Seas—continuing the President's commitment to expand and rebuild the U.S. Navy fleet, the Budget increases the total number of ships by procuring 10 ships in 2019 to deter threats and maintain control of the sea.

- Developing and Procuring Advanced Aircraft—the Budget request supports continued development and procurement of advanced fighter aircraft, bombers, tankers, and other support aircraft. The Air Force's investment focuses on modernization of its tactical fighter aircraft fleet with the advanced F-35A stealth fighter, development of the next generation stealthy bomber, and procurement of the KC-46 aerial refueling tanker. The Budget would enable the Air Force to grow its fighter force from 55 combat squadrons to 58 squadrons by the end of the five-year planning period and would increase procurement of Air Force F-35 fighters from 250 in the five years of the 2018 Budget request to 258 in the five years of the 2019 Budget request. The Budget also accelerates the modernization of the existing F-16 fleet with active electronically scanned array antennas, radar warning systems, and the multifunctional information distribution Line 16 tactical airborne terminal system. The major priority for the Navy and Marine Corps is to modernize their fighter aircraft fleets with procurement of the F-35B and C, and to reduce the strike fighter shortfall through procurement of additional F/A-18E/Fs.

**Innovates at the Speed of Relevance.** Worldwide advances in technology are regularly changing the nature of the threats America faces and proliferating threats to new actors. Nations that are best able to adapt and integrate new technologies—in order to create speed and surprise across multiple domains in the fight—would prevail. The Budget's key areas of focus include artificial intelligence, autonomous systems, and hypersonics. The Budget requests more than $84 billion in research, engineering, and prototyping activities to maintain technical superiority.

**Grows the Military.** The Budget increases military personnel by 16,400 servicemembers compared to the end strength level authorized in the National Defense Authorization Act for 2018. These additional servicemembers would allow DOD to fill gaps in combat formations and serve as critical enablers in America's national defense strategy.

**Invests in Innovative Defense Intelligence Capabilities**. The Budget restores funding to combat support agencies to improve intelligence support to the warfighter and grows the analytical capacity at the Combatant Command Intelligence Centers. The Budget invests in intelligence, surveillance, and reconnaissance capabilities that would expand the competitive space through a more lethal, rapidly innovating defense intelligence enterprise.

**Bolsters Missile Defenses.** The Budget supports the President's initiative to accelerate and expand urgent missile defeat and defense enhancements, and continues priority investments proposed by the Administration and enacted by the Congress in the Department of Defense Missile Defeat and Defense Enhancements Appropriations Act, 2018. The Budget increases the capability and capacity of the United States to detect, defeat, and defend against any North Korean use of ballistic missiles against the United States, its deployed forces, allies, and partners. For missile defense, the Budget supports the procurement of 20 additional Ground-Based Interceptors (GBIs). The Administration plans to increase the number of deployed GBIs to 64, including the new GBI missile field at Fort Greely, Alaska, to protect the homeland against North Korean and other intermediate- and long-range ballistic missile threats.

**Prevents the Resurgence of the Islamic State of Iraq and Syria (ISIS), al Qaeda, and other Jihadist Terrorists.** The Budget requests the funding necessary to ensure the lasting defeat of ISIS. Building on ISIS's territorial defeat in Iraq and Syria, DOD would prevent any resurgence by working with partner forces and agencies to stabilize liberated cities, secure borders, retain territorial control, and disrupt ISIS's capability to attack the U.S. homeland and America's allies. The Budget also requests funding for DOD to address the threat from ISIS branches outside Iraq and Syria, and to protect the United States against a resurgence of al Qaeda.

**Promotes Stability and Security in South Asia.** The Budget furthers the U.S. goal of a stable and secure South Asia by supporting the Afghan government and security forces in their fight against Taliban insurgents and jihadist terrorist organizations such as al Qaeda and ISIS. The Budget requests more than $5 billion for continued U.S. training and assistance for the Afghan security forces and would enable U.S. forces to conduct counterterrorism operations to ensure that the region cannot be used by jihadist terrorist groups to plot transnational attacks against the U.S. homeland, citizens overseas, or allies and partners. The Budget also continues to include funding to support America's partnership with Pakistan, contingent on Pakistan taking appropriate action to expand cooperation in areas where interests converge and to address areas of divergence, in line with the Administration's South Asia strategy.

**Renews the Nation's Leadership and Freedom of Action in Space.** The Budget accelerates investments in space situational awareness, the Global Positioning System, defensive measures, and other areas to improve the resiliency of DOD space systems in the face of increasing adversarial threats. In combination with architectural diversity and proliferation, the Budget preserves space capabilities for national leaders and combatant commanders in order to maintain strategic stability and ensure battlefield dominance across the spectrum of conflict.

**Prioritizes Cyber Activities.** The Budget continues to place a high priority on cyber security and those responsible for providing it by requesting more than $8 billion in 2019 to advance DOD's three primary cyber missions: safeguarding DOD's networks, information and systems; supporting military commander objectives; and defending the Nation. This investment would also provide the necessary resources to sustain the 133 Cyber Mission Force (CMF) teams established at Cyber Command. Since their inception in 2013, the CMF teams have grown in capability and capacity, and all teams are on track to be fully operational by the end of 2018.

### *Enhances the Quality of Life of Servicemembers and their Families*

**Provides Fair Compensation for Servicemembers and Supporting Military Families.** Military compensation must be competitive to recruit and retain the most qualified men and women to serve in an All-Volunteer Force. The Budget proposes a calendar year 2019 military pay raise of 2.6 percent—the largest increase since 2010. The Budget also requests funding for a full range of compensation programs, from monthly incentive pays to recently expanded retirement benefits. In addition, the Budget requests funding to continue important programs that improve the quality of life for military families, and ensure they receive the support they need throughout every stage of their family members' service.

**Improves TRICARE.** DOD continues to modernize TRICARE to provide greater flexibility and access to medical care for servicemembers and their families. TRICARE Select would replace TRICARE Standard and Extra. As a result, beneficiaries would notice improved coverage for preventive services with TRICARE. The current three Managed Care Regions would be combined into two Managed Care Regions, providing beneficiaries expanded access to network providers. The rollout of GENESIS, DOD's integrated medical and dental electronic health record, would accelerate the sharing of patients' records across military treatment facilities and provide an electronic health record that focuses on quality, safety, and patient outcomes.

### *Drives Resource Discipline and Accountability*

**Reforms the Department to Reinvest Resources in Warfighter Priorities.** DOD management and support functions must enable and empower the warfighter with the knowledge, equipment, and support systems to fight and win the Nation's wars. DOD will adapt its organizational and support structures to best support the joint force and achieve savings that can be reinvested in higher priority needs, such as force readiness and modernization. For example, DOD is leveraging the scale of its operations to drive greater efficiency in procurement of materials and services, saving billions in 2019. At the same time, DOD is pursuing opportunities to consolidate and streamline contracts for logistics, information technology, and other support services. The Department will also identify options to reduce excess property and infrastructure.

**Audits the Department.** Better management begins with effective financial stewardship. With more than $2.4 trillion in assets spread across 26 stand-alone reporting entities, the Department's full financial statement audit is the largest ever undertaken by an agency of the U.S. Government. DOD has committed to performing annual financial statement audits to bolster accountability and public confidence in the Department's fiscal discipline and to modernize its business practices and systems. The Budget will mark the release of results from DOD's first-ever consolidated financial statement audit. The Department anticipates this audit will identify procedural and system deficiencies, consistent with the initial audits of other large Chief Financial Officers Act agencies and not unusual for an audit of this scale and complexity. Accordingly, DOD has shifted its focus from audit preparation to remediation of audit findings. Upon release of the audit report, the Department will address findings by holding the military departments and defense agencies accountable for the development and implementation of their corrective actions, with a goal of meaningful, persistent progress toward a clean audit opinion. Armed with audit findings and remediation plans, DOD will provide more sound data to inform decision-making, while enhancing internal controls and business procedures to improve efficiency and effectiveness.

# DEPARTMENT OF EDUCATION

**Highlights:**

- The Department of Education promotes excellence and access to opportunity in elementary, secondary, and postsecondary education. The Department focuses its mission on supporting States and school districts in their efforts to provide high-quality education to all students, on streamlining and simplifying funding for college, and on expanding access to new postsecondary options.

- The Budget maintains funding for essential K-12 formula grant programs that support the Nation's neediest students, while also delivering on the President's commitment to ensure that every child has the opportunity to attend a high-quality school that meets their unique educational needs.

- The Budget proposes to ensure students can successfully pursue various pathways of postsecondary education and training. The Budget invests in career and technical education, streamlines student loan repayment, and offers the opportunity to use Pell Grants for high-quality, short-term training.

- The Budget requests $59.9 billion for the Department of Education, a $7.1 billion or 10.5-percent decrease from the 2017 enacted level.

## The President's 2019 Budget:

Quality education exists when parents have a voice in choosing their child's K-12 schools and students have the tools they need to succeed. Decades of investments and billions of dollars in spending have shown that an increase in funding does not guarantee high-quality education. While the Budget reduces the overall Federal role in education, the Budget makes strategic investments to support and empower families and improve access to postsecondary education, ensuring a future of prosperity for all Americans.

### *K-12 Education*

The Budget request for elementary and secondary education reflects the restoration of local control in education provided by the Congress in the reauthorization of the Elementary and Secondary Education Act (ESEA) by the Every Student Succeeds Act (ESSA). ESSA reauthorized the ESEA for the first time in 14 years and recognized that the primary responsibility for creating, improving, and sustaining education systems lies with States and local school districts. The Budget builds on these principles by ensuring the Department focuses on returning decision-making power back to States and districts and by giving parents more control over addressing their child's unique education needs.

The Budget maintains funding for essential formula grant programs that support the Nation's neediest students, including those in low-income communities and students with disabilities. The Budget also streamlines and refocuses the Federal investment in K-12 education by eliminating funding for 17 programs totaling $4.4 billion that are duplicative, ineffective, or more appropriately supported through State, local, or private funds.

**Empowers Families to Choose the Schools that are Best for Their Children.** The Budget invests $1.1 billion in school choice programs to expand the range of high-quality public and private school options for students, putting more decision-making power in the hands of parents and families. This investment serves as a down payment toward achieving the President's goal of an annual Federal investment of $20 billion—for a total of an estimated $100 billion when including matching State and local funds—in school choice funding. The Budget requests $500 million to establish a new school choice grant program to support a wide range of innovative approaches to school choice. These include expanding existing private school choice programs to serve more low-income and at-risk students, developing new private school choice models, or supporting school districts' efforts to adopt student-based budgeting and open enrollment policies that enable Federal, State and local funding to follow the student to the public school of his or her choice. In addition, States and districts would have opportunities to leverage funding from Title I grants to support public school choice. The Budget requests $500 million to fund the opening, expansion, and replication of high-quality public charter schools and the financing of charter school facilities. The Budget invests $98 million to expand the number of public magnet schools, which offer specialized curricula and instructional programming. In addition, the Tax Cut and Jobs Act expands school choice by enabling families to use 529 savings plans to pay for private school tuition and home schooling costs.

**Provides High-Quality Special Education Services to Children with Disabilities.** To support State and local education agencies in providing high-quality special education services to more than 6.8 million children with disabilities, the Budget maintains the Federal investment in the Individuals with Disabilities Education Act (IDEA) formula and discretionary grant programs. The Budget invests $12.8 billion for IDEA formula grants to States to support special education and early intervention services. In addition, the Budget requests $222 million for discretionary grants to States, institutions of higher education, and other nonprofit organizations to support research, demonstrations, technical assistance and dissemination, and personnel preparation and development. These investments would ensure that high-quality special education and related services would meet the unique needs of children with disabilities and their families.

**Supports Implementation of School-based Opioid Abuse Prevention Strategies.** The opioid crisis has devastated families across the United States and strained the capacity of schools in affected communities to meet the academic and mental health needs of their students. To address these issues, the Budget invests $43 million for School Climate Transformation grants to help school districts implement multi-tiered, evidence-based strategies to prevent opioid misuse and address associated behavioral and academic challenges through interventions such as trauma counseling, violence prevention, and targeted academic support. This funding would also support technical assistance centers that develop and provide opioid abuse prevention and treatment resources that would be publicly available to all schools and institutions of higher education.

### Higher Education

The Budget continues support for Federal programs that help prepare low-income and minority students for postsecondary education, targeted student financial aid that helps students and families pay rising college costs, and programs that strengthen postsecondary institutions serving large proportions of minority students. The Budget also includes proposals that address student debt by simplifying student loan repayment and redirecting inefficiencies in the student loan program to prioritize debt relief for undergraduate borrowers. These proposals would support congressional efforts to reauthorize the Higher Education Act to address student debt and higher education costs while reducing the complexity of student financial aid.

**Requires Colleges and Universities to Have Shared Accountability for Repayment of Federal Student Loans.** Investing in higher education generally provides strong value for students and taxpayers. However, some institutions consistently fail to deliver a quality education that enables students to successfully repay Federal student loans—leaving borrowers and taxpayers holding the bill. A better system would require postsecondary institutions accepting taxpayer funds to share a portion of the financial risk associated with student loans, in consideration of the actual loan repayment rate to ensure that the substantial taxpayer investment in higher education continues to provide strong value for students and the economy. The Administration looks forward to working with the Congress to address these issues.

**Reforms Student Loan Programs.** In recent years, income-driven repayment (IDR) plans, which offer student borrowers the option of making affordable monthly payments based on factors such as income and family size, have grown in popularity. However, the numerous IDR plans currently offered to borrowers overly complicate choosing and enrolling in the right plan. The Budget proposes to streamline student loan repayment by consolidating multiple IDR plans into a single plan. The single IDR plan would cap a borrower's monthly payment at 12.5 percent of discretionary income. For undergraduate borrowers, any balance remaining after 15 years of repayment would be forgiven. For borrowers with any graduate debt, any balance remaining after 30 years of repayment would be forgiven.

To support this streamlined pathway to debt relief for undergraduate borrowers, and to generate savings that help put the Nation on a more sustainable fiscal path, the Budget eliminates the Public Service Loan Forgiveness program, establishes reforms to guarantee that all borrowers in IDR pay an equitable share of their income, and eliminates subsidized loans. To further improve the implementation and effectiveness of IDR, the Budget proposes auto-enrolling severely delinquent borrowers and instituting a process for borrowers to consent to share income data for multiple years. To facilitate these program improvements and to reduce improper payments, the Budget proposes to streamline the Department of Education's ability to verify applicants' income data held by the Internal Revenue Service. These student loan reforms would reduce inefficiencies and waste in the student loan program, and focus assistance on needy undergraduate student borrowers instead of high-income, high-balance graduate borrowers. All student loan proposals would apply to loans originating on or after July 1, 2019, except those provided to borrowers to finish their current course of study.

**Expands Pell Grant Eligibility for Short-Term Programs.** There are many paths to a successful career in addition to a four-year degree. The Budget expands Pell Grant eligibility to include high-quality short-term programs. This would help low-income and out-of-work individuals access training programs that can equip them with skills to secure well-paying jobs in high-demand fields more quickly than traditional two-year or four-year degree programs.

**Improves Grantmaking and Maintains Support for Minority-Serving Institutions (MSIs) and Historically Black Colleges and Universities (HBCUs).** The Budget maintains important investments to support improvements in academic quality, institutional management and capacity, infrastructure, and student support services for MSIs and HBCUs. In particular, the Budget proposes to improve grantmaking by consolidating six MSI programs into a $147.9 million formula grant, providing funds more institutions can count on and yielding program management efficiencies. The Budget continues to recognize the extraordinary contributions of HBCUs and requests more than

$642 million to support HBCU-focused programs that strengthen their capacity to provide the highest quality education.

**Invests in Evidence-Based Postsecondary Preparation Programs.** The Budget proposes to restructure and streamline the TRIO and GEAR UP programs by consolidating them into a $550 million State formula grant. These grants would support evidence-based postsecondary preparation programs designed to help low-income students progress through the pipeline from middle school to postsecondary opportunities. Given the statutory prohibition limiting the Department's ability to evaluate overall TRIO program effectiveness using the most rigorous methodologies, as well as budget constraints, the Budget supports a restructuring of the programs that leverages evidence-based activities and allows States more flexibility in meeting the unique needs of their students.

**Supports a Reauthorized Higher Education Act (HEA).** The Administration looks forward to working with the Congress to encourage colleges, universities, and other educational institutions to offer every student an accessible, affordable, and innovative education tailored to their needs that prepares them for lifelong learning and success. The Administration's principles for an HEA reauthorization include:

- expand Pell Grant eligibility for short-term programs;

- reform Federal student loan and repayment options;

- recalibrate the grant allocation process;

- ensure institutional accountability;

- reduce regulatory burdens;

- improve transparency;

- offer administrative updates and financial flexibility; and

- promote free speech on college campuses.

## *Workforce*

In today's rapidly changing economy, it is more important than ever to prepare workers to fill both existing and newly created jobs and to prepare workers for the jobs of the future. The U.S. education system must provide access to affordable and quality education and training that includes career and vocational tracks. The Budget supports reforms to programs that would help students graduate with the skills necessary to secure high-paying jobs in today's workforce and contribute to the Nation's robust economy.

**Supports Career and Technical Education (CTE).** As part of the Administration's commitment to supporting the Nation's workforce, the Budget maintains $1.1 billion in funding for CTE. This investment recognizes that students should have access to a full menu of postsecondary educational options including certificate programs, community colleges, and apprenticeships. At the secondary and postsecondary levels, CTE prepares students with the skills necessary to succeed in a broad array of careers and provides an alternate pathway to a traditional four-year degree. The Administration also looks forward to working with the Congress to reauthorize the Carl D. Perkins Act. The Administration's principles for Perkins reauthorization include ensuring that CTE programs prepare students for careers in science, technology, engineering, and mathematics fields and other high-demand areas; promoting partnerships between schools, businesses, and other community organizations; and expanding access to apprenticeship and other work-based learning.

**Revamps Federal Work Study to Emphasize Workforce Development.** The Budget proposes to reform the Federal Work Study program to support workforce and career-oriented training opportunities for low-income undergraduate students, not just subsidized employment as a means of financial aid, in order to create pathways to high-paying jobs. The program would allocate funds to schools based in part on enrollment of Pell recipients. Schools could fund individual students through subsidized employment, paid internships, or other designs, so long as the placements were career or academically relevant. Schools could also fund broader programs that serve multiple students that expose students to or build their preparedness for careers.

**Promotes Science, Technology, Engineering, and Mathematics (STEM) Education.** Consistent with the 2017 Presidential Memorandum on STEM education, the Budget provides a path forward to direct at least $200 million to STEM education. Supporting STEM education is imperative to better equip America's young people with the relevant knowledge and skills that would enable them to secure high-paying, stable jobs throughout their careers. As the role of technology grows in driving the American economy, many jobs will increasingly require skills in STEM. The Budget supports STEM education through a variety of programs including those that test and replicate what works in education and a new, $20 million grant program for STEM-focused career and technical education programs.

> *"As part of my Administration's commitment to supporting American workers and increasing economic growth and prosperity, it is critical that we educate and train our future workforce to compete and excel in lucrative and important STEM fields."*
>
> STEM Presidential Memorandum
> September 25, 2017

**Modernizes and Makes Government More Efficient.** The Budget reflects a number of reform proposals aimed at streamlining the Department of Education's internal organization and improving the Department's services to States, districts, postsecondary institutions, and the public, while reducing its workforce.

The Budget supports Federal Student Aid (FSA) in undertaking a monumental student loan servicing upgrade. FSA is reorganizing its fragmented servicing and operating infrastructure in order to provide an innovative, world-class financial services experience for its customers. The Next Generation Financial Services Environment at FSA will start with a mobile-first, mobile-complete engagement layer for all customer interactions that will link with an integrated but nimble new system. Integrated into every aspect of this modernization effort will be state-of-the-art cybersecurity protection. This technical reorganization and modernization effort will provide better service for the over 40 million customers served by FSA, including students and institutions, across the student loan lifecycle. The new environment will help increase awareness and understanding of Federal student aid opportunities and responsibilities, improve FSA's operational flexibility, and enhance cost and operational efficiency, producing better outcomes for students and taxpayers.

**Reduces Waste: Streamlines or Eliminates Ineffective or Redundant Programs.** The Budget eliminates funding for 29 discretionary programs that do not address national needs, duplicate other programs, are ineffective, or are more appropriately supported with State, local, or private funds. These eliminations would decrease taxpayer costs by $5.9 billion and include the Supporting Effective Instruction State Grants, 21st Century Community Learning Centers, and Federal Supplemental Educational Opportunity Grant programs.

The Budget also reduces funding or consolidates 13 programs to yield program management efficiencies, focus on activities that are supported by the highest levels of available evidence, and empower

States and local entities to meet the unique needs of their students. These efficiencies for programs such as those supporting Minority Serving Institutions, TRIO, GEAR UP, and Federal Work Study would reduce costs by $1.8 billion and support more targeted and effective uses of Federal resources. Overall, the Budget reduces waste in 41 discretionary programs, saving taxpayers more than $7.7 billion.

# DEPARTMENT OF ENERGY

---

**Highlights:**

• The mission of the Department of Energy is to advance U.S. security and economic growth through transformative science and technology innovation that promotes affordable and reliable energy and meets America's nuclear security and environmental clean-up challenges.

• The Budget protects American prosperity by making strategic investments to maintain global leadership in scientific and technological innovation and aggressively modernize the nuclear security enterprise that underpins the safety and security of Americans, both at home and abroad.

• The Budget requests $29 billion for DOE, a more than 3-percent decrease from the 2017 enacted level.

---

**The President's 2019 Budget:**

American leadership in science and technology is critical to achieving the Administration's highest priorities: national security; economic growth; and job creation. American ingenuity combined with free-market capitalism have driven, and will continue to drive, tremendous technological breakthroughs. The Budget for the Department of Energy (DOE) demonstrates the Administration's commitment to American energy dominance, making hard choices, and reasserting the proper role of the Federal Government. The Budget focuses resources on early-stage research and development (R&D) of energy technologies and reflects an increased reliance on the private sector to fund later-stage demonstration and commercialization activities. In so doing, the Budget emphasizes energy technologies best positioned to enable American energy independence and domestic job-growth in the near- to mid-term.

The Budget also reflects the critical role DOE has in protecting the safety and security of the American people, including by ensuring that nuclear and radiological materials worldwide remain secured against theft by those who might use them against the U.S. homeland or U.S. interests abroad. The Budget funds the modernization of nuclear weapons and ensures that the U.S. nuclear force is second-to-none. The Budget ensures continued progress on cleaning up sites contaminated from nuclear weapons production, and energy R&D. The Budget also continues support for a robust interim storage program and the licensing of the Yucca Mountain geologic repository, demonstrating the Administration's commitment to nuclear waste management.

In addition to the priorities laid out below, the Budget proposes the elimination of the Title XVII Innovative Technology Loan Guarantee Program, the Advanced Technology Vehicle Manufacturing Loan Program, and the Tribal Energy Loan Guarantee Program because the private sector is better positioned to finance the deployment of commercially viable energy and advanced vehicle manufacturing projects. The Budget also proposes the elimination of Advanced Research Projects Agency-Energy, recognizing the private sector's primary role in taking risks to commercialize breakthrough energy technologies with real market potential.

The Budget includes several reforms that realign, consolidate, or merge functions within the Department to improve efficiency and effectiveness, such as the consolidation of program-level international affairs activities into a single headquarters office. In addition, the Budget proposes a realignment of DOE program offices to elevate cybersecurity and energy security as priorities within the Department, with the goal of ensuring the security of the American people. DOE is also committed to eliminating waste, fraud, and abuse. For example, the Budget would avoid $10 to $12 billion in waste by terminating construction of the Mixed Oxide Fuel Fabrication Facility in favor of a plutonium disposition alternative. DOE will also continue to improve contract management and oversight to address potential fraud and abuse risks raised by the Government Accountability Office.

**Modernizes the Nuclear Arsenal.** The Budget for DOE nuclear security programs is aligned with Department of Defense requirements for deterring 21st Century threats and reassuring U.S. allies and partners. The Budget increases investments in the nuclear stockpile to guarantee it is modern, robust, flexible, safe, and effective. Specifically, the Budget supports completing production of the W76-1 Life Extension Program (LEP), preparing the B61-12 LEP and the W88 Alteration 370 for production in 2020, and continuing development of the W80-4 LEP.

**Revitalizes the Nuclear Security Enterprise's Aging Infrastructure.** Safe, secure, and modern infrastructure at the National Nuclear Security Administration's (NNSA) national laboratories, production plants, and Nevada National Security Site is essential to maintaining the U.S. nuclear deterrent and accomplishing DOE's other national security missions. The Budget makes significant investments in design and construction of facilities, with an emphasis on infrastructure related to strategic materials (e.g., uranium, plutonium, tritium, lithium) that are critical to the nuclear weapons stockpile. NNSA infrastructure is also an important part of a whole-of-government approach to supply chain assurance in microelectronics. NNSA must have a modern, secure, streamlined complex that would meet military requirements, keep the nuclear deterrent safe and effective, and enhance worker and public safety.

**Reduces Global Nuclear Threats.** Nuclear terrorism and the spread of nuclear weapons constitute two of the most critical threats to American safety and prosperity. The Budget invests in nonproliferation, counterterrorism, and emergency response programs to provide for the safety and security of the American people. The Budget accelerates the Cesium Irradiator Replacement Program, which would reduce the threat of radiological terrorism by permanently removing cesium sources that could be used in dirty bombs. The Budget begins procurement of replacement aircraft for NNSA's Aerial Measuring System to ensure the Nation maintains its radiation detection capabilities for emergency preparedness and response missions. In addition, the Budget supports the removal of additional nuclear materials from around the world and helping countries develop strong programs to secure those that remain, reducing opportunities for terrorists to acquire such material for use in a nuclear weapon.

**Maintains Safe Naval Nuclear Propulsion.** The Budget provides $1.8 billion to support a strong U.S. Navy through NNSA's Naval Reactors (NR) program. NR works to provide the U.S. Navy with safe, reliable nuclear propulsion plants for submarines and aircraft carriers. The Budget includes major investments to modernize NR's spent fuel handling infrastructure and develop the reactor systems for the *Columbia*-class ballistic missile submarine.

**Supports Cutting-Edge Research and Invests in Leading Scientific User Facilities to Enable Future Breakthroughs in Energy.** The Budget provides $4.2 billion for the Office of Science to continue its mission to focus on early-stage research, operate the national laboratories, and continue high priority construction projects. Within this amount, $445 million is for Exascale computing to help secure a global leadership role in supercomputing. The Budget would continue to ensure access to critical scientific user facilities including $100 million for the Long Baseline Neutrino Facility/Deep Underground Neutrino Experiment and $75 million to complete the Facility for Rare Isotope Beams.

**Continues Support for Cyber and Energy Security Initiatives across the Department.** Ranging from cybersecurity of the electrical grid to prioritization of early-stage R&D focused on hardening energy infrastructure, the Budget prioritizes the energy security for all Americans through continued investments that address cyber threats across the Nation's electrical grid. To ensure robust cybersecurity programs across the energy sector, the Budget Request provides funding in multiple programs, including slightly more than $95 million in the reorganized Office of Cybersecurity, Energy Security, and Emergency Response with a renewed focus on early-stage activities that improve cybersecurity and resilience to harden and evolve critical grid infrastructure. These activities include early-stage R&D at national laboratories to develop the next generation of cybersecurity control systems, components, and devices including a greater ability to share time-critical data with industry to detect, prevent, and recover from cyber events.

**Unleashes an Era of Energy Dominance through Strategic Support for Innovation.** The United States has among the most abundant and diverse energy resources in the world, including oil, gas, coal, nuclear, and renewables. The ability of entrepreneurs and businesses to commercialize technologies that take full advantage of those resources is paramount to promoting U.S. economic growth, security, and competitiveness. That is why the Budget provides more than $1.7 billion across the applied energy programs at DOE, which support early-stage R&D that enables the private sector to deploy the next generation of technologies and energy services that usher in a more secure, resilient, and integrated energy system.

> "When it comes to the future of America's energy needs, we will find it, we will dream it, and we will build it."
>
> President Donald J. Trump
> June 29, 2017

Within this amount, the Budget provides $757 million for the Office of Nuclear Energy, prioritizing support for early-stage R&D on advanced reactor technologies, including small modular reactors, and advanced instrumentation and manufacturing methods. The Budget also provides more than $300 million for R&D by the Office of Fossil Energy to support national laboratory research on clean, efficient fossil fuels and systems, and bolster early-stage critical materials R&D. In addition, the Budget provides more than $180 million for the Department's Grid Modernization Initiative, a joint effort funded by the Office of Electricity Delivery, the Office of Energy Efficiency and Renewable Energy, and the new Office of Cybersecurity, Energy Security, and Emergency Response. The initiative aims to maintain progress on innovative technologies and operational approaches for achieving a more reliable, resilient, and secure electricity delivery system integrated with energy storage, renewable generation, smart buildings, and electric vehicles.

**Implements Reforms in the Environmental Management Program to Accelerate Clean Up of Waste and Contamination from Nuclear Weapons Production.** The Budget includes $6.6 billion for 16 sites remaining to be completed. The Budget provides $150 million to carry forward the 2018 Budget initiative to accelerate deactivation and decommissioning of selected high-risk excess facilities to protect human health and the environment, and support modernization of the Nuclear Security Enterprise.

**Proposes to Divest Federally Owned and Operated Transmission Assets and Authorize the Power Marketing Administrations (PMAs) to Charge Market Based Rates for Power.** The Budget proposes to sell the transmission assets owned and operated by PMAs, including those of Southwestern Power Administration, Western Area Power Administration, and Bonneville Power Administration. The Budget also proposes to authorize PMAs to charge rates based on comparable rates charged by for-profit investor-owned utilities, rather than being limited to cost-based rates, for electricity. The vast majority of the Nation's electricity needs are met through investor owned utilities. Reducing or eliminating the Federal Government's role in electricity transmission infrastructure ownership—thereby increasing the private sector's role—and introducing more market-based incentives, including rates, for power sales from Federal dams, would encourage a more efficient allocation of economic resources and mitigate risk to taxpayers.

# DEPARTMENT OF HEALTH AND HUMAN SERVICES

---

**Highlights:**

- The Department of Health and Human Services (HHS) works to enhance the health and well-being of Americans by providing effective health and human services and by fostering sound, sustained advances in the sciences underlying medicine, public health, and social services.

- The Budget supports critical investments to enable HHS to deliver on its mission, while also reducing funding or eliminating programs that are ineffective, inefficient, or duplicative. The Budget saves taxpayer dollars and helps move toward the President's vision of an accountable Government that is effective and efficient in its delivery of programs.

- The Budget addresses some of the Nation's most pressing public health needs, investing in efforts to combat the devastating opioid epidemic, making new investments in programs to treat individuals suffering from severe mental illness, and accelerating work on ending infectious diseases. The Budget invests in biomedical research, increases accountability for research dollars, and enhances the Government's preparedness for responding to infectious disease outbreaks or other man-made disasters. The Budget also includes proposals to lower drug costs, strengthen and protect the Medicare program, repeal and replace Obamacare, and provide States more flexibility in Medicaid.

- The Budget continues to invest in key programs and proposes innovative solutions that promote child well-being, build stronger families, and help low-income Americans move from welfare to work.

- The Budget requests $68.4 billion for HHS, a $17.9 billion or 21-percent decrease from the 2017 enacted level. This Budget funding level includes additional funds for program integrity and implementing the 21st Century CURES Act and the 2017 enacted funding levels do not include actual fee collections and contract support costs. The Budget proposes $295 billion in mandatory savings, helping to put Federal spending on a sustainable path. In addition, the Budget includes $675 billion in net mandatory savings across HHS and the Department of the Treasury to repeal and replace Obamacare.

---

**The President's 2019 Budget:**

The Budget shows a clear commitment to a better future for all Americans and funds the highest priority HHS activities, such as addressing the opioid crisis, serious mental illness, and emergency preparedness. The Budget strengthens Medicare, repeals and replaces Obamacare, comprehensively reforms Medicaid, and includes a strong focus on program integrity for all health programs.

The Budget delivers on the President's vision to reorganize the Government to improve efficiency, effectiveness, and accountability by putting forward proposals to reorganize HHS. These include: improving the management of the Strategic National Stockpile; streamlining the administrative functions at the National Institutes of Health (NIH); and improving efficiency through examining the effectiveness of the U.S. Public Health Service Commissioned Corps. The Budget also integrates the research of three programs—the Agency for Healthcare Research and Quality, the National Institute for Occupational Safety and Health, and the National Institute on Disability, Independent Living, and Rehabilitation—within NIH to improve coordination and outcomes. Initially, these activities would be established as separate Institutes, but NIH will assess the feasibility of integrating these research activities more fully into existing NIH Institutes and Centers over time.

**Combats the Opioid Epidemic.** The Budget significantly strengthens efforts to combat the opioid epidemic by including $5 billion in new resources over the next five years. Approximately 64,000 people died in 2016 as the result of drug overdoses, the largest increase in drug deaths ever recorded in a single year in the United States. Deaths from drug overdoses have almost doubled in the last 10 years, and drug overdose is the leading cause of unintentional injury deaths for Americans under the age of 50. A major driver of this crisis is opioids, a class of drugs that includes both legal and illicit drugs such as certain prescription painkillers, heroin, and synthetic opioids such as fentanyl.

The Budget builds upon the Administration's continued efforts—in 2017, the Administration declared a nationwide public health emergency and provided nearly $500 million to States to prevent and treat opioid abuse and addiction; in addition, the 2018 Budget requested another $500 million. The Budget requests $1 billion in new resources for 2019 and a total of $5 billion over the next five years to combat the opioid epidemic by preventing abuse and helping those who are addicted get access to overdose reversal drugs, treatment, and recovery support services.

The Administration will increase awareness of the dangers of opioids through a national media campaign,

---

**Where to find help for addiction to opioids and other substances**

The Substance Abuse and Mental Health Service Administration's National Helpline, 1-800-662-HELP (4357) provides a free, 24-hour-a-day, 365-day-a-year, information (in English and Spanish) for individuals and family members facing mental illness and/or substance abuse issues. This confidential service provides referrals to local treatment facilities, support groups, and community-based organizations. Callers can also order free publications and other information. Callers are not asked for any personal information other than their zip code or other geographic information in order to accurately identify the local resources appropriate to the caller's needs. Referral information can also be searched online at *https://findtreatment.samhsa.gov/*.

---

encourage safer prescribing practices to reduce unnecessary prescriptions, and help States improve their Prescription Drug Monitoring Programs. The Administration will continue its work to develop innovative technologies to replace the use of opioids in pain management and to prevent addiction to opioids. In addition, the Administration supports more rigorous research to better understand how existing programs or policies might be contributing to or mitigating the opioid epidemic.

For Medicaid, the Budget proposes expanding coverage of comprehensive and evidence-based Medication Assisted Treatment options, previews forthcoming guidance from the Centers for Medicare & Medicaid Services (CMS) that would set minimum standards for State Drug Utilization Reviews to reduce clinical abuse, and requires States to track and act on high prescribers and utilizers of prescription drugs.

For Medicare, the Budget proposes to test and expand nationwide a bundled payment for community-based medication assisted treatment, including, for the first time, comprehensive Medicare reimbursement for methadone treatment. The Budget also proposes to prevent prescription drug abuse in Medicare Part D and protect beneficiaries from potentially harmful drugs by requiring plan participation in a program to prevent prescription drug abuse, which would promote sound public health policy and help keep premiums down for seniors.

In addition, the Budget proposes to authorize the Secretary to work with the Drug Enforcement Administration to revoke a provider's certificate (which allows a provider to prescribe controlled substances) when that provider is barred from billing Medicare based on a pattern of abusive prescribing.

**Reforms Drug Pricing and Payment.** The goal of the Administration's comprehensive strategy is to address the problem of high drug prices, provide greater access to lifesaving medical products, and ensure that the United States remains the leader in biomedical innovation. The Budget proposes new strategies to address high drug prices, increase access to lifesaving medicines, rationalize the current payment incentive structure in Medicare Part D and Part B, and foster greater competition among generic pharmaceutical firms.

- Tests Innovative Medicaid Drug Coverage and Financing Reforms—the Budget calls for new Medicaid demonstration authority for up to five States to test drug coverage and financing reforms that build on private sector best practices. Participating States would determine their own drug formularies, coupled with an appeals process to protect beneficiary access to non-covered drugs based on medical need, and negotiate drug prices directly with manufacturers. HHS and participating States would rigorously evaluate these demonstrations, which would provide States with new tools to control drug costs and tailor drug coverage decisions to State needs.

- Speeds Development of More Affordable Generics—the Budget proposes to give the Food and Drug Administration (FDA) greater ability to bring generics to market faster by incentivizing more competition among generic manufacturers. This would lead to greater access for consumers to safe, high-quality, and affordable generic drugs and would improve health and quality of life through FDA's advances in shaping medical practices. The proposal ensures that first-to-file generic applicants who have been awarded a 180-day exclusivity period do not unreasonably and indefinitely block subsequent generics from entering the market beyond the exclusivity period. Under this proposal, when a first-to-file generic application is not yet approved due to deficiencies, FDA would be able to tentatively approve a subsequent generic application, which would start the 180-day exclusivity clock, rather than waiting an indefinite period for the first-to-file applicant to fix the deficiencies in its application. Triggering the start of the 180 day-exclusivity period for first-to-file applicants who "park" their exclusivity would speed delivery of generic drugs and provide substantial cost savings to American consumers.

- Modernizes the Medicare Part D Drug Benefit and Modifies the Part B Drug Payment—the Budget addresses the misaligned incentives of the Part D drug benefit structure and better equips plans with the tools necessary to manage spending. Proposed changes are designed to: lower beneficiary costs at the pharmacy counter by requiring plans to share at the point of sale a portion of rebates that plans receive from drug manufacturers; enhance Part D plans' negotiation power with manufacturers by allowing for additional flexibilities in formulary management; encourage utilization of higher value drugs by eliminating cost-sharing for generic drugs for beneficiaries who receive the low-income subsidy; modify the Part D payment structure to discourage drug manufacturers' price and rebate strategies that increase spending for both beneficiaries and the Government; and provide beneficiaries with more predictable annual drug expenses through the creation of a new out-of-pocket spending cap. In addition, the Budget modifies payment for Part B drugs to discourage manufacturers from increasing prices faster than inflation and improve payment accuracy. The Budget also modifies hospitals' payment for drugs acquired through the 340B drug discount program by rewarding hospitals that provide charity care and reducing payments to hospitals that provide little to no charity care.

**Repeals & Replaces Obamacare and Reforms Medicaid Financing.** Obamacare, which substantially shifted regulatory power from the States to the Federal Government in order to standardize coverage, has wreaked havoc on the individual insurance market. Average premiums increased 105 percent from 2013 to 2017 while choices have dwindled. In 2017, people in one-third of U.S. counties only had a single insurer from which to purchase a plan on an exchange. For 2018, approximately 30 percent of enrollees only had choices from a single insurer.

*"We will deliver relief to American workers, families, and small businesses, who right now are being crushed by Obamacare, by increasing freedom, choice, and opportunity for the American people."*

President Donald J. Trump
March 10, 2017

While many people with expensive medical conditions and those with income sufficiently low enough—below 200 percent of the Federal poverty level—to receive large subsidies have obtained coverage, the exchanges have failed to attract healthier individuals and families with somewhat higher incomes that want affordable options that meet their needs. In addition, the Patient Protection and Affordable Care Act's (PPACA) Medicaid expansion has cost significantly more than expected. For example, in 2015, CMS actuaries increased their estimates of Federal spending for the average Medicaid expansion enrollee in that year by almost 50 percent. Overall, the cost per newly insured individual is far more than what was expected.

The Budget supports a two-part approach to repealing and replacing Obamacare, starting with enactment of legislation modeled closely after the Graham-Cassidy-Heller-Johnson (GCHJ) bill as soon as possible, followed by enactment of additional reforms to help set Government healthcare spending on a sustainable fiscal path that leads to higher value spending. The President is committed to rescuing States, consumers, and taxpayers from the failures of Obamacare, and supporting States as they transition to more sustainable healthcare programs that provide appropriate choices for their citizens. The Budget also provides a path for States and consumers to be relieved from many of the PPACA's insurance rules and pricing restrictions that have resulted in one-size-fits-all plans with soaring premiums and deductibles. This would allow people to buy insurance plans that work for them and that are fairly priced, a substantial benefit to middle class families who do not receive coverage through the workplace.

The Market-Based Health Care Grant Program would provide more equitable and sustainable funding to States to develop affordable healthcare options. The block grant program would promote structural reforms to improve the functioning of the healthcare market through greater choice and competition, with States and consumers in charge rather than the Washington bureaucracy. The Budget would allow States to use the block grant for a variety of approaches in order to help their citizens, including those with high cost medical needs, afford quality healthcare services. The block grant approach also reflects the Administration's view that Government subsidies are better targeted to States and consumers rather than funneled through insurance companies as with the PPACA.

The President is also committed to the comprehensive Medicaid reform in the GCHJ bill, including the repeal of the Obamacare Medicaid expansion and reducing State gimmicks, such as provider taxes, that raise Federal costs. Medicaid financing reform would empower States to design individual, State-based solutions that prioritize Medicaid dollars for the most vulnerable and support innovations such as community engagement initiatives for able-bodied adults. National healthcare spending trends are unsustainable in the long term and the Budget includes additional proposals to build upon the GCHJ bill to make the system more efficient, including proposals to align the Market-Based Health Care Grant Program, Medicaid per capita cap, and block grant growth rates with the Consumer Price Index (CPI-U) and to allow States to share in program savings.

This two-part approach in the Budget ensures that States have the financial support they need to transition away from Obamacare, while allowing greater choice and competition in healthcare markets and more sustainable Government health spending over the long term.

**Provides States with Flexibility to Modernize Medicaid.** In addition to the program flexibilities included in the Budget proposal to repeal and replace Obamacare, and building on the recent Administration guidance allowing States to explore community engagement requirements for able-bodied adults in Medicaid, the Budget proposes to empower States to further modernize Medicaid benefits and eligibility. The Budget would give States additional flexibility around benefits and cost-sharing, allow States to consider savings and other assets when determining Medicaid eligibility, and reduce waste by counting lottery winnings as income for Medicaid eligibility. These proposals enable the Federal and State governments to be partners in greater fiscal responsibility which would preserve and protect the Medicaid program for Americans who truly need it.

**Improves Program Integrity for Medicare, Medicaid, and the Children's Health Insurance Program (CHIP).** The Budget includes legislative proposals and administrative actions to strengthen the integrity and sustainability of Medicare, Medicaid, and CHIP. Combined with additional funding investments, these policies would provide CMS with additional resources and tools to combat fraud, waste, and abuse and to promote high-quality and efficient healthcare.

To improve fiscal integrity and transparency in Medicaid payment policy, CMS will propose guidance to improve timely and complete data collection on Medicaid supplemental payments, including the financing of such payments. In addition, current law allows States to make Medicaid provider payments far in excess of actual service costs. States have used this additional money to leverage Federal reimbursements in excess of their Medicaid matching rate or for other purposes. To avoid this misuse of funds, the Budget also proposes to limit reimbursement to Government providers to no more than the cost of providing services to Medicaid beneficiaries.

> **Health Care Fraud and Abuse Control: $5 returned for every $1 spent**
>
> Additional funding for the Health Care Fraud and Abuse Control (HCFAC) program has allowed CMS in recent years to shift away from a "pay-and-chase" model toward identifying and preventing fraudulent or improper payments from being paid in the first place. The return on investment for the HCFAC account was $5 returned for every $1 expended from 2014-2016. The Budget proposes HCFAC discretionary funding of $770 million in 2019, which is $45 million higher than the 2017 enacted level.

**Strengthens and Protects the Medicare Program.** Consistent with the President's commitment to protect Medicare, the Budget proposes to improve program efficiency, enhance program integrity, and bolster program solvency to ensure the sustainability of the Medicare program for current and future generations. To accomplish this, the Budget works to restructure and bring transparency and accountability to payments that do not directly relate to Medicare's health insurance role, by financing them outside the Hospital Insurance trust fund and modifying their growth rate. The Budget ensures payments accurately align with the costs of care to address perverse payment incentives identified by non-partisan experts that drive overutilization or clinically inappropriate use of more expensive sites of care. This would improve the quality of care seniors receive and better protect them from excessive out-of-pocket costs. The Budget also supports the Administration's commitment to reduce provider burden by providing hospitals and physicians freedom to use electronic health records as they deem best by removing ineffective Federal penalties and requirements, eliminating reporting burden and low-value metrics in performance-based payment for physicians, improving incentives for physicians to participate in advanced payment models that reward high-value healthcare delivery, and providing CMS with greater flexibility in beneficiary education and quality assurance. The Budget creates a new option for Medicare beneficiaries to save for out of pocket healthcare expenses by allowing tax deductible contributions to health savings accounts associated with high deductible health plans offered by employers or Medicare Advantage. The Budget would extend Medicare's solvency by roughly eight years.

**Serves Older Americans.** The Budget prioritizes funding for programs that address the needs of older Americans, many of whom require some level of assistance to continue living independently or semi-independently within their communities. This funding provides critical help and support to seniors and caregivers. These programs provide direct services such as respite care, transportation assistance, and personal care services. These services also include $838 million for senior nutrition programs. This funding is estimated to provide 222 million meals to 2.4 million older Americans nationwide.

**Improves Treatment for Serious Mental Illness.** The Budget requests new investments to improve treatment for individuals suffering from serious mental illness. Approximately 35 percent of the more than 10 million adults in the United States that suffer from serious mental illness did not receive mental health services in the past year. The Budget requests new investments to ensure more adults with serious mental illness receive Assertive Community Treatment, an evidence-based practice that provides a comprehensive array of services to reduce costly hospitalizations. The Budget also increases funding to improve mental health services for seriously mental ill individuals who are involved with the criminal justice system. The Budget maintains funding for the Community Mental Health Services Block Grant, which requires States to support services for first episode psychosis, which is vitally important to ensuring that individuals with serious mental illness receive appropriate treatment in a timely manner.

**Enhances Emergency Preparedness and Health Security.** The Budget proposes to transfer the Strategic National Stockpile to the HHS' Assistant Secretary for Preparedness and Response from the Centers for Disease Control and Prevention (CDC). This move consolidates strategic decision-making around the development and procurement of medical countermeasures, and streamlines leadership to enable nimble responses to public health emergencies. The Budget also prioritizes funding for the Biomedical Advanced Research and Development Authority, BioShield, and pandemic influenza, to continue to build on investments to protect the civilian population in the event of public health emergencies related to infectious disease outbreaks, and other man-made crises. A disease threat anywhere is a disease threat everywhere, so the United States will continue to support capacity building in other countries so that they can stop outbreaks at their source before they reach the U.S. homeland. Through CDC, the Budget proposes new investments via the Global Health Security Agenda to strengthen countries' abilities to respond to infectious disease outbreaks whether naturally occurring, accidental, or deliberate.

**Accelerates Progress on Infectious Disease Elimination.** Progress on fighting infectious diseases such as HIV/AIDS, viral hepatitis, sexually transmitted disease, and tuberculosis continues, but much work remains—approximately 40,000 Americans are newly infected with HIV each year and there were more than two million cases of chlamydia, gonorrhea, and syphilis reported in the United States in 2016—the highest number ever recorded. The Budget requests $40 million for a new demonstration initiative within CDC focused on jointly eliminating multiple infectious diseases using intensive prevention, screening, and treatment/referral as treatment efforts. This initiative would focus on at least five States/jurisdictions, particularly those that are seeing a rise in infectious diseases related to opioid abuse. The Budget also includes a focus on accelerating the elimination of perinatal HIV transmission in the United States.

**Reauthorizes the Ryan White HIV/AIDS Program.** The Ryan White HIV/AIDS Program provides a comprehensive system of primary medical care, treatment, and supportive services to over half a million people living with HIV, which is more than half of the people in the United States who have been diagnosed with HIV. The Budget supports reauthorizing the Ryan White program to ensure Federal funds are allocated to address the changing landscape of HIV across the United States. Reauthorization of the Ryan White Program should include data-driven programmatic changes as well as simplifying and standardizing certain requirements and definitions. These changes would ensure Federal funds may be allocated to populations experiencing high or increasing levels of HIV infections/diagnoses while continuing to support Americans already living with HIV across the Nation.

**Addresses Overlapping and Burdensome Food Regulation.** FDA will continue to work with the U.S. Department of Agriculture to streamline regulatory and inspection activities to ease burden on the industry by reducing the number of businesses that are inspected by both agencies. FDA will also support development of a State-based safety infrastructure by evaluating whether States will have an increased role in conducting inspections on larger farms on behalf of FDA and continuing outreach and education to small farms as they prepare for their upcoming compliance dates.

**Reforms Federal Investments in the Healthcare Workforce.** The Budget proposes to improve the effectiveness of Federal investments in the healthcare workforce to better address provider shortages. To better target Federal spending on graduate medical education (GME) and increase transparency and accountability, the Budget consolidates GME spending in Medicare, Medicaid, and the Children's Hospital GME Payment Program into a new mandatory GME capped grant program. Funding would be distributed to hospitals that are committed to building a strong medical workforce and would be targeted to address medically underserved communities and health professional shortages. The Budget also proposes to eliminate $451 million in other health professions and training programs, which lack evidence that they significantly improve the Nation's health workforce. The Budget continues to fund high value health workforce activities, such as the National Health Service Corps, that provide scholarships and loan repayment in exchange for service in areas of the United States where there is a shortage of health professionals.

**Modernizes How the Government Employs Public Health Professionals.** The U.S. Public Health Service Commissioned Corps (Corps) consists of over 6,500 uniformed public health professionals who work alongside their equivalent civilian counterparts performing the same day jobs but often receiving higher total compensation. The Corps receives military-like benefits, but has not been incorporated into the Armed Forces since 1952 and generally does not meet the Department of Defense's criteria for the military compensation system. Further, the Corps' mission assignments and functions have not evolved in step with the public health needs of the Nation. It is time for that to change. HHS is committed to providing the best public health services and emergency response at the lowest cost, and is undertaking a comprehensive look at how the Corps is structured. The specific recommendations and plans resulting from this analysis will be released in the months ahead and could range from phasing out unnecessary Corps functions to reinventing the Corps into a smaller, more targeted cadre focused on providing the most vital public health services and emergency response.

The goal of this proposal is to modernize how the Government employs public health professionals and how HHS responds to public health emergencies, saving Federal funds, and reducing duplication while safeguarding the well-being of the Nation.

**Prioritizes Direct Health Services for American Indians and Alaska Natives.** The Budget increases access to direct health services for American Indians and Alaska Natives by funding the staffing and operations of newly constructed facilities, extending services to three newly recognized Tribes, and increasing resources available for accreditation emergencies to address ongoing health-care delivery challenges in the Great Plains area.

**Prohibits Certain Abortion Providers from Receiving Federal Funds.** The Budget includes provisions prohibiting certain abortion providers from receiving Federal funds from HHS, including those that receive funding under the Title X Family Planning program and Medicaid, among other HHS programs.

**Supports Children and Families in Achieving Their Potential.** The Budget continues to invest in programs that help American families and children thrive. The Budget supports States in providing key services to children and youth by increasing State flexibilities and reducing administrative burdens in foster care. These child welfare reforms focus on preventing the need for foster care unless absolutely necessary to ensure families can remain intact. The Budget also helps working families afford and access child care by maintaining Federal funding for key HHS child care programs and using these investments to leverage additional State support for child care. In addition, the Budget promotes evidence-building and innovation to strengthen America's safety net, proposes improvements to the Temporary Assistance for Needy Families program, and supports efforts to get noncustodial parents to work. Together, these proposals reflect the Administration's commitment to helping low-income families end dependency on Government benefits and promote the principle that gainful employment is the best pathway to financial self-sufficiency and family well-being.

**Rightsizes the Proper Role of the Federal Government.** The Budget continues the 2018 Budget proposals to eliminate low-performing or ineffective programs, such as the Low Income Home Energy Assistance Program (LIHEAP) and the Community Services Block Grant (CSBG). Many States and utility companies currently provide energy assistance services, reducing the need for a distinct Federal program to fulfill this role. Further, LIHEAP is unable to demonstrate strong performance outcomes, and the Government Accountability Office has raised concerns about fraud and abuse in the program in the past. CSBG also has difficulty in demonstrating effective outcomes. In addition, eligible entities that receive funding from CSBG receive funding from many other sources, including other Federal sources. CSBG accounts for just five percent, on average, of total funding that these eligible entities receive, and these funds are distributed by a formula that is not directly tied to performance and outcomes.

# DEPARTMENT OF HOMELAND SECURITY

---

**Highlights:**

- The mission of the Department of Homeland Security (DHS) is to secure the Nation from the many threats it faces. DHS safeguards the American people, the homeland, and America's values by: preventing terrorism and enhancing security; managing the borders; administering immigration laws; securing cyberspace; and ensuring disaster resilience.

- The Budget requests $46 billion in discretionary appropriations for DHS, a $3.4 billion or 8-percent increase from the 2017 enacted level (excluding updated 2017 receipts). In addition, $6.7 billion is available to help communities overwhelmed by major disasters.

- Critical investments include $1.6 billion for construction of the border wall and $782 million to hire and support 2,750 additional law enforcement officers and agents at U.S. Customs and Border Protection (CBP) and U.S. Immigration and Customs Enforcement (ICE). The Budget also requests $2.5 billion for detaining up to 47,000 illegal aliens on a daily basis.

- The Budget ensures the appropriate use of taxpayer dollars by reducing Federal programs that support activities that are primarily the responsibility of State and local governments.

---

**The President's 2019 Budget:**

In the years since the 9/11 terrorist attacks, the Nation has faced numerous ongoing and emerging threats. U.S. adversaries continue to devise new ways to attack and undermine the American way of life. DHS is continuously vigilant in its efforts to protect the Nation, strengthen communities' preparedness and resilience, and respond to and recover from emergencies that occur. The Budget increases funding for border security, immigration enforcement, cybersecurity, and law enforcement capabilities. The Budget fully funds DHS's critical operations to provide the American people the security they expect and deserve.

**Secures the Borders of the United States.** Each day, DHS works to protect the American people and economy by preventing the illegal movement of people and contraband across U.S. borders, including the materials that could be used to produce weapons of mass destruction. CBP and the U.S. Coast Guard (USCG) patrol more than 5,000 miles of border with Canada, 1,900 miles of border with Mexico, and 95,000 miles of shoreline to intercept threats originating beyond the Nation's borders. The Budget invests in border security to protect the American people, while facilitating

*"I could not be prouder to serve alongside the men and women of the Department of Homeland Security. And we, as a Nation, owe them a debt of gratitude for taking on some of the toughest, most important jobs in America. While you're having your morning coffee, the Coast Guard is pulling a fisherman aboard after his boat capsized in stormy seas. While you're deciding what you want for lunch, the Federal Law Enforcement Training Center is teaching law enforcement officers how to respond to an active shooter... While you're zoning out on your commute home, Homeland Security Investigators are closing in on a dangerous child predator. While you're binge-watching Mad Men on Netflix, TSA is stopping an actual mad man with a loaded gun from boarding a flight to Disney World."*

John F. Kelly
White House Chief of Staff, as DHS Secretary
April 18, 2017

legitimate trade and travel to advance American prosperity.

As shown in the chart below, since the start of the Administration in 2017, apprehensions of illegal border crossers have dropped between ports of entry. At the same time, DHS has accelerated its apprehension of illegal aliens within the United States.

The Budget follows through on the President's commitments on border security. As part of the Administration's proposal for $18 billion to fund the border wall, the Budget requests $1.6 billion to construct approximately 65 miles of border wall in south Texas. The Budget also provides funding to hire 2,000 additional ICE law enforcement officers and 750 Border Patrol agents. The Budget makes these significant investments while continuing to fund surveillance and other border security technologies and initiatives.

The Budget also continues to modernize USCG's vessels and aircraft that patrol the waters off the Nation's coasts. These vessels and aircraft serve as America's first line of defense at sea. USCG works every day to stop illegal aliens traveling by maritime routes, and disrupts the flow of cocaine and other illegal drugs well before they can poison communities. New assets deployed by USCG, such as the National Security Cutter, are also much more effective at detecting threats and stopping them before they reach American shores.

**Ensures the Immigration System Works.** The Budget invests in critical law enforcement programs that would ensure the immigration system works, including hiring 2,000 new ICE law enforcement officers in 2019. This doubles the number of new ICE officers who would be hired in 2018. These new law enforcement personnel would help fulfill the President's commitment to apprehend and deport illegal aliens, dismantle smuggling networks, and enhance public safety.

In addition, in order to combat immigration fraud, the Budget proposes a new approach to fund ICE investigators by collecting $208 million in fees from immigration

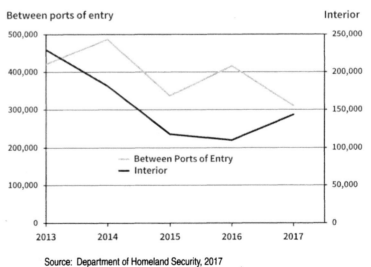

## Fewer Illegal Border Apprehensions and Increased Interior Apprehensions

Between ports of entry                          Interior

Source: Department of Homeland Security, 2017

applicants. These funds would ensure ICE has what it needs to disrupt criminal enterprises conducting document and benefit fraud, while also stopping unscrupulous employers that hire illegal aliens and undermine job opportunities for Americans.

Companies that employ illegal aliens violate the law, harm U.S. workers, and fuel other crimes such as human smuggling, document fraud, identity theft, money laundering, and labor violations. In order to crack down on illegal employers, the Budget continues to call for mandatory, nationwide use of the E-Verify system. E-Verify is an online tool that allows businesses to determine the eligibility of their employees to work in the United States, can be used at no cost to employers, and has an over 99-percent accuracy rate.[1] The Administration continues to enforce E-Verify use by Federal contractors, which has been required for many years.

**Secures Cyberspace.** The President has affirmed the important role that DHS plays in combating cyber-attacks and protecting the Nation's critical infrastructure. The Budget includes $1.0 billion to support DHS's efforts to safeguard the Federal Government's civilian information technology systems against cybersecurity threats. These funds also support DHS efforts to share cybersecurity information with State, local, and tribal governments, as well as with international partners and the private sector. As these threats continue to evolve, DHS cybersecurity programs are more important than ever.

**Secures the Nation's Transportation Systems.** The Transportation Security Administration (TSA) ensures the security of the Nation's various transportation systems. In addition to screening more than two million passengers and millions more bags daily, TSA supports security of air cargo, mass transit systems, passenger and freight railways, pipelines, highways, and ports. In 2016, TSA discovered 3,391 firearms in carry-on bags at checkpoints across the United States, averaging more than nine firearms per day. Of those, 83 percent were loaded. The Budget provides approximately $7.7 billion to support the TSA employees and technology that ensure the free movement of people and commerce.

---

**National Flood Insurance Program's Reinsurance Purchase Pays Off During Hurricane Harvey**

In January 2017, FEMA purchased reinsurance coverage for the National Flood Insurance Program, which would provide up to $1 billion in payment to FEMA if flood insurance claims from a single event exceeding $4 billion. The reinsurance overage paid off when Hurricane Harvey hit the coast of Texas in August of 2017. This investment gave FEMA nearly $7 for every $1 of reinsurance coverage purchased, keeping the program from falling further into debt and protecting taxpayer funds. FEMA plans to continue purchasing reinsurance as a way to protect against losses resulting from catastrophic disasters.

---

**Protects against Emerging Threats.** Within TSA, the Budget invests $71 million in new technology to make airport screening more effective and faster. Computed tomography, used for years in hospital and industrial applications, is being adapted for aviation checkpoints to address emerging threats to passenger flights. The technology provides high-definition 3D images that screeners can zoom and rotate to identify and remove suspicious items before they get onto an airplane.

The Budget also enhances DHS's ability to counter the threat to the homeland from weapons of mass destruction including efforts overseas and domestically. The Budget supports DHS's plans to establish a new Countering Weapons of Mass Destruction Office, which would unify the Department's various chemical, biological, radiological, and nuclear counter-threat missions. This reorganization would allow the Department to protect the United States from weapons of mass destruction more efficiently and effectively.

---

[1] *https://www.uscis.gov/e-verify/about-program/performance*

*"State, local, tribal, and territorial governments, along with the residents in the impacted areas, are the true first responders."*

Brock Long
FEMA Administrator
October 31, 2017

**Strengthens State and Local Investments in National Preparedness.** The Budget requests $1.9 billion for the Federal Emergency Management Agency (FEMA) for its programs that award grants to State and local governments. These funds help equip emergency responders so they can be prepared for natural or manmade disasters. Responding to and recovering from any disaster is a whole community effort that relies on the strength of Federal agencies such as FEMA, State, local, and tribal governments, and non-governmental entities and individuals. The Budget also supports efforts by communities to invest their own resources by establishing a non-Federal cost share for certain FEMA grant programs, and proposing to eliminate the National Domestic Preparedness Consortium.

**Assists Communities when Disaster Strikes.** The Budget proposes $6.9 billion for the FEMA Disaster Relief Fund to ensure effective response to and recovery from emergencies and major disasters. This funding helps survivors get back on their feet while restoring essential community services and facilities. Within these amounts, the Budget provides $24 million to the DHS Office of the Inspector General to exercise robust oversight of disaster-related spending, ensuring accountability for taxpayer dollars.

Catastrophic storms in the fall of 2017 demonstrated the importance of flood insurance in helping individuals quickly recover. However, flood claims for damages from the storms drove the National Flood Insurance Program (NFIP) deeper into debt. The Administration recognizes that flood insurance rates must increase so that policyholders' premiums reflect the risk of living in flood zones. The Administration has proposed various reforms to the Congress that would ensure the continued financial stability of the NFIP while maintaining affordability for low-income policyholders, and expand the private market to get the Federal Government out of the flood insurance business.

**Protects the Nation's Leaders by Strengthening the Secret Service.** The Budget provides $2.2 billion for the U.S. Secret Service, fully supporting the Agency's dual missions of protecting the Nation's leaders while securing America's financial systems. The Budget proposes hiring an additional 450 special agents, officers, and professional staff at the Secret Service. This would keep the Agency on a path to reach its staffing goal of 7,600 employees by the end of 2019, the highest level ever (see chart). This increase fulfills key recommendations from independent reviews of Secret Service operations, continuing the Administration's progress toward improving the morale of this critical law enforcement agency.

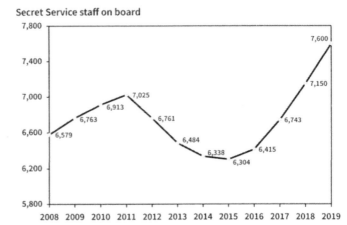

**Strengthening Protection of U.S. Leaders**

Secret Service staff on board

Source: Office of Personnel Management (FedScope), 2017.

**Improves the Efficiency of the Federal Government.** The Budget proposes transferring operational responsibility for the National Bio and Agro-Defense Facility (NBAF) from the DHS Science and Technology Directorate to the United States Department of Agriculture (USDA). Given that USDA is already responsible for the research programs that would be at this facility once construction is completed, it makes sense for USDA to manage the facility itself. DHS would oversee construction through completion and support USDA transition. Shifting NBAF operations to USDA would allow the Science and Technology Directorate to focus on its primary research and development mission.

# DEPARTMENT OF HOUSING AND URBAN DEVELOPMENT

---

**Highlights:**

• The Department of Housing and Urban Development (HUD) promotes decent, safe, and affordable housing for Americans and provides access to homeownership opportunities.

• The Budget reflects the President's commitment to fiscal responsibility by reforming programs to encourage the dignity of work and self-sufficiency while supporting critical functions that provide assistance to vulnerable households. The Budget recognizes a greater role for State and local governments and the private sector to address community and economic development needs and affordable housing production.

• The Budget requests $39.2 billion in gross discretionary funding for HUD, an $8.8 billion or 18.3-percent decrease from the 2017 enacted level.

---

**The President's 2019 Budget:**

HUD promotes affordable housing for low-income families and supports access to homeownership. A secure, healthy housing situation is a foundation on which families can establish economic security, improve their quality of life, and form strong communities. In a fiscally constrained environment, the Budget strategically invests $39.2 billion in programs to support HUD's core functions, and ensures HUD programs remain a vital resource to the most vulnerable households and first-time homeowners. The Budget provides $33.8 billion for HUD's rental assistance programs and requests legislative reforms to place these programs on a more fiscally sound path while encouraging work and self-sufficiency for tenants. The Budget also continues to support efforts across the United States to reduce homelessness and remove lead and other hazards from over 9,500 homes. For first-time and low- to moderate-income homebuyers, HUD's Federal Housing Administration (FHA) remains a critical source of mortgage financing.

The Budget also eliminates programs that are duplicative or have failed to demonstrate effectiveness, such as the Community Development Block Grant (CDBG) program, and devolves responsibility for community and economic development to State and local governments that are better equipped to respond to local conditions.

**Reforms Rental Assistance.** The Budget requests $33.8 billion across HUD's rental assistance programs, a decrease of 11.2 percent relative to the 2017 enacted level. To address the increasing and unsustainable Federal costs of rental assistance, the Budget requests legislative reforms that would produce significant cost savings. In addition to these reforms, the Budget proposes program-specific savings in the Housing Voucher and Public Housing programs. The Budget does not request funding for the Public Housing Capital Fund, as the provision of affordable housing should be a responsibility more fully shared with State and local governments. These funding levels, while significantly reduced from the 2017 enacted level, should support currently assisted households while strategically decreasing the Federal footprint of HUD's rental assistance programs over time.

**Encourages Work Among HUD-Assisted Households.** The Budget proposes legislative reforms to encourage work and self-sufficiency across its core rental assistance programs, consistent with broader Administration goals. Currently, tenants generally pay 30 percent of their adjusted income toward rent. The Administration's reforms require able-bodied individuals to shoulder more of their housing costs and provide an incentive to increase their earnings, while mitigating rent increases for the elderly and people with disabilities. The Administration's legislative proposal would also reduce administrative and regulatory burdens and allow communities further flexibility to develop tenant rent requirements that are consistent with local needs and objectives.

**Leverages Private Capital for Housing Improvements.** The Budget provides investments and statutory authorities to facilitate a shift from the Public Housing funding platform to Housing Vouchers and Project-Based Rental Assistance (PBRA). The Voucher and PBRA programs benefit from greater private sector involvement and are able to leverage private financing to modernize their units, generally resulting in higher quality housing for assisted low-income families. To further this objective, the Budget requests $100 million for the Rental Assistance Demonstration, which supports the redevelopment of Public Housing units through conversion to the Housing Voucher and PBRA funding platforms. Additional authorities in the Public Housing program, such as tenant protection vouchers and the strategic release of certain public housing assets, would also assist in this effort.

**Establishes EnVision Centers for a Holistic Approach to Self-Sufficiency.** On December 7, 2017, Secretary Ben Carson announced the launch of EnVision Centers to help HUD-assisted households achieve self-sufficiency and deliver on the President's commitment to a better future. Detroit, Michigan is home to the first of 10 sites that will be part of this demonstration. EnVision Centers will provide communities with a centralized hub for HUD's four pillars of self-sufficiency: 1) Economic Empowerment; 2) Educational Advancement; 3) Health and Wellness; and 4) Character and Leadership. Through partnerships with non-profits, corporations, and State and local governments, these EnVision Centers would leverage private and public resources for maximum community impact. The Budget requests funding to evaluate these EnVision Centers, and adjust the program design and improve implementation if needed to achieve better outcomes for individuals and communities.

> "We need to think differently about how we can empower Americans to climb the ladder of success. EnVision Centers are designed to help people take the first few steps towards self-sufficiency."
>
> Ben Carson
> Secretary
> December 7, 2017

**Promotes Economic Mobility and Improves Quality of Life.** The Budget requests $75 million for the Family Self-Sufficiency program and $10 million for the Jobs-Plus Initiative. By connecting HUD-assisted households to social services and employment resources, these programs help tenants maximize their earning potential and improve their financial situations and quality of life. Rigorous evaluations have shown that the Jobs-Plus program produces lasting increases in the wage earnings of tenants.

**Continues Supporting Communities in their Efforts to Reduce Homelessness.** The Budget requests $2.4 billion for the Homeless Assistance Grants (HAG) program, equal to the 2017 enacted level. HAG primarily funds the Continuum of Care program, which is designed to be a coordinated community-based network of programs to prevent and address local homelessness. HUD uses its annual grant competition to encourage grantees to allocate funds to evidence-based and cost-effective strategies. These policies have encouraged communities to increasingly support evidence-based interventions such as permanent supportive housing rather than models such as transitional housing that have been proven less effective. The Budget also requests $255 million for Emergency Solutions Grants, which would enable municipalities to support emergency shelter, rapid re-housing, and homelessness prevention.

**Beds Available for Homeless and Formerly Homeless People**

Number of beds

Source: HUD's 2017 Annual Homeless Assessment Report to the Congress, December 2017.

**Reduces Lead Exposure for Low-Income Children.** Lead paint in housing presents a significant threat to the health, safety, and future productivity of America's next generation. The Budget continues to make progress to promote healthy and lead-safe homes by requesting $145 million, equal to the 2017 enacted level, for the mitigation of lead-based paint and other hazards in low-income homes, especially those in which children reside. This funding level also includes resources for enforcement, education, and research activities to further support this goal. Research suggests that this program generates high returns on investment due to higher wages and reduced medical costs.

**Supports Sustainable Homeownership Opportunities and Upgrades FHA Operations.** The Budget preserves access to sustainable homeownership opportunities for creditworthy borrowers through FHA and Ginnie Mae credit guarantees. FHA provides a crucial source of mortgage financing for first-time homebuyers, who accounted for over 80 percent of FHA-insured home purchase loans in 2017. FHA's activities enable these new homeowners to build wealth and establish economic security. The Budget requests an additional $20 million above the 2017 enacted level of $130 million for FHA to upgrade its operations by investing in information technology and contract support. This additional funding is fully offset by a modest new fee on FHA lenders, better aligning the responsibilities for the costs and benefits of this program.

**Eliminates Major Block Grants.** Similar to the 2018 Budget, the Administration continues to propose eliminating funding for programs that lack measureable outcomes and are ineffective. The Budget eliminates HUD's community and economic development as well as affordable housing production programs. The Budget eliminates CDBG, a program that has expended more than $150 billion since its inception in 1974, but has not demonstrated sufficient impact. Studies have shown that the allocation formula, which has not been updated since 1978, is ineffective at targeting funds to the areas of greatest need, and many aspects of the program have become outdated. The Budget also eliminates the HOME Investment Partnerships Program, which has not been authorized since 1994. The Budget devolves responsibility to State and local governments, which are better positioned to assess local community needs and address unique market challenges.

# DEPARTMENT OF THE INTERIOR

---

**Highlights:**

- The Department of the Interior (DOI) conserves and manages natural resources and cultural heritage for the benefit and enjoyment of the American people, provides scientific and evidence-based information about America's natural resources and hazards, supports safe and responsible development of Federal energy resources, and honors the Nation's trust responsibilities and special commitments to American Indians, Alaska Natives, and U.S.-affiliated island communities to help them prosper.

- The Budget request for DOI prioritizes energy development programs, infrastructure improvements on public lands, and DOI-wide reorganization efforts. The Budget eliminates funding for unnecessary or duplicative programs while reducing funds for lower priority activities, including land acquisition and various grant programs.

- The Budget requests $11.3 billion for DOI, a $2.2 billion or 16-percent decrease from the 2017 enacted level. This funding level includes changes in mandatory programs.

---

**The President's 2019 Budget:**

DOI's mission affects the lives of all Americans. The Department protects and manages the Nation's natural resources and cultural heritage, manages development of energy and mineral resources on Federal lands and waters, provides scientific and other information about the Nation's natural resources, manages water infrastructure, honors trust responsibilities to American Indians and Alaska Natives, and fulfills commitments to Insular areas. The Budget reflects the Administration's commitment to promoting economic and energy security by developing domestic energy resources. These efforts put the safety and security of America first by reducing U.S. dependency on energy from foreign nations. The Budget also makes investments to improve public lands and water infrastructure, reorganize and reform Departmental operations, streamline administrative functions, improve public access to outdoor recreation, and uphold unique tribal trust responsibilities. At the same time, the Budget reflects the President's commitment to fiscal responsibility by eliminating unnecessary or low priority programs and reducing administrative overhead costs.

**Strengthens America's Energy Security.** The Budget increases funding for DOI programs that support safe and responsible development of energy on public lands and offshore waters. DOI has proposed an aggressive strategy for leasing offshore oil and gas under its Draft Proposed Program for 2019-2024. Onshore, the Administration is taking steps to initiate oil and gas leasing in

> *"It's important that the taxpayers and Tribes get the full and fair value of traditional and renewable energy produced on public lands and offshore areas."*
>
> Ryan Zinke
> Secretary
> September 1, 2017

the coastal plain of the Arctic National Wildlife Refuge, which was recently authorized by the Congress. The Department will also continue to make new areas available for renewable energy development—both onshore and offshore—and will prioritize renewable project permitting consistent with industry demand. The Budget also maintains funding for scientific research and data collection to inform responsible energy and mineral development, while minimizing the environmental impacts of these activities. Combined with administrative reforms to streamline permitting processes, these efforts would provide industry with access to the energy resources America needs, while ensuring that taxpayers receive a fair return from the development of these public resources.

**Supports Historic Effort to Reorganize DOI.** The Budget provides $18 million to help initiate DOI's internal reform plan, which would move away from the current bureau and State-based regional system of management toward an integrated Federal land and water management approach organized around watersheds. This "one-agency model" approach proposes to improve cross-bureau collaboration, reduce duplication, and move resources closer to land management units. DOI's reform plan breaks silos among bureaus by creating a common regional structure, co-locating regional offices, and improving coordinated decision-making. On the whole, these efforts are expected to facilitate better management of important resources such as watersheds, wildlife corridors, trail systems, infrastructure assets, and recreational systems.

**Launches Public Lands Infrastructure Fund.** Interior manages an infrastructure asset portfolio with a replacement value exceeding $300 billion, which includes buildings, housing, trails, roads, water systems, and Bureau of Indian Education (BIE) schools. Many of these assets are deteriorating, with older assets becoming more expensive to repair and maintain in good condition. The Budget would establish a new Public Lands Infrastructure Fund to help pay for repairs and improvements in national parks, wildlife refuges, and at BIE schools, which have more than $12 billion in deferred maintenance. The fund would be derived from 50 percent of incremental energy leasing receipts over 2018 Budget projections that are not otherwise allocated for other purposes. As DOI works to expand Federal energy development on Federal lands and waters, this initiative has the potential to generate up to $18 billion over 10 years for parks and other public lands infrastructure. This investment would significantly improve the Nation's most visible and visited public facilities that support a multi-billion dollar outdoor recreation economy.

**Invests in Preservation of National Park Service Assets for Future Generations.** For over 100 years, the National Park Service (NPS) has preserved assets in parks and historic sites that represent America's unique history. The Budget provides $257 million to help address the $11 billion NPS deferred maintenance backlog. In conjunction with the mandatory funding provided by the Public Lands Infrastructure Fund, these investments would lead to measurable upgrades on NPS's highest priority assets.

**Streamlines Permitting and Reviews.** DOI administers several foundational environmental and historic preservation statutes and manages more than 20 percent of the Nation's lands, making it responsible for the review and permitting of actions affecting those responsibilities. The Budget commits to a better future by reducing inefficiencies in the environmental review and permitting processes, which would allow the American people to enjoy improved infrastructure sooner. For example, the Budget maintains core funding for Fish and Wildlife Service Endangered Species Act consultations and related activities; these consultations help facilitate the delivery of infrastructure projects while ensuring the protection of imperiled species. The Budget also strengthens the Bureau of Land Management's ability to efficiently facilitate and administer development of energy transmission projects.

**Improves DOI's Procurement of Goods and Services and Management of Administrative Functions.** DOI will realize $50 million in savings through consolidation and sharing of administrative services, such as acquisitions and human resources, and procurement reforms, including multiagency "Best in Class" contracts that leverage the Federal Government's buying power to bring more value and efficiency to how taxpayer dollars are used.

**Proposes a Comprehensive Solution to Wildfire Suppression Funding.** The Budget responsibly funds 100 percent of the rolling 10-year average cost for wildfire suppression in the Departments of Agriculture and the Interior within discretionary budget caps. Similar to how unanticipated funding needs for other natural disasters are addressed, the Budget proposes a separate fund that would include an annual cap adjustment appropriation for wildfire suppression operations, in order to ensure that adequate resources are available to fight wildland fires, protect communities, and safeguard human lives during the most severe wildland fire seasons. In addition, the Administration believes that meaningful forest management reforms to strengthen our ability to restore the Nation's forests and improve their resilience to destructive wildfires should be part of any permanent solution.

**Prioritizes Land Management Operations of the National Park Service, Fish and Wildlife Service, and Bureau of Land Management.** The Budget streamlines operations and eliminates waste while providing the necessary resources for DOI to continue to protect and conserve America's public lands and beautiful natural resources, provide access to public lands for the next generation of outdoor enthusiasts, and ensure visitor safety. The Budget provides $4 billion for land management operations.

**Supports Tribal Sovereignty and Self-Determination across Indian Country.** The Budget addresses Federal trust responsibilities and tribal needs related to education, social services, infrastructure, and stewardship of land, water, and other natural resources. The Budget prioritizes core funding and services that support tribal government operations, such as full funding for contract support costs. The Budget maintains programmatic eliminations proposed in the 2018 Budget, which reduced funding for more recent demonstration projects and initiatives that only serve a few Tribes, and eliminates additional programs that are not fundamental to the missions of the Bureau of Indian Affairs (BIA) or BIE.

**Eliminates Unnecessary, Lower Priority, or Duplicative Programs.** The Budget includes elimination of discretionary Abandoned Mine Land grants that overlap with existing mandatory grants, National Heritage Areas that are more appropriately funded locally, and National Wildlife Refuge fund payments to local governments that are duplicative of other payment programs.

**Reduces Funding for Land Acquisition.** The Budget continues the 2018 Budget proposal to reduce funding for land acquisitions, so that available resources can support existing lands and assets managed by DOI. The Budget reduces land acquisition funding to $8 million, including balance cancellations, and would instead focus available discretionary funds on investing in and maintaining existing national parks, refuges, and public lands.

**Supports Law Enforcement capabilities.** DOI is the steward of over 600 million acres of public lands, including over 12 million acres on the United States-Mexico border. The Budget supports law enforcement efforts on the Nation's public lands to keep visitors and natural resources safe, including DOI's efforts to collaborate with other agencies supporting border security efforts. The Budget also invests in the United States Park Police, who safeguard lives and protect America's national treasures. In addition, the Budget invests in Fish and Wildlife Service law enforcement capacity to combat illegal wildlife trafficking, in support of the President's Executive Order on combatting transnational criminal organizations.

**Invests in Essential Science Programs.** The Budget maintains funding for the Landsat 9 ground system, as well as research and data collection that informs sustainable energy and mineral development, responsible resource management, and natural hazard risk reduction.

**Expands Access and Bolsters the Outdoor Recreation Economy.** Hundreds of millions of people visit U.S. national parks, wildlife refuges, and other public lands each year to hunt, fish, hike, view wildlife, and participate in other outdoor recreation opportunities. Visitors to public lands spend money in local gateway regions, and these expenditures generate and support economic prosperity within these local economies. In addition, through the purchases of licenses and equipment—and associated excise taxes—sportsmen and women have generated billions of dollars to support conservation of wildlife and habitat. To better serve these visitors, the Budget supports expanded public access to lands and waters administered by DOI. The Budget also invests in increased access to encourage sportsmen and women conservationists, veterans, minorities, and underserved communities that traditionally have low participation in outdoor recreation activities. To further boost hunting opportunities, the Budget invests $34 million in North American Wetlands Conservation Act grants, a program that finances conservation of wetlands and associated uplands habitat to benefit waterfowl.

> *"Hunting and fishing is a cornerstone of the American tradition and hunters and fishers of America are the backbone of land and wildlife conservation"*
>
> Ryan Zinke
> Secretary
> September 15, 2017

**Invests in Water Resources and Infrastructure.** The Budget invests in the safe, reliable, and efficient management of water resources throughout the United States. The Budget requests $1 billion for the Bureau of Reclamation. The Budget does not propose any new starts for the Bureau of Reclamation, but rather focuses resources on operating, maintaining, and rehabilitating existing infrastructure. Through the Bureau of Reclamation and BIA, the Budget requests $172 million for the implementation of enacted Indian water rights settlements in support of Federal trust responsibilities to Tribes. The Budget also invests $179 million in water-related science, monitoring, research, and development to better understand the water resources challenges facing the Nation, and develop new technologies to respond to those challenges.

# DEPARTMENT OF JUSTICE

---

**Highlights:**

- The Department of Justice defends the interests of the United States and protects all Americans as the chief enforcer of Federal laws.

- The Budget focuses on the Nation's most pressing security needs to reduce violent crime, enforce immigration laws, and continue combatting the opioid epidemic. In light of the Nation's long-term fiscal challenges, the Budget also maintains prior year spending restraints, supports administrative reorganization, and focuses resources on key priorities.

- The Budget requests $28 billion for the Department of Justice, a $345 million or 1.2-percent decrease from the 2017 enacted level. Targeted funding increases are provided to support public safety and national security while identifying savings opportunities.

---

**The President's 2019 Budget:**

The Department of Justice is charged with enforcing the laws and defending the interests of the United States, ensuring public safety against foreign and domestic threats, providing Federal leadership in preventing and controlling crime, seeking just punishment for those guilty of crimes, and ensuring the fair and impartial administration of justice for all Americans. With violent crime rates rising across the Nation, the work of the men and women at the Department is more important than ever. The Department is committed to dismantling criminal networks, halting the flow of illegal drugs, and restoring law and order to communities. The Budget requests a total of $28 billion to expand the capacity of key law enforcement agencies and strengthen the Department's ability to address the most pressing public safety needs.

The Department will expand the highest priority programs that have been proven to reduce violence and drug-related crime nationwide, including the Organized Crime Drug Enforcement Task Force and the International Organized Crime Intelligence Operations Center. While today's overall crime rates are near historic lows, recent trends indicate that those levels are on the rise. In addition, national and cyber security threats persist and continue to evolve, reinforcing the Department's commitment to safeguarding American citizens. The Budget includes resources to confront each of these rising threats to the Nation while making challenging decisions to reprioritize funds from lower priority or less effective initiatives.

**Tackles the Opioid Epidemic.** Today, the United States faces the deadliest drug overdose crisis in American history. Approximately 64,000 Americans lost their lives to drug overdoses in 2016. Over 42,000 of these tragic deaths were caused by fentanyl, heroin, or prescription opioids. The Department of Justice recognizes its critical role in combating opioid misuse and heroin and fentanyl use. The Budget provides $2.2 billion in discretionary resources for the Drug Enforcement Administration (DEA), including an additional $41 million over the $26 million currently provided for specialized efforts to end the opioid epidemic. The Budget also provides $421 million in fee-funded resources for DEA's Diversion Control Fee Account to combat the diversion of licit drugs and precursor chemicals. In addition, the Budget includes $103 million for opioid-related State and local assistance including: $20 million for the Comprehensive Opioid Abuse Program to support a variety of activities such as treatment and recovery support services, diversion, and alternative to incarceration programs; $59 million for Drug Courts, Mental Health Courts, and Veterans Treatment Courts; $12 million for Residential Substance Abuse Treatment; and $12 million for Prescription Drug Monitoring Programs.

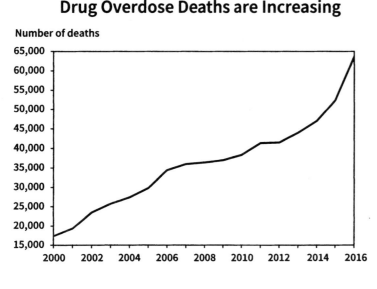

**Drug Overdose Deaths are Increasing**

Number of deaths

Source: Centers for Disease Control WONDER.

**Targets Drug Trafficking Organizations.** To further enhance the Department's efforts to concentrate law enforcement resources on drug traffickers in the most critical regions, the Budget proposes to transfer the High Intensity Drug Trafficking Areas program from the Office of National Drug Control Policy to the DEA. Consolidating anti-drug law enforcement efforts in the DEA would better focus resources on the most dangerous, complex, and interjurisdictional drug trafficking organizations in the United States.

**Combats Violent Crime.** As violent crime rates continue to climb, the Department of Justice aims to restore public safety to communities by providing Federal resources where most needed and most effective. The Budget provides $14.2 billion to Federal law enforcement agencies, including the Federal Bureau of Investigation (FBI), the DEA, the United States Marshals Service, the Bureau of Alcohol, Tobacco, Firearms, and Explosives (ATF), and the Organized Crime and Drug Enforcement Task Forces. This represents an increase of 2.4 percent from the 2017 enacted level, and supports the Department's ability to respond to national security crises; investigate violent- and drug-related crime; and apprehend, detain, and prosecute offenders.

ATF would transfer the entirety of its alcohol and tobacco regulatory and enforcement responsibilities to the Alcohol and Tobacco Tax and Trade Bureau (TTB) in the Department of the Treasury. This transfer would enable the ATF to hone its focus on activities that protect U.S. communities from violent criminals and criminal organizations, while consolidating duplicative alcohol and tobacco enforcement mechanisms within the TTB. In addition, the operating capability of the DEA's highly successful Special Investigative Unit program would retain its critical role in enhancing the Federal Government's ability to pursue threat networks to their source, as prioritized in the National Security Strategy.

The Budget also supports key State and local assistance programs, including $333 million for the Byrne Justice Assistance Grants Program, which provides State and local governments with crucial Federal funding to prevent and control crime. These resources also contribute to important officer safety programs serving State and local law enforcement such as the Bulletproof Vest program.

In addition, $70 million is provided for the Violent Gang and Gun Crime Reduction/Project Safe Neighborhoods (PSN) program. PSN is designed to create safer communities through sustained reductions in gang violence and gun crime by leveraging Federal, State, and local partnerships. The Budget also supports $230 million for State and local juvenile justice programs, including programs aimed at delinquency prevention, intervention, and making improvements to the juvenile justice system. Another $5 million is set aside to support the National Public Safety Partnership program, which leverages the Department's resources to reduce violence in cities with the highest violent crime rates in the Nation.

**Enforces Immigration Laws.** The Administration is committed to strengthening the Nation's security through a more robust enforcement of the Nation's immigration laws. As a result of increased enforcement, this past year the Executive Office for Immigration Review received an approximate 25-percent increase in case receipts from 2016, bringing the pending caseload to over 650,000 cases. In addition, the Agency continues to struggle with a wholly paper-based system that is both cumbersome and inefficient. The Budget provides funding for 75 additional immigration judge teams, as well as $25 million for information technology modernization, including the expansion of electronic case processing. Taken together, these enhancements would expand capacity, improve efficiency, and remove impediments to the timely administration of justice.

**Maintains Domestic and Foreign Security.** The FBI has responsibility for protecting U.S. citizens from harm both at home and abroad. The Budget supports an increase of $148 million for the FBI to continue to carry out its important dual missions of enforcing the Nation's laws and protecting national security. The FBI fights terrorism and combats foreign intelligence threats, prevents the spread and use of weapons of mass destruction and other emerging threats, and fights cyber-based attacks and high-technology crimes. In addition, the FBI fights public corruption, protects civil rights, combats homegrown violent extremism and domestic terrorism, and fights transnational criminal organizations, white-collar crime, violent crime, and gangs. To protect against biological threats, the Budget proposes a cost-sharing agreement between the FBI and the Department of Homeland Security for the National Biodefense Analysis and Countermeasures Center. The National Security Division is also provided with an additional $5 million more than the 2017 enacted level to continue expanding coordination between the Federal intelligence communities to combat terrorism.

**Increases Prosecutorial Support.** Increased Assistant United States Attorney hiring in prior years has helped to expand immigration and violent crime prosecutions across the Nation. The Budget provides the United States Attorneys with $2.1 billion, $70 million above the 2017 enacted level, to support retention of these hires and to allow for $4.7 million in additional paralegal support.

**Reprioritizes Prison Spending.** The Bureau of Prisons (BOP) is responsive to Federal efforts to fight violent crime and prosecute high priority offenders. Recent declines in the prison population coupled with the continuation of contracts with privately-operated facilities ensure that BOP has the necessary space to absorb population fluctuations. The Budget maintains this capacity by funding BOP at $7.1 billion, approximately equal to the 2017 enacted level. In addition, the Budget proposes to leverage economies of scale by closing two standalone minimum security camps and instead transferring inmates to larger Federal complexes. The Budget also proposes to realign regional offices to eliminate duplication and reduce bureaucracy.

**Expanding Apprenticeships in America**

*"Today's apprentices will construct the roads and bridges that move our citizens, they will bend the metal and steel that shape our cities, and they will pioneer the new technology that drives our commerce."*

President Donald J. Trump
June 15, 2017

The Presidential Executive Order "Expanding Apprenticeships in America," directed agencies to prioritize effective, evidence-based workforce development programs through the promotion of apprenticeship. Accordingly, the Budget provides $10 million for expansion of effective apprenticeship programs in the Bureau of Prisons, giving inmates the necessary skills for lucrative employment in the sectors employers—and our economy—most need.

**Strengthens Prisoner Reentry Programming.** In addition to prosecuting crime and enforcing the Nation's laws, the Administration proposes to promote public safety by preventing individuals who have reentered society from returning to criminal activity. Approximately 95 percent of people in State or Federal prison will be released at some point, and two-thirds are rearrested for a new offense within three years. The Administration is committed to breaking this cycle of crime and preparing returning citizens for lives as responsible, contributing members of society. The Budget provides approximately $739 million for reentry programming in BOP, including funding for education, career and technical training, substance abuse, and residential reentry centers. In addition, through State and local assistance programs, the Budget provides $48 million for the Second Chance Act Grant program to reduce recidivism and help ex-offenders return to productive lives.

**Expands Efforts to Combat Violence Against Women.** The Budget provides $486 million to reinforce efforts to combat and respond to violent crimes against women, including $215 million for Services, Training, Officers, and Prosecutors Grants. Domestic and sexual violence persist as serious threats to community safety and public health, with current estimates showing that 19.1 percent of women and 1.5 percent of men have been raped, and 23.2 percent of women and 13.9 percent of men have experienced severe physical violence by an intimate partner at some point in their lives. These grants play a critical role in helping to create a coordinated community response to this problem.

**Prioritizes Evidence-Based Practices that Work.** The Budget increases the set-aside for research, evaluation, and statistics at the Office of Justice Programs. In addition, the Budget supports the National Crime Statistics Exchange Initiative to develop nationally representative crime statistics. The Budget also continues to invest in *CrimeSolutions.gov*, a "what works" clearinghouse for best practices in criminal justice, juvenile justice, and crime victim services. These investments bolster the Administration's efforts to ensure that more Federal funding flows to evidence-based activities.

# DEPARTMENT OF LABOR

---

**Highlights:**

- The Department of Labor (DOL) fosters the well-being of wage earners, job seekers, and retirees.

- Given the budget constraints the Nation faces after decades of reckless spending, and the current need to rebuild the Nation's military without increasing the deficit, the Budget focuses DOL on its highest priority functions and disinvests in activities that are duplicative, unnecessary, unproven, or ineffective. The Budget also takes steps to reorganize and modernize the Agency's operations so scarce taxpayer dollars are spent well.

- The Budget requests $9.4 billion for DOL, a $2.6 billion or 21-percent decrease from the 2017 enacted level.

---

**The President's 2019 Budget:**

DOL promotes the well-being of American workers, job seekers, and retirees by helping them improve their skills, find work, and get back on their feet after job loss, injury, or illness, as well as safeguarding their working conditions, health and retirement benefits, and wages. Workers are the backbone of the American economy, and the Nation needs a skilled and productive workforce to keep its economy growing. The Budget improves the quality of life for all workers by making targeted, evidence-based investments to help workers get ahead and by eliminating duplicative, wasteful, and non-essential activities.

*"Not only will our apprentices transform their lives, but they will also transform our lives in the truest sense. Today's apprentices will construct the roads and bridges that move our citizens, they will bend the metal and steel that shape our cities, and they will pioneer the new technology that drives our commerce."*

President Donald J. Trump
June 15, 2017

## *Building a Highly Skilled and Competitive Workforce*

**Expands Access to Apprenticeship.** The Budget invests $200 million in apprenticeships, a proven earn-while-you-learn strategy that equips workers with the skills they need to fill open, high-paying jobs. Apprenticeship is a great solution for employers looking for a skilled workforce and workers looking for an affordable path to a secure future, yet currently only

550,000 individuals—less than half of one percent of the workforce—participate in apprenticeships each year. As part of implementing the President's Executive Order "Expanding Apprenticeships in America," the Department is establishing a new industry-recognized apprenticeship system to modernize and expand the U.S. approach to apprenticeships. DOL is working to empower employers, educational institutions, labor-management organizations, trade associations, States, and other third parties to collaborate to create new, industry-driven apprenticeship solutions. The Department is also pursuing ways to expand apprenticeship opportunities in high-growth sectors where apprenticeships are underutilized, including healthcare, information technology, and advanced manufacturing.

**Develops a Plan to Reorganize and Consolidate the Nation's Workforce Development Programs.** The Federal Government has more than 40 workforce development programs spread across 14 agencies with a total annual cost of approximately $17 billion. Despite changes in the recent reauthorization of the Workforce Innovation and Opportunity Act, the system remains fragmented at the Federal level, perpetuating unnecessary bureaucracy and complicating State and local efforts to meet the comprehensive needs of Americans seeking workforce-related services. The Secretaries of Labor and Education, who administer most of the programs, are working on a comprehensive plan to consolidate and reorganize Federal workforce development programs to ensure that American workers receive the highest quality services possible and are prepared to fill the high-growth jobs of today and tomorrow. The plan will be released as part of a spring 2018 Government reorganization package.

**Reforms Job Corps.** Job Corps trains and educates approximately 50,000 disadvantaged youth at 125 primarily residential centers across the United States. The Budget takes aggressive steps to improve Job Corps for the youth it serves by: closing centers that do a poor job educating and preparing students for jobs; focusing the program on the older youth for whom the program is more effective; improving center safety; and making other changes to sharpen program quality and efficiency. As part of this reform effort, the Budget ends the Department of Agriculture's (USDA) role in the program, unifying responsibility in DOL. Workforce development is not a core USDA role, and the 26 centers it operates are overrepresented in the lowest performing cohort of centers. The Budget also announces other reforms to the program, including shifting the outreach and admissions function to States and piloting the use of cooperative agreements with non-profits that have expertise in serving youth to operate centers. These reforms would save money and improve results by eliminating ineffective centers and finding better ways to educate and train youth.

### *Modernizing the Unemployment Safety Net to Emphasize Work*

**Reduces Waste, Fraud, and Abuse While Getting Claimants Back to Work More Quickly.** The Budget expands Reemployment Services and Eligibility Assessments, an evidence-based activity that saves an average of $536 per claimant in unemployment insurance (UI) benefit costs by reducing improper payments and getting claimants back to work more quickly and at higher wages. The Budget proposes to create a permanent program that would allow each State to provide these services to one-half of its UI claimants as well as all of its transitioning servicemembers. The Budget also reduces waste, fraud, and abuse in the UI program with a package of program integrity proposals. These proposals would require States to use the tools already at their disposal for combatting improper payments while expanding their authority to spend certain UI program funds on activities that reduce waste, fraud, and abuse in the system.

**Focuses Trade Adjustment Assistance on Apprenticeship and Other Work-Based Training.** The Trade Adjustment Assistance (TAA) program, which provides cash benefits and training to workers who have been displaced by international trade, is in need of reform. A rigorous 2012 evaluation of the program demonstrated that workers who participated in the program had lower earnings than the comparison group at the end of a four-year follow-up period,[1] in part because they were more likely to participate in long-term job training programs rather than immediately reentering the workforce. However, this training was not targeted to in-demand industries and occupations—only 37 percent of participants became employed in the occupations for which they trained. The Budget proposes to refocus the TAA program on apprenticeship and on-the-job training, earn-as-you-learn strategies that ensure that participants are training for relevant occupations. States would also be encouraged to place a greater emphasis on intensive reemployment services for workers who are not participating in work-based training, getting those workers back into the workforce more quickly.

**Strengthens the Unemployment Safety Net.** States are responsible for funding the benefits they provide under the State-administered UI program. In order to avoid raising taxes on employers in the middle of a recession, States should build balances that would allow them to cover benefits when unemployment spikes. Despite years of recovery since the Great Recession, many States' UI accounts are still not adequately financed—as of September 30, 2017, only 24 States had sufficient reserves to weather another recession. The Budget proposes to strengthen the incentive for States to prepare for the next recession and adequately fund their UI systems by reducing Federal tax credits in States with particularly low reserve balances.

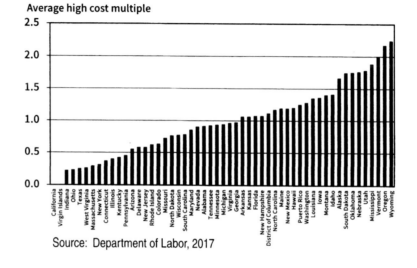

**Unemployment Insurance Reserves by State**

Average high cost multiple

Source: Department of Labor, 2017

## Protecting American Workers

**Secures Safe and Healthy Workplaces.** The Budget maintains targeted investments in the Occupational Safety and Health Administration (OSHA) and Mine Safety and Health Administration aimed at preventing worker fatalities, injuries, and illnesses through enforcement, outreach, and compliance assistance. The Budget increases OSHA Federal Compliance Assistance to assist employers who want help protecting their workers through cooperative programs.

**Makes Health Insurance More Affordable for Small Businesses.** The President's Executive Order "Promoting Healthcare Choice and Competition Across the United States" directed the Secretary of Labor to expand access to health coverage by allowing more employers to form Association Health Plans (AHPs), arrangements under which small businesses may band together to offer competitive and affordable health insurance to their employees. The Budget supports this initiative by increasing funding for the Employee Benefits Security Administration to develop policy and enforcement capacity to expand access to AHPs.

---

[1] *https://www.mathematica-mpr.com/our-publications-and-findings/publications/the-evaluation-of-the-trade-adjustment-assistance-program-a-synthesis-of-major-findings*

**Rebuilds DOL's Role in Overseeing Union Integrity.** To help safeguard labor union democracy and financial integrity, the Budget takes steps to restore the Office of Labor-Management Standards' investigative workforce, which has fallen by more than 40 percent during the past 10 years. The Budget would strengthen protections for union members by supporting more audits and investigations to uncover flawed officer elections, fraud, and embezzlement.

**Protects Americans' Pensions.** The Pension Benefit Guaranty Corporation's multiemployer program, which insures the pension benefits of 10 million workers, is at risk of insolvency by 2025. As an important step to protect the pensions of these hardworking Americans, the Budget proposes to add new premiums to the multiemployer program, raising approximately $16 billion in premiums over the 10-year window. At this level of premium receipts, the program is more likely than not to remain solvent over the next 20 years, helping to ensure that there is a safety net available to workers whose multiemployer plans fail.

**Reforms the Federal Employees' Compensation Act.** The Budget proposes to reform the Federal Employees' Compensation Act program, which provides workers' compensation benefits to Federal employees injured or killed on the job and their survivors. The proposed reform would save taxpayer dollars by modernizing program administration, simplifying benefit rates, and introducing controls to prevent waste, fraud, and abuse.

**Puts American Workers First.** DOL handles the labor certification component of foreign temporary work visa programs, which ensure that American workers are not unfairly displaced or disadvantaged by foreign workers. The certification programs lack a reliable workload-based source of funding, which has created recurring seasonal backlogs for employers and hindered DOL's ability to enforce protections for workers. The Budget proposes to establish fees to create a workload-based funding source and place responsibility for funding this work on the program's users rather than taxpayers.

## Supporting Working Families

**Provides for Paid Family Leave for New Parents.** The Budget invests in a better future for Americans with a fully paid-for proposal to provide six weeks of paid family leave to new mothers and fathers, including adoptive parents, so all families can afford to take time to recover from childbirth and bond with a new child. Using the UI system as a base, the proposal would allow States to establish paid parental leave programs in a way that is most appropriate for their workforce and economy. The Administration looks forward to working with the Congress to advance policies that would make paid parental leave a reality for families across the Nation.

## Making Government More Efficient

**Tackles Duplication and Inefficiency at the Department of Labor.** DOL is acting to implement in-house reforms consistent with the President's directive to reorganize and improve the Federal Government. Many of DOL's administrative activities, including procurement, human resources, financial management, and physical security, are separated across its subcomponents, creating duplication and wasting resources that would be better spent on core mission-related work. As part of its plan, DOL is centralizing these activities to improve oversight, eliminate duplication, save money, and achieve economies of scale. In addition, the Budget gives more tools to DOL's Chief Information Officer to modernize the Department's antiquated information technology systems by reallocating base resources.

# DEPARTMENT OF STATE AND OTHER INTERNATIONAL PROGRAMS

**Highlights:**

- The Department of State, the U.S. Agency for International Development (USAID), and other international programs help to advance the national security interests of the United States by building a more democratic, secure, and prosperous world.

- The Budget for the Department of State and USAID's diplomatic and development activities supports the strategic objectives of the United States, including those outlined in the 2018 Budget and the newly released National Security Strategy of the United States. In addition, the Budget supports Agency reform and critical investments that improve accountability, effectiveness, and efficiency in using taxpayer dollars to advance U.S. foreign affairs and national security goals. By pursuing a more balanced share of international spending and holding Departments and international organizations accountable for results, the Budget supports U.S. interests abroad, which would lead to a more prosperous and secure America.

- The Budget requests $25.8 billion in base funding for the Department of State and USAID, a $9 billion or 26-percent decrease from the 2017 enacted level. The Budget also requests $12 billion as Overseas Contingency Operations funding for extraordinary costs, primarily in war areas such as Syria, Iraq, and Afghanistan, for an Agency total of $37.8 billion, which is a $191 million increase from the 2018 Budget. The Budget also requests $1.4 billion for Department of the Treasury international programs, a $354 million or 20-percent reduction from the 2017 enacted level.

## The President's 2019 Budget:

The Budget supports the missions of the Department of State, USAID, and other international programs to advance the national security interests of the United States. The Budget promotes the development of more resilient and democratic societies, leading to a more secure and prosperous world. The Budget requests sufficient resources for the Department of State and other international programs to carry out their responsibilities under the National Security Strategy to protect the American people, preserve peace and security, promote American prosperity, and advance American influence. The Budget would enable the United States to compete for influence against those who do not share America's values or interests, catalyze conditions to help aspiring partners achieve mutually beneficial economic and security goals, and respond to the emerging era of great power competition across political, economic, and information domains. In addition, the Budget prioritizes diplomatic and development activities that provide maximum policy benefits, while making efficient, effective, and accountable use of taxpayer resources. Furthermore, the Budget upholds

*"America is a sovereign Nation and our first priority is always the safety and security of our citizens. We are not here to lecture—we are not here to tell other people how to live, what to do, who to be, or how to worship. Instead, we are here to offer partnership—based on shared interests and values—to pursue a better future for us all."*

President Donald J. Trump
May 21, 2017

U.S. commitments to partners and allies, while emphasizing the critical role of other donors to advance shared priorities.

**Provides a Platform of over 275 Embassies, Consulates, and Diplomatic Missions Around the World for the Development and Implementation of U.S. Foreign Policy, and to Carry out Visa and Passport Programs to Protect the American People.** The Budget requests $8.2 billion for Diplomatic Programs and the Information Technology (IT) Central Fund, which would support the critical day-to-day operations of the Department's overseas staff. In addition, the Budget is investing in more efficient and effective business processes for the Department of State. Specifically, the Budget requests $96 million for human capital investments in order to integrate a comprehensive approach to attracting, developing, and enabling personnel to have the resources and capabilities required for improved performance, leadership, and accountability. The Budget requests an additional $150 million to address key IT investments that would modernize legacy systems and software, allow the workforce to be more agile and resourceful—regardless of their location—and accelerate cloud-based solutions. The Budget also requests $1.3 billion for USAID Operations to support USAID personnel in 87 missions.

**Prioritizes the Safety and Security of American Diplomats and Staff Overseas.** The Budget requests $4.6 billion to protect overseas personnel and facilities. This funding level includes the Department's share of the $2.2 billion requested Government-wide in the Budget for new, secure embassy construction, as recommended by the Benghazi Accountability Review Board report. This would continue the upward trend of housing overseas personnel in safer diplomatic facilities. With the proposed level of funding, the Department of State would continue to protect American personnel representing more than 30 agencies, as well as provide services to Americans overseas, in a safe and secure environment.

**Promotes a Free and Open Indo-Pacific.** The United States' future security and prosperity depends on maintenance of free-and-open access to the Indo-Pacific. The Budget supports the Administration's commitment to U.S. leadership in this dynamic region through advancing democracy and good economic governance, supporting U.S. private sector competitiveness, promoting exports of U.S. goods and services, and sustaining the role of the United States as the region's preferred security and economic partner.

**Advances American Interests in the Middle East.** The Budget fully supports the new, 10-year Memorandum of Understanding between the United States and Israel, including $3.3 billion in Foreign Military Financing grant assistance to bolster Israel's capacity to defend itself and maintain its qualitative military edge. The Budget also requests $1.3 billion in economic and security assistance to support a long-term commitment to Jordan in recognition of the critical U.S.-Jordan strategic partnership. This extraordinary level of commitment contributes to Jordan's stability and security, and to shared goals of peace and prosperity in the Middle East and beyond. The Budget also dedicates significant security and economic assistance to other key partners in the region, including Egypt. In addition, the Budget supports the President's strategy to counter the destabilizing influence of the Iranian regime in the Middle East and beyond.

**Keeps the Islamic State of Iraq and Syria (ISIS) and Other Violent Extremist Organizations on the Path to Lasting Defeat.** The Budget for the Department of State and USAID supports the global strategy to defeat ISIS and other terrorist organizations, in coordination with the Global Coalition working to defeat ISIS as well as other partner countries. The Budget provides targeted assistance to address sources of regional instability and support partner country efforts to re-establish security and stability within their borders. These efforts constitute conditions for the long-term defeat of violent extremists, and protect U.S. interests in the region.

**Supports the President's Strategy in Afghanistan and South Asia.** The Budget's more than $630 million for civilian assistance supports the President's new strategy to empower the people of Afghanistan to take ownership of their future. In addition, the Budget strengthens and sustains improvements in education, health, governance, and other sectors that are essential for securing a stable and prosperous Afghanistan. The Budget also allows the United States to honor the pledge made at the Brussels conference on Afghanistan, which anticipated gradually declining assistance levels. The Budget requests $256 million for Pakistan in economic and other assistance to help increase stability, promote economic growth, and create opportunities for U.S. businesses. In addition, the Budget requests $80 million in Foreign Military Financing assistance to enhance Pakistan's counterterrorism and counterinsurgency capabilities, contingent on Pakistan taking appropriate action to expand cooperation in areas where U.S.-Pakistan interests converge and to address areas of divergence, in line with the Administration's South Asia strategy.

**Counters the Proliferation of Weapons of Mass Destruction.** The Budget prioritizes efforts to secure, eliminate, and prevent the proliferation of weapons of mass destruction and their delivery systems. Through diplomatic engagement, and bilateral and multilateral programs, the United States continues to promote strategic stability. These efforts build the international coalitions necessary to stop the spread of materials and expertise that aid state and non-state proliferators, and ensure that those who seek to build and use these weapons are held accountable.

**Proposes a Reformed, Consolidated U.S. Development Finance Institution to Expand U.S. Influence Abroad.** During his November 2017 trip to Asia, the President committed to reforming U.S. development finance institutions to better incentivize private sector investment in developing nations, counter America's competitors, and provide better alternatives to State-directed initiatives. The Budget builds on this commitment and acts on the President's call for a streamlined, more effective Government. Specifically, the Budget consolidates several private sector mobilization and development finance functions at various agencies, such as the Overseas Private Investment Corporation (OPIC) and USAID's Development Credit Authority, into a new, enhanced U.S. Development Finance Institution (DFI). The DFI would not only reduce fragmentation, achieve operational efficiencies, and provide cost savings to the taxpayer, but it would also improve coordination and policy alignment. The DFI also includes reformed and modernized tools to ensure that U.S. development finance effectively catalyzes, but does not displace, private sector resources, and does not create undue risk for the U.S. taxpayer. A reformed, consolidated DFI more effectively supports economic growth and development outcomes in emerging markets. It would also advance U.S. national security interests, and support U.S. companies, jobs, and exports.

**Ensures that Trade is Fair and Reciprocal.** The Budget requests $63 million for the Office of the U.S. Trade Representative (USTR) in support of the President's ambitious trade agenda. By renegotiating outdated agreements and pursuing opportunities for new trade deals, the Administration is working to ensure that trade grows the economy and brings jobs back to America's shores. The Administration further protects American workers and businesses by identifying trade violations, and pursuing all enforcement options at its disposal to end these abuses, many of which went unaddressed for years.

**Levels the Playing Field for America's Exporters.** The Budget supports a fully functioning Export-Import Bank (ExIm) to help level the playing field for America's exporters and help America compete, while ensuring that ExIm does not displace the private sector. The Budget would allow ExIm to play an important role in supporting the Administration's job creation agenda by facilitating exports where market gaps would otherwise exist, while ensuring that ExIm does not unnecessarily distort the market. ExIm would focus its efforts on market segments where U.S. support is critical to compete, including in areas of national security importance, and on supporting small and medium-sized American exporters that are the engines of economic growth and U.S. job creation.

**Targets Foreign Assistance to Promote Developing Countries' Self-Reliance and Ultimately End their Need for Aid.** The Budget reflects the Administration's goal to encourage and advance partner countries' self-reliance in order to become tomorrow's trading and security partners. Working with partners to help them reach their development goals advances common interests and values, strengthens stability in key regions, boosts U.S. economic opportunities, and establishes the conditions for a more secure and prosperous world. The Budget supports new efforts to track countries' development progress from fragility through self-reliance to lasting prosperity. Going forward, agencies would use this information to guide resource requests, program approaches, incentivize critical reforms, and measure program performance to support partner countries' progress along the development pathway and toward a transition away from the need for aid. The Budget also emphasizes aid approaches that bring in private capital and innovation, foster fair and reciprocal trading relationships, and empower reform-minded governments and people who share the same goals to develop their own capabilities and resources.

**Concentrates Efforts Against HIV/AIDS.** In September, Secretary Tillerson launched the President's Emergency Plan for AIDS Relief's (PEPFAR) new Strategy for Accelerating HIV/AIDS Epidemic Control (2017-2020). The Budget supports the new impact strategy by continuing support in more than 50 countries and strengthening U.S. investment in a subset of countries, which represent the most vulnerable communities to HIV/AIDS and have the potential to achieve control by 2020. In addition, the Budget requests $925 million to complete a three-year commitment to the Global Fund to Fight AIDS, Tuberculosis and Malaria, fully funding the U.S. Government's Fifth Replenishment pledge to match $1 for every $2 provided by other donors. At the funding level requested in the Budget, the United States would provide sufficient resources to maintain all current patient levels on HIV/AIDS treatment. U.S. efforts to control the HIV/AIDS epidemic are a direct reflection of U.S. leadership abroad and the goodwill, compassion, and generosity of the American people.

**Helps Prevent Public Health Emergencies through the Global Health Security Agenda (GHSA) and Advances Maternal and Child Health.** Containing the spread of deadly diseases overseas is a vital U.S. national security interest. To prevent, detect, and respond to infectious disease threats abroad, the Budget request supports an array of global health security activities through the GHSA. The Budget also requests nearly $2 billion for lifesaving health interventions through USAID, including the President's Malaria Initiative, programs that address tuberculosis, polio eradication, and Neglected Tropical Diseases, and the U.S. contribution to Gavi, the Vaccine Alliance. With the Protecting Life in Global Health Assistance policy now in place, the Budget request includes U.S. investments in family planning and reproductive health, with an emphasis on evidence-based methods, including fertility awareness. These services would save thousands of lives and support women's empowerment.

**Improves Food Security and Resilience.** To help address global hunger and poverty, the Budget includes bilateral funding for agriculture-led food security programs. Increased emphasis on resilience and evidence-based programs that aim to address root causes of vulnerability would help prevent future famines in regions that face recurrent crises, particularly in Sub-Saharan Africa.

Resilience and targeted programs have been shown to be effective in helping vulnerable populations withstand severe weather and other shocks, which limits the need for emergency food and other humanitarian assistance. Beyond resilience, this funding is focused on strengthening the capacity of developing countries with extreme poverty that have strong potential to address their severe food insecurity, through activities such as improvements in smallholders' agricultural productivity, markets, and nutrition, and which commit to undertake policy reforms as part of robust country-led strategies.

**Maintains U.S. Global Humanitarian Leadership While Expecting Others to do More.** The Budget requests significant humanitarian assistance resources enabling the United States to remain the largest single humanitarian donor. The Budget request also enables the United States to address major humanitarian crises, including those driven by conflict, such as in Syria, Yemen, and Iraq. The Budget relies on a new approach to relief that includes new efforts to influence other donors to give a greater share. The Budget also demands improved performance by United Nations (UN) organizations and other implementers to maximize the benefit for recipients of assistance. This approach supports the priority to impose greater accountability on international partners along with donor burden sharing that is more balanced, while reducing suffering and meeting the needs of refugees and displaced persons close to their homes until they can safely return.

> *"To honor the people of our nations, we must ensure that no one and no member state shoulders a disproportionate share of the burden, and that's militarily or financially. We also ask that every peacekeeping mission have clearly defined goals and metrics for evaluating success. They deserve to see the value in the United Nations, and it is our job to show it to them."*
>
> President Donald J. Trump
> September 18, 2017

**Mobilizes Partner Countries' Domestic Resources, a Critical Step on the Path to Self-Reliance and Transitioning Away from Aid Assistance.** Domestic resource mobilization (DRM) presents a long-term path to sustainable development finance by encouraging countries to adopt effective, transparent, and accountable systems for mobilizing their own resources to invest in their own development. The U.S. Government's DRM activities are funded by USAID, Treasury's Office of Technical Assistance, the Millennium Challenge Corporation (MCC), and PEPFAR. USAID's new centrally-managed DRM initiative would equip and challenge partner countries to more effectively mobilize and manage domestic public and private resources, leverage other available financing sources, and sustainably lead their own development. USAID is building on the experiences and successes of DRM efforts in countries such as El Salvador, where improvements in tax collection over the last decade have increased government revenues by $350 million per year. Assistance would be provided to local governments to mobilize and manage public revenues, as well as private capital via local capital markets, to finance their own development and decrease aid dependency. This initiative would strive to ensure partner country commitment, a robust graduation strategy, rigorous monitoring and evaluation, and enhanced public-private dialogue.

**Ensures U.S. Leadership at Multilateral Development Banks (MDBs).** The Budget requests $1.4 billion in funding for MDBs, including the World Bank's International Development Association, the African Development Fund, and the Asian Development Fund. As a leading donor in these institutions, the United States demands high performance, reforms in line with U.S. values, and strategic investments in projects that serve U.S. development, foreign policy, and national security goals.

**Advances U.S. Interests and Values in Multilateral Organizations.** The United States will compete and be a leader in multilateral organizations so that American interests and principles are protected. The Administration remains committed to the need for greater transparency and reform in international bodies and for other donors to invest more. The Budget requests more than $2 billion for contributions to the UN Secretariat and technical agencies, UN peacekeeping, and other international organizations while signaling intent to pursue greater accountability and emphasize shared responsibility among members throughout the international system. In support of these goals, the Department of State and USAID will review multilateral aid and contributions to evaluate how each multilateral organization to which the United States belongs advances American interests.

**Reforms International Affairs Agencies to Strengthen Implementation of their Strategic Missions.** The Administration is committed to making the Federal Government more effective, more efficient, and more accountable. In 2019, the Department of State and USAID will continue to implement an in-depth redesign process to adapt U.S. diplomacy and development to the 21$^{st}$ Century, and better position each Agency for the future. More than 35,000 State and USAID professionals provided comments about which strengths to build on and which inefficiencies to remedy, including information technology and human capital management. The Budget also supports USAID's efforts to realign its strategies, programs, and processes to improve project design and procurement, diversify its portfolio of partners, and build local capacity to prepare countries to progress beyond the need for traditional assistance. The Budget further proposes consolidating small grants assistance currently managed by the U.S. African Development Foundation and the Inter-American Foundation into USAID, in order to improve alignment while also elevating locally driven development in poor and remote communities.

# DEPARTMENT OF TRANSPORTATION

---

**Highlights:**

- The mission of the Department of Transportation (DOT) is to ensure that: the Nation has the safest, most efficient, and modern transportation system in the world; the system improves the quality of life for all American people and communities, from rural to urban; and the system increases the productivity and competitiveness of American workers and businesses.

- The Budget request for DOT streamlines the Department to focus on its vital Federal safety mission, and provides critical investments necessary for regionally and nationally significant projects. The Budget also ensures taxpayer dollars are spent prudently, by reducing, eliminating, and reforming programs that are ineffective, inefficient, and unaccountable, or lack a clear Federal nexus and fail to encourage innovation.

- The Budget requests $15.6 billion in discretionary budget authority for 2019, a $3.7 billion or 19-percent decrease from the 2017 enacted base discretionary level of $19.3 billion (which excludes supplemental emergency relief funding). The Budget also provides $60.9 billion in mandatory funds and obligation limitations. For programs funded from the Highway Trust Fund, the Budget is consistent with the fourth year of the Fixing America's Surface Transportation Act (FAST Act) of 2015.

---

## The President's 2019 Budget:

DOT oversees the safety, security, mobility, efficiency, and interconnectedness of the Nation's vast transportation networks. DOT's highest priority is the safety of the American people. The Budget reflects this priority by providing DOT the resources necessary for ensuring that the Nation's air, surface, and maritime transportation systems are safe. Another top priority is improving the condition and performance of the Nation's transportation infrastructure. The Budget ensures that DOT would continue to advance nationally and regionally significant projects, via Federal financial assistance and timely, prudent regulatory and permitting decision-making. While providing the funds to support these and other important priorities, the Budget also reflects reductions and eliminations of programs that are inefficient, ineffective, or should be carried out by States, local government, or the private sector.

**Ensures the Safety of the Nation's Transportation System.** The Budget prioritizes the resources necessary for fulfilling the Department's safety missions. The human and economic costs of transportation accidents are severe, and DOT is committed to preventing as many accidents as possible through its educational outreach, investments, and oversight of safety standards. The vast majority of transportation-related fatalities occur on the Nation's highways: 37,461 in 2016. The Budget provides

**Promise Made:**

*"Our infrastructure will again be the best in the world."*

President Donald J. Trump
August 15, 2017

**Promise Kept:**

To dramatically modernize the Nation's infrastructure, and make it the best in the world, the Administration is proposing a comprehensive Infrastructure Initiative. The initiative is designed to: spur additional State, local, and private infrastructure investment by awarding incentives to project sponsors for demonstrating innovative approaches that would generate new revenue streams, modernize procurement practices, and improve project performance; support bold, innovative, and transformative infrastructure projects that can significantly improve existing conditions; support rural economic competitiveness through a Rural Formula Grant program; and accelerate the delivery of nationally and regionally significant projects with increased Federal loan support. The Administration is also advocating for transformational reform to the environmental permitting process, to shorten the timelines it takes to permit a project, while still maintaining good environmental outcomes. These programs would support additional investment in highways, bridges, airports, rail, ports, and other types of infrastructure in urban and rural America.

$2.6 billion to the Federal Highway Administration's (FHWA) Highway Safety Improvement Program, to assist States in the implementation of their safety plans. The Budget also funds other FHWA, National Highway Traffic Safety Administration (NHTSA), and Federal Motor Carriers Safety Administration (FMCSA) safety programs, to prevent highway fatalities. In addition, the Budget provides resources to support the development of autonomous vehicles and infrastructure, which hold promise to dramatically improve highway safety and deliver many other benefits. The Budget also supports the continued emphasis on ensuring that the air, rail, transit, and pipeline systems are the safest in the world.

**Continues Investment in Surface Transportation.** Americans' quality of life and long-term economic prosperity depend, in part, on the condition and performance of the Nation's transportation infrastructure. To address these challenges, the Budget requests $57.4 billion in mandatory funds and obligation limitation to improve the Nation's highways, bridges, and transit systems. The Budget includes $46 billion for highway infrastructure and safety programs, $9.9 billion for transit infrastructure, and $1.4 billion for NHTSA and FMCSA safety programs. These levels match the authorized amounts in the FAST Act.

**Reforms Air Traffic Control.** Consistent with the 2018 Budget, the Budget includes a multiyear reauthorization proposal to shift the air traffic control function of the Federal Aviation Administration to a non-governmental, independent air traffic services cooperative, making the system more efficient and innovative while maintaining safety. Similar to successful efforts in many other developed countries, the goal is to create a system that can respond to changing air travel demand by deploying cutting-edge technology and giving airlines, general aviation users, and passengers a system that is a good steward of their financial resources.

**Reforms the Essential Air Services (EAS) Program.** EAS was designed as a temporary program nearly 40 years ago. However, today many EAS flights are not full and have high per passenger subsidy costs. Several EAS eligible communities are relatively close to major airports. The Budget includes a legislative reform proposal to modify the definition of essential air service, to ensure that Federal funds are efficiently targeted at the communities most in need. These reforms aim to reduce support for service that results in high per passenger subsidies (often hundreds of dollars per passenger) and end subsidies to communities that are relatively close to other airports. The Budget requests $93 million in discretionary resources, a reduction of $57 million from the 2017 enacted level of $150 million.

**Reforms Amtrak Long Distance Services.** While Amtrak has in recent years improved its ridership and revenue on the Northeast Corridor and State Supported Routes, Amtrak continues to rely exclusively on Federal subsidies to operate long distance train routes, which have large operating losses and serve a small number of passengers. The Budget proposes reforms to Amtrak to improve efficiencies in long distance services and reduce reliance of the Federal Government. In particular, the Budget proposes that States begin to share the operating subsidy costs of Long Distance routes with the Federal Government. This would make States more equal partners with the Federal Government, and would strengthen the responsiveness of Amtrak to the communities they serve. State contributions to long distance routes is only one tool in the menu of options for reform the Administration will be exploring to improve the current system and reduce Federal subsidies in the Long Distance network.

**Eliminates Discretionary Grant Programs.** Consistent with the 2018 Budget, the Budget eliminates funding for the unauthorized Transportation Investment Generating Economic Recovery discretionary grant program, which awards grants to projects that are generally eligible for funding under existing surface transportation formula grant and loan programs. In addition, DOT's Infrastructure For Rebuilding America grant program, authorized by the FAST Act, supports larger highway and multimodal freight projects with demonstrable national or regional benefits. The Budget also proposes to wind down the Federal Transit Administration's Capital Investment Grant program (known as New Starts), by limiting funding to projects with existing full funding grant agreements only. The President's Infrastructure Initiative is designed to incentivize States and localities to raise new revenue and funding dedicated for infrastructure investment, via competitive Federal grant awards and other incentives. Those new State and local funds would be available for transportation projects prioritized by those communities, which are better equipped to understand their infrastructure needs. The Federal Government would continue to be a partner in advancing large, regionally- or nationally-significant projects via expanded Federal credit support.

**Reorganizes the Department of Transportation.** The Budget includes proposals in response to Executive Order 13781, which requires each agency to prepare a plan to reorganize the agency, if appropriate, in order to improve its efficiency, effectiveness, and accountability. One such proposal is to modernize Air Traffic Control. Another proposal to increase effectiveness is to explore the transfer of certain surface transportation job training programs to the Department of Labor, the Federal Agency with the most expertise in job training programs. The Department is also undertaking a major shared services effort to consolidate acquisitions, human resources, and information technology functions within the Department.

---

**Large Increase in 2017 Loans for Transportation Infrastructure Renewal**

(Dollars in millions)

|                   | 2015    | 2016    | 2017     |
|-------------------|---------|---------|----------|
| Loans Closed      | 7       | 6       | 12       |
| TIFIA Assistance  | $2,384  | $2,180  | $3,851   |
| Total Project Costs | $8,776 | $6,793 | $14,602  |

Source: DOT

DOT's Build America Bureau provides innovative financing support for large, complex transportation infrastructure projects. One of the major financial tools the Bureau executes is the Transportation Infrastructure Finance and Innovation Act (TIFIA) loan program. TIFIA loans leverage substantial non-Federal investment to support nationally or regionally significant transportation projects. In 2017, the Bureau provided $3.9 billion in TIFIA assistance, $1.7 billion or 77 percent more than in 2016. This assistance supported $14.6 billion in infrastructure improvements, $7.8 billion or 115 percent more than in 2016. Examples of recently financed projects include construction of a bridge and roadways connecting Indiana and Kentucky; a public-private partnership toll road project in Harris County, Texas; and a 17.6-mile tunnel connecting the Norfolk/Virginia Beach areas to Virginia's eastern shore.

# DEPARTMENT OF THE TREASURY

---

**Highlights:**

- The Department of the Treasury (Treasury) manages the U.S. Government's finances, promotes conditions that enable stable economic growth, protects the integrity of the financial system, and combats financial crimes and terrorist financing.

- The Budget requests the resources necessary to responsibly manage the Nation's debt and efficiently collect revenue while reallocating funding from non-mission critical areas to invest in the financial enforcement tools that would safeguard the financial system and bring maximum economic pressure against North Korea and other national security threats.

- The Budget requests $12.3 billion in base discretionary resources for Treasury's domestic programs, a $392 million or 3-percent decrease from the 2017 enacted level. This program level excludes mandatory spending changes involving the Treasury Forfeiture Fund.

- The Budget also proposes a program integrity initiative to narrow the gap between taxes owed and taxes paid that is estimated to reduce the deficit by approximately $29 billion over the next 10 years.

---

**The President's 2019 Budget:**

The Budget capitalizes on Treasury's ongoing drive for efficiencies, and would improve stewardship of taxpayers' dollars, by focusing on the Department's core economic and financial responsibilities. The Budget prioritizes resources to combat terrorist financing, proliferation financing, and other forms of illicit finance and supports Treasury's role as chair of the Committee on Foreign Investment in the United States (CFIUS) to address current and future national security risks. In addition, the Budget maintains Treasury's mission-critical functions as the Federal Government's revenue collector, financial manager, and economic policymaker. The foundation of American prosperity rests with the people, not the Federal Government, and the Budget would ensure that taxpayers, investors, and job-creators operate in an economy that is secure, fair, and free from unnecessary bureaucratic impediments.

**Prioritizes Safeguarding Markets and Protecting Financial Data.** Treasury's Office of Terrorism and Financial Intelligence (TFI) possesses a unique set of authorities and tools to combat terrorists, rogue regimes, proliferators of weapons of mass destruction, and other illicit actors by denying their access to the financial system, disrupting their revenue streams, and degrading their capabilities. Likewise, the Financial Crimes Enforcement Network's (FinCEN) role in linking the law enforcement and intelligence communities with financial institutions and regulators helps these entities uncover and prosecute illegal activities and money-laundering schemes. In addition, consistent with the National Security Strategy, the Budget supports Treasury's leading role as chair of the CFIUS. The Administration will work with the Congress to modernize and strengthen this essential national security tool.

The Budget requests $159 million for TFI, a $36 million increase from the 2017 enacted level, to continue its critical work safeguarding the financial system from abuse and combatting other national security threats using non-kinetic economic tools. These additional resources would be deployed to economically isolate North Korea, complete the Terrorist Financing Targeting Center in Saudi Arabia, and increase sanctions pressure on Iran, including through the implementation of the Countering America's Adversaries Through Sanctions Act.

The Budget requests $118 million for FinCEN, a $3 million increase from the 2017 enacted level, to administer the Bank Secrecy Act and focus on the prevention of terrorist financing, money laundering, and other financial crimes in new sectors and through new pathways. This increase would also enable FinCEN to further utilize its unique authorities—FinCEN would expand investigations into financial institutions that may be facilitating the illicit activities of national security threats such as North Korea, terrorist organizations, and drug trafficking organizations that are fueling the opioid crisis.

The Budget also requests $25 million to proactively and strategically protect Treasury information technology (IT) systems that carry out these activities as well as those that account for, and process, trillions of dollars in revenue and payments against cybersecurity threats. These funds are requested in addition to bureau-level investments, and would be centrally managed to strengthen the security of Treasury's most critical IT assets and improve Treasury's response and recovery capabilities. The funds would also allow Treasury to leverage enterprise-wide services and capabilities and help the Department nimbly respond to cybersecurity incidents.

**Preserves Funding for Essential Revenue Collection Operations.** The tax reforms enacted last year were the most significant changes to the Nation's tax code in more than 30 years. They achieved the President's goals of: 1) cutting taxes for middle-income families; 2) simplifying the tax code for individuals; and 3) reducing business taxes so American employers can create jobs, raise wages for their workers, better compete with foreign businesses, and bring back money that is currently held offshore. By investing in the modernization of Internal Revenue Service (IRS) systems, the Budget would help make the implementation of tax reform successful and support the President's vision of making tax filing simpler for hardworking Americans.

The IRS collects approximately $3.4 trillion in tax revenue annually and processes more than 246 million tax returns and forms resulting in more than $437 billion in tax refunds. The Budget proposes $11.1 billion in base funding for the IRS including $2.3 billion for running key tax filing and compliance IT applications and $110 million for IT modernization efforts. The Budget also requests additional funds for new and continuing investments to expand and strengthen the enforcement of tax law to ensure that all Americans are paying the taxes they owe. These additional investments proposed over the next 10 years are estimated to generate approximately $44 billion in additional revenue at a cost of $15 billion, yielding a net savings of $29 billion over 10 years.

Approximately 90 percent of individual taxpayers file their tax returns electronically and more than 278 million taxpayers use the Where's My Refund application to check the status of their refunds rather than calling the IRS. However, for many interactions, the IRS relies on antiquated tax processing systems (many of which date back to the 1960s) and handles most of its interactions with taxpayers, other than tax filing, through the mail. Modernizing IRS systems would allow IRS staff to have up-to-date, accurate information about taxpayer accounts when they work with taxpayers.

The Budget also includes several proposals to ensure that taxpayers comply with their obligations, that tax refunds are only paid to those taxpayers who are eligible for them, and that taxpayer dollars are protected from criminals seeking to commit fraud:

- Increasing oversight of paid tax preparers—taxpayers are increasingly turning to paid tax return preparers to assist them in meeting their tax filing obligations. Ensuring that these preparers understand the tax code would help taxpayers get higher quality service and prevent unscrupulous tax preparers from exploiting the system and vulnerable taxpayers.

- Giving the IRS the authority to correct more errors on tax returns before refunds are issued—this would keep refunds from being issued to taxpayers who are not eligible. The Budget would also allow the IRS to resolve simple issues quickly without having to direct enforcement resources away from more difficult cases.

- Requiring a valid Social Security Number for work in order to claim the Child Tax Credit and Earned Income Tax Credit—this proposal would ensure that only individuals authorized to work in the United States could claim these credits.

**Manages the Nation's Finances More Effectively.** The Bureau of the Fiscal Service (Fiscal Service) conducts all Treasury debt financing operations, provides central payment services for Federal agencies, runs Government-wide accounting and reporting services, and manages the collection of delinquent debt. In 2017, the Fiscal Service issued approximately $8.6 trillion in marketable Treasury securities, processed the collection of more than $4 trillion in Federal receipts, and distributed more than $3.4 trillion in payments, including Social Security payments, IRS tax refunds, and veterans' benefits.

The Fiscal Service performs the vast majority of payment and collection transactions electronically, but in 2017, it still issued almost 60 million paper checks and collected more than $500 billion in payments by mail or in person. The Budget supports Treasury's ongoing digitization of payments that would reduce burden and bureaucracy while increasing options and accessibility for citizens and customers to conduct transactions with the Federal Government in a secure, electronic environment.

As the Federal Government's central payment provider, the Fiscal Service is also responsible for helping agencies identify, prevent, and reduce improper payments. To improve Treasury's efforts to help agencies prevent and detect improper payments, the Budget includes administrative actions and legislative proposals that would:

- remove costly barriers to data sharing across the Government;

- allow for more cost-effective and efficient use of data sources;

**Doing More with Less**

The Budget proposes $331 million for Fiscal Service operations, approximately $100 million less than the 2010 level. This reduction is the result of the successful consolidation of two bureaus and significant administrative actions including the closing or re-purposing of two payments centers, consolidating five data centers into two, and decreasing the Bureau's footprint. During the same period, the Fiscal Service has maintained, and in many cases improved, its performance of core services and taken on a number of new Government-wide initiatives.

- provide centralized access and use of the National Directory of New Hires and the Social Security Administration's full death file;

- create a central repository for death records from Federal agencies; and

- facilitate partnerships with non-Federal partners.

The Budget also includes two legislative proposals that would help to improve these efforts by authorizing an additional mechanism to recover delinquent Federal non-tax debt and streamlining recovery of unclaimed assets owed to the United States.

**Rationalizes the Financial Regulatory Framework.** The Administration is committed to reforming the Nation's financial system and rolling back the regulatory excesses mandated by the Dodd-Frank Act, as demonstrated by Executive Order 13772, "Core Principles for Regulating the United States Financial System" (Core Principles EO).

Since issuance of the Core Principles EO in February 2017, Treasury has published several reports making numerous recommendations for administrative and statutory reforms. These reviews included evaluation of the Financial Stability Oversight Council (FSOC) and the Office of Financial Research (OFR), both established by the Dodd-Frank Act. The Budget proposes to impose appropriate congressional oversight of these functions by subjecting all Treasury FSOC and OFR activities to the normal appropriations process. The Budget reflects continued reductions in OFR spending commensurate with the renewed fiscal discipline being applied across the Federal Government. Treasury is also working to increase the transparency of FSOC decision-making procedures and to implement more rigorous cost-benefit analysis standards.

**Increases Treasury's Efficiency and Effectiveness by Streamlining Operations.** The Budget eliminates funding for the Community Development Financial Institutions (CDFI) Fund's discretionary grant and direct loan programs, a savings of $234 million from the 2017 enacted level. The CDFI Fund was created more than 20 years ago to jump-start a now mature industry. In addition, private institutions should have ready access to the capital needed to extend credit and provide financial services to underserved communities. However, the Budget maintains funding for administrative expenses to support ongoing CDFI Fund program activities, including the New Markets Tax Credit program. The Budget also proposes to extend the CDFI Bond Guarantee Program, which offers CDFIs low-cost, long-term financing at no cost to taxpayers, as the program requires no credit subsidy.

In addition, the Budget proposes to transfer all alcohol and tobacco responsibilities from the Department of Justice's Bureau of Alcohol, Tobacco, Firearms and Explosives (ATF) to Treasury's Alcohol and Tobacco Tax and Trade Bureau (TTB). This transfer would leverage TTB's resources and expertise relating to the alcohol and tobacco industries and allow ATF to continue to focus on its firearms and explosives mandates, enabling both agencies to more efficiently and effectively carry out their core mission of protecting the public.

The U.S. Mint and the Bureau of Engraving and Printing (BEP) are responsible for assuring that the Nation retains its status as producing the world's most accepted currency, that U.S. currency is secure against counterfeiting efforts, and that U.S. currency is produced efficiently and at the lowest cost. The Budget includes two legislative proposals that would enable BEP to lower costs and improve the security of official documents issued by States:

- providing BEP with the authority to vacate its aging production facility, purchase land, and construct a new facility in the National Capital Region which would result in estimated 10-year savings of $579 million in lower project costs, ultimately lowering operating costs; and

- authorizing BEP to offer its specialized printing services to States for a fee which would allow States to leverage the U.S. Government's secure document production capabilities to print birth, marriage, and death certificates. Many States want to use this technology but cannot find an American printing firm to produce the documents and are instead turning to foreign companies or lowering their security standards.

In addition, the U.S. Mint and BEP are consolidating their acquisition and sales activities to share a common sales platform and gain efficiencies from similar procurement needs and expertise.

# DEPARTMENT OF VETERANS AFFAIRS

---

**Highlights:**

- The Department of Veterans Affairs (VA) provides veterans of the Armed Forces and their survivors with a wide variety of benefits including but not limited to healthcare, mental health services, homelessness programs, service-connected disability compensation, readjustment counseling, vocational rehabilitation, education, and home loan guaranties.

- The Budget provides resources to implement a multi-faceted strategy to modernize and transform VA to meet a growing demand for access to healthcare, improve the timeliness and effectiveness of non-medical benefit delivery, and promote internal accountability to reduce waste, fraud, and abuse.

- The Budget requests $83.1 billion for VA, an $8.7 billion, or 11.7-percent increase from the 2017 enacted level. In addition, $75.6 billion is requested for advance medical care appropriations for 2020 to ensure the Department has the resources to continue providing high-quality medical services to veterans. In addition, the Budget also requests new legislative authorities and $122.7 billion in mandatory budget authority, including $121 billion in 2020 advance appropriations, for other veteran and survivor benefits.

---

**The President's 2019 Budget:**

VA fulfills President Lincoln's promise to care for America's veterans, their families, and survivors—men and women who have responded when their Nation needed help. The Budget would provide the resources for the Nation to meet its obligations to those who have served in the Armed Forces. With this funding, VA would: deliver premier care through one of the largest integrated healthcare systems in the United States to approximately 9.3 million enrollees; deliver compensation benefits to approximately 4.9 million veterans and 432,000 survivors; administer pension benefits for approximately 469,000 veterans and their survivors; provide servicemember and veteran group life insurance plans to approximately six million enrollees; provide educational assistance to slightly more than 950,000 beneficiaries; manage a home mortgage program with slightly more than 3.1 million active loans,

> *"As Commander-in-Chief, I will not accept substandard service for our great veterans."*
>
> President Donald J. Trump
> March 17, 2017

guaranteed by VA; and provide memorial and burial benefits to approximately 141,000 veterans and their family members in 2019.

## Agency Reforms

**Improves Veteran Experience.** The Budget focuses on four priorities to enhance veterans' quality of life and demonstrate the Administration's commitment to a better future. These priorities include: a greater focus on identifying at-risk veterans and providing them targeted interventions to prevent suicide; enhancing healthcare in the community; simplifying access to and knowledge of non-medical benefits; and implementing a new appeals framework. These objectives are essential to VA's efforts to enrich veterans' experiences and become the service provider of choice.

In addition, the Budget supports initiatives to modernize and reform VA:

- $4.2 billion to leverage emerging technology, modernize and maintain infrastructure, and provide greater choices and benefits to veterans;

- $172 million for the Office of the Inspector General to strengthen accountability, promote transparency, and reduce waste, fraud, and abuse; and

- in 2019 VA will continue implementing a long-term strategic plan that would further streamline service delivery, improve the efficiency of the Federal Government, and ensure that veterans are receiving the benefits they need.

## Veterans Health Administration

**Improves Veterans' Access to Medical Care.** The Budget provides $70.7 billion, a 9.6-percent increase above the 2017 enacted level, to provide high-quality healthcare services to veterans and eligible beneficiaries. The Budget also proposes $75.6 billion in advance appropriations for VA medical care programs in 2020, a 6.9-percent increase above the 2019 request. In addition, $11.9 billion would be used to enhance and expand veterans' access to high-quality community care, by consolidating multiple community care programs, including the Veterans Choice Program, into one unified program. This new program, the Veteran Coordinated Access & Rewarding Experiences program, would place the veteran and his or her physician at the center of the decision-making process and offer options for veterans to use a network of walk-in clinics for minor illnesses and injuries. Overall, the Budget is designed to improve veterans' experiences with and access to healthcare, building on the best features of VA's existing community care programs and strengthening VA's ability to furnish care in its own facilities.

> *"I intend to build a system that puts veterans first and allows them to get the best possible health care and services wherever they may be—in VA or in the community."*
>
> David Shulkin
> Secretary
> February 1, 2017

**Combats the Opioid Epidemic.** Fighting the opioid epidemic is a top priority of this Administration, and VA is at the forefront of combatting this public health emergency. The Budget provides $381 million in critical investments to reduce over-reliance on opioids for pain management and to promote the safe and effective use of opioid therapy. Funding supports multidisciplinary approaches in opioid prevention and treatment, including investments in: provider training to assess risk and manage treatment; mental health outpatient and residential treatment programs; opioid overdose, recognition, rescue and response training programs; medication assisted therapy for opioid use disorders; patient advocacy; and distribution of naloxone kits.

**Provides Critical Funding for Mental Health and Suicide Prevention.** The Budget provides slightly more than $8.6 billion to expand and transform VA's focus on mental health services to ensure veterans receive timely and appropriate care that is tailored to the unique needs of each person. As part of its effort, VA is focusing on earlier identification and intervention for at-risk veterans to link them with the health services they need. VA would also continue to provide emergent mental healthcare treatment for veterans with other-than-honorable discharges. Suicide prevention is VA's number one clinical priority, and the Budget supports VA's efforts across five key domains: improve transition; know all veterans; partner across communities; reduce easy access to dangerous substances and objects; and improve access to care.

**Continues Efforts to End Veteran Homelessness.** The Budget supports VA's commitment to ending veteran homelessness by sustaining funding levels and providing opportunities to improve the targeting of intervention for veterans impacted by homelessness. Specifically, the Budget requests $1.8 billion for veteran homelessness programs including Supportive Services for Veteran Families and VA's component of the Department of Housing and Urban Development—VA Supportive Housing Program. These programs provide critical wrap-around care to help address and prevent veteran homelessness.

### *Veterans Benefits Administration and Board of Veterans Appeals*

**Streamlines Delivery of Veteran Benefits.** VA provides veterans and eligible dependents with benefits including disability compensation, pension, GI Bill, educational assistance, vocational rehabilitation, and home loan guaranties among others. The Budget invests $2.9 billion, a 1-percent increase from the 2017 enacted level for these programs. These benefits directly support the economic security of veterans and their families, and reflect a greater commitment to a better future.

**Modernizes the Claims Appeals Process.** Of the amount requested, $183.5 million is for the Board of Veterans Appeals and related information technology (IT) initiatives to enhance ongoing efforts to reduce the pending appeals inventory and modernize VA's appeal process by establishing a new framework that is designed to provide quicker decisions on appeals for the veteran. The new framework would provide veterans with choices to obtain resolution of their appeals based on the option that best serves the individual veteran's circumstances. The new options are designed to improve the timeliness of appeals decisions.

> *"This is about making benefits work better for veterans and transforming the Department of Veterans Affairs to do better for years, and for generations [of] future veterans."*
>
> David Shulkin
> Secretary
> November 6, 2017

**Enhances and Expands Access to Post-9/11 GI Bill Education Benefits.** The Budget complements and supports continued implementation of the Harry W. Colmery Veterans Educational Assistance Act of 2017 (the "Forever GI Bill") which represents one of the most sweeping changes to the Post-9/11 GI Bill since its inception, expanding access to veterans and eligible dependents. In addition to the benefit payments, requested funding would also fund IT investments to effectively implement all provisions of the new law.

## National Cemetery Administration

**Increases Access to Burial and Memorial Benefits.** The Budget includes $315.8 million, a 10.4-percent increase from the 2017 enacted level, to expand veteran access to memorial benefits, deliver premier service to veterans' families, and provide perpetual care for slightly more than 3.8 million gravesites. The National Cemetery Administration consistently receives high satisfaction ratings from veterans and their families for the care of VA cemeteries as National Shrines. In addition to sustaining 139 cemeteries and 33 other sites, the Budget supports the initial activation of nine new cemeteries in California, Idaho, Indiana, Maine, New York (two), North Dakota, Wisconsin, and Wyoming. In 2019, VA anticipates providing slightly more than 141,000 interments for veterans and family members.

## Infrastructure Revitalization

**Provides Critical Funding for Construction and Modernization of VA Facilities.** The Budget provides $1.8 billion for 91 major and minor construction projects including new medical care facilities, national cemeteries, and projects at regional offices. The Budget also provides $1.4 billion for non-recurring maintenance projects to maintain and modernize medical facilities. These investments enhance the safety and security of VA facilities and help VA programs and services keep pace with modern technologies.

- Approximately $1.1 billion funds major construction projects, including construction of a community living center and domiciliary at Canandaigua, New York; construction of a facility that would specialize in spinal cord injuries at Dallas, Texas; and expansion of four national cemeteries that would provide slightly more than 80,000 new gravesites. This funding also includes $400 million to address critical seismic issues at VA facilities.

- In addition, $707 million funds minor construction projects, including corrections and additions to Veterans Health Administration facilities, gravesite expansions at national cemeteries, and renovations at regional offices.

- VA would use the $1.4 billion in funding for non-recurring maintenance to address infrastructure needs in its medical facilities.

**Invests in IT Infrastructure to Improve Services.** The Budget provides $4.2 billion for the Office of Information Technology. Of this amount, $204 million would support recapitalizing VA's legacy IT systems with new enterprise and business-line specific IT solutions to better support veteran focused initiatives. These investments are essential to better integrate processes, adopt modern technology solutions, improve security, and reduce long-term sustainment costs. In support of VA's goal to provide a comprehensive source to simplify veterans' access to and understanding of their benefits and services available to them, the Budget includes funding for a Navigator interface to navigate veterans to those entities best equipped to meet their needs. In addition to the amount requested for enterprise-wide IT infrastructure enhancements, $1.2 billion is included in a separate budget account for the acquisition of a replacement Electronic Health Records system. This is a substantive investment for this critical initiative, which would help facilitate a seamless transition for servicemembers as they leave the Armed Forces.

# CORPS OF ENGINEERS—CIVIL WORKS

---

**Highlights:**

- The Army Corps of Engineers civil works program (Corps) develops, manages, restores, and protects water resources primarily through the construction, operation and maintenance, and study of water-related infrastructure projects. The Corps is also responsible for regulating development on navigable waters of the United States and works with other Federal agencies to help communities respond to and recover from floods and other natural disasters.

- The Budget focuses Federal investment where it is most warranted. The Budget also proposes reforms to how the Nation invests in water resources projects, reducing the reliance on Federal funding and control and providing States and local government, as well as the private sector, more flexibility to make investments they deem a priority.

- The Budget requests $4.8 billion for the Corps, a more than 20-percent decrease from the 2017 enacted level.

---

**The President's 2019 Budget:**

The Corps has three main missions: flood and storm damage reduction; commercial navigation; and aquatic ecosystem restoration. The Corps also regulates development in navigable waters and wetlands. While the Agency has had a significant impact on water resources development throughout its history, current approaches to funding, constructing, and maintaining projects are not delivering benefits in either a timely or cost effective manner. The current paradigm for investing in water resources development is not sustainable; it can deter rather than enable local communities, States, and the private sector from making important investments on their own, even when they are the primary beneficiaries. The Budget supports the Administration's infrastructure proposal and lays the groundwork for: modernizing the Nation's approach to water resources; broadening the pool of capital for infrastructure investments; reducing bureaucratic red tape; and empowering State, local, and private decision-making. The Budget does this by focusing Federal investment where it is most warranted and proposing reforms to provide States and communities greater flexibility to make the investments that they deem priorities.

## *Provides Accountability to the American Taxpayer*

**Emphasizes Investments in Ongoing Construction of Projects with High Economic or Environmental Returns while Addressing Public Safety.** The Budget keeps the Federal Government's promise to complete ongoing construction projects, which provide a high return to the Nation or address a significant risk to public safety, more quickly and cost effectively. By proposing to not start any new construction projects, the Budget enables the Corps to focus on completing these ongoing priority projects faster for less cost, allowing the affected communities to see their benefits sooner. The Budget also recognizes the need for a change in the way future construction investments are funded, with less reliance on Federal appropriations. For example, the Budget proposes to accelerate repairs of the Herbert Hoover Dike through an innovative partnership between the Federal Government and the State of Florida using a combination of appropriations from the Federal Government and the State of Florida.

**Prioritizes Operating and Maintaining Existing Infrastructure.** The Budget gives priority to operating and maintaining existing infrastructure, improving its reliability, and improving its resilience to cyber-related attacks. Maintenance of key infrastructure is funded; this includes navigation channels that serve the Nation's largest coastal ports and the inland waterways with the most commercial use, such as the Mississippi and Ohio Rivers, and the Illinois Waterway.

**Increases Transparency for the American Taxpayer.** The Budget establishes clear priorities based on objective criteria for investment decisions. This approach ensures the best overall use of available funds and allows the American taxpayer to understand how Federal resources are allocated. For example, the Budget begins to fund dam safety studies and dredged materials disposal plans within the investigations account where they appropriately belong. The Budget also classifies the Poplar Island project, which serves as the primary dredged material disposal site for the Port of Baltimore, as a navigation project. The Administration believes new Federal investment decisions should be clearly identified by both the Administration and the Congress before funds are spent. Consistent with this approach, the Budget does not propose any new starts. In addition, the Budget proposes revisions to the appropriations language for the Construction, Operations and Maintenance, and Mississippi River and Tributaries accounts and the Harbor Maintenance and Inland Waterways Trust Funds to enable greater transparency in how these funds are spent.

## *Promotes American Economic Prosperity*

**Reforms Inland Waterways Funding.** The Budget proposes to reform the laws governing the Inland Waterways Trust Fund, including an annual per vessel fee for commercial users, to help finance future capital investments on these waterways and a portion of the cost of operating and maintaining them. The current diesel fuel tax is insufficient to support the users' share of these costs.

## *Increases Flexibility for State and Local Communities to Make Investment Decisions*

**Reduces the Harbor Maintenance Tax.** The Budget proposes to reduce the Harbor Maintenance Tax as a step toward providing ports greater flexibility to finance their capital and operating costs on their own. By reducing the tax burden on users of ports, ports would have greater flexibility to determine appropriate fees for services they provide, in order to help finance their operations.

**Divests the Washington Aqueduct.** The Budget proposes to sell the Washington Aqueduct, the wholesale water supply system for Washington, District of Columbia; Arlington County, Virginia; the City of Falls Church, Virginia; and parts of Fairfax County, Virginia. The Corps owns and operates the Aqueduct, which is the only local water supply system in the Nation owned and operated by the Corps. Ownership of local water supply is best carried out by State or local government or the private sector, where there are appropriate market and regulatory incentives. Selling the Aqueduct to a public or private utility would contribute to American economic prosperity through a more efficient allocation of economic resources.

# ENVIRONMENTAL PROTECTION AGENCY

---

**Highlights:**

- The Environmental Protection Agency (EPA) is responsible for implementing and enforcing statutes designed to protect human health and the environment.

- The Budget continues the Agency's work to protect the air, land, and water from pollution, while reducing and eliminating lower priority activities and voluntary programs. Focusing on the core mission supports overall efforts to restrain Federal spending and promote operational efficiencies that enhance the Agency's performance.

- The Budget requests $5.4 billion for EPA, a $2.8 billion or 34-percent decrease from the 2017 enacted level.

---

**The President's 2019 Budget:**

Environmental protection and public health are key to U.S. prosperity and essential to America's quality of life. EPA was created in 1970 to consolidate into one agency the Federal Government's activities to protect human health and the environment. Through cooperative federalism, EPA works with States and Tribes, as well as local governments, businesses, and the public to protect clean air, water, and land.

Since its creation, the work of EPA and its partners has led to significant reductions in the risks from pollution and has helped to meaningfully improve the lives of all Americans:

- emissions of the major air pollutants identified in the Clean Air Act of 1970 have decreased by 70 percent;

- approximately 90 percent of the U.S. population served by community water systems receives drinking water that meets all applicable water quality standards; and

- more than 2,700 of the most contaminated Superfund and other hazardous waste sites have a remedy in place to reduce human exposure to hazardous substances.

In recognition of the significant environmental and public health gains that have already been made, the Budget would maintain key environmental achievements while furthering work in core mission areas. EPA would continue to invest in protecting the air, land, and water as well as address exposure to toxic chemicals.

---

## EPA Answers the Call to Action

In 2017, faced simultaneously with three major hurricanes, a tropical storm, and major wildfires spanning over eight States and two Territories, EPA provided crucial front line support to its Federal, State, territorial, and tribal partners by:

- evaluating slightly more than 6,300 drinking water systems and close to 500 wastewater systems;

- assessing approximately 250 Superfund sites and 1,700 oil and chemical facilities;

- providing technical assistance as needed to damaged facilities;

- responding to approximately 275 spills and recovering more than 2,000 vessels and 48,600 orphaned containers;

- advising on waste management and debris disposal mechanisms; and

- utilizing its laboratory network, along with specialized equipment such as the Airborne Spectral Photometric Environmental Collection Technology airplane and Trace Atmospheric Gas Analyzer mobile laboratories to monitor the air and water quality in the affected communities.

EPA's support delivered vital data on the potential risks and hazards to first responders and the public.

---

To achieve these goals, the Budget continues to propose a number of strategic reforms. The Budget eliminates many voluntary and lower priority activities and programs, and invests in process improvements and other operational enhancements to bring greater efficiency and cost-effectiveness to the work of the Agency. EPA is also in the midst of implementing sweeping regulatory reforms. The President's Executive Orders 13771, "Reducing Regulation and Controlling Regulatory Costs," and 13783, "Promoting Energy Independence and Economic Growth," are guiding the Agency to find new approaches to protecting the environment and human health while also ensuring consideration of economic security, as consistent with law. As EPA continues to focus on its fundamental responsibilities, and strengthens its relationships with States and Tribes on the implementation of Federal environmental laws, there is an opportunity to reshape the Agency's workforce, ensuring that EPA operates efficiently while maintaining critical skills and expertise.

**Empowers State Environmental Priority-Setting.** States are the primary implementers of many Federal environmental statutes and critical partners in protecting the Nation's environment and human health. States have long sought flexibility to direct grant resources to their individual priorities, rather than receiving funding only through grants dedicated to specific programs. The Budget recognizes and responds to this need by providing $27 million for "Multipurpose Grants" within EPA's Categorical Grant portfolio totaling $597 million. States would be able to spend this funding on any statutorily mandated delegated duty. This proposal would enable each State to set its own environmental priorities and quickly respond to new threats as they arise.

**Invests in Water Infrastructure Construction, Repair, and Replacement.** The Budget funds water infrastructure through the State Revolving Funds and the Water Infrastructure Finance and Innovation Act (WIFIA) credit program. The 2019 capitalization of the State Revolving Funds would supplement the approximately $80 billion currently revolving at the State level; in addition, the WIFIA credit subsidy would support more than $1 billion in direct loans, resulting in more than $2 billion in total investment. These resources would complement State and local drinking water and wastewater infrastructure investments as well as funding provided through other Federal channels, including the President's Infrastructure Initiative.

**Accelerates the Clean Up of the Nation's Most Complex Hazardous Waste Sites.** The Budget provides $762 million for the Hazardous Substance Superfund Account to address the release of hazardous substances and the clean up of hazardous waste sites. The Budget also supports the recommendations made in EPA's Superfund Task Force Report to identify impediments to expeditious clean up at sites with significant exposure risks and to bring more private funding to the table for redevelopment. Revitalizing contaminated land improves the quality of life for communities around the United States and is part of EPA's core mission.

**Enhances Monitoring of America's Significant Watersheds.** The Budget funds programs to measure and assess the health of the Great Lakes and Chesapeake Bay. These watersheds require coordination and collaboration among numerous States, Tribes, and local governments. In the case of the Great Lakes, international coordination with Canada is also necessary. Effective coordination and collaboration among these stakeholders relies on accurate and continuous data. The Budget provides funds to support basin-wide monitoring in these watersheds, which would assist decision-making on health and economic issues including harmful algal blooms and invasive species management. The Budget also supports cooperative federalism by building State and local capacity to conduct monitoring, while recognizing that the primary responsibility for local ecosystem restoration rests with States and local groups.

**Ensures Consistent Enforcement and Enhanced Compliance Assistance.** The

### Restoring the Land to Productive Use

The Budget prioritizes funding for Brownfields site assessment grants in order to accelerate investment in local communities. The EPA Brownfields program provides competitive grants to local communities to address sites where redevelopment is challenged by the presence or potential presence of contamination. EPA's Brownfields program site assessment grants provide useful information to communities about the extent of contamination at a property. Real estate developers use this information to estimate future clean-up costs and to plan for redevelopment of the property. EPA Brownfields grantees report that approximately 30 percent of brownfield properties that are assessed using EPA Brownfields funding do not require remediation for the intended reuse of the property; although, in some cases, institutional controls may be required. Finding that remediation is not necessary for the intended reuse of the site means faster redevelopment and the return of the property to productive use.

Budget continues to concentrate EPA's enforcement objectives on programs that are not delegated to State, local, and tribal partners. EPA will work with partners to maintain a consistent and effective enforcement program to avoid duplication and give the regulated community an even playing field for conducting business. To specifically assist the oil and chemical industries in their compliance with EPA regulations, the Budget proposes to institute a voluntary fee that can be paid by a facility to have EPA provide on-site compliance assistance.

**Strengthens Protections from Toxic Chemicals.** In 2016, the Congress passed the Frank R. Lautenberg Chemical Safety for the 21st Century Act to modernize the Toxic Substances Control Act (TSCA). TSCA, as amended, requires EPA to make an affirmative finding of safety on all new chemicals introduced into commerce. EPA must also prioritize and evaluate existing chemicals in commerce and manage chemicals when EPA finds they do not to meet safety standards that are in place to protect people and the environment from unreasonable risks. In 2019, EPA will continue to set up new protocols to implement the modernized TSCA and evaluate the risks of new and existing chemicals in commerce as part of the Agency's commitment to provide for the safety and security of all Americans.

**Fee-Funds the Popular ENERGY STAR Program.** ENERGY STAR is a trusted resource for consumers and businesses that want to purchase products that save them money and help protect the environment. The Budget includes a proposal to authorize EPA to administer the ENERGY STAR program through the collection of user fees. Product manufacturers that seek to label their products under the program would pay a modest fee to support EPA's work to set voluntary energy efficiency standards and to process applications. Fee collections would begin after EPA undertakes a rulemaking process to determine which products would be covered by fees and the level of fees, and to ensure that a fee system would not discourage manufacturers from participating in the program or result in a loss of environmental benefits.

**Reinforces Emergency Preparedness and Response Capabilities.** The 2017 hurricane season reminded the Administration of how important it is for all levels of government to be ready to assist residents in the face of natural disasters. EPA plays a critical role in this capacity, providing technical assistance to drinking water and waste water utilities, responding to the release of hazardous substances, and advising on disease vector control and waste disposal. The Budget further supports EPA's efforts by providing $6 million to the Critical Infrastructure Protection program and $45 million for key emergency response equipment and training under the Homeland Security Preparedness Response & Recovery program. Protecting the safety and security of the American people is a Federal priority that ensures a prosperous Nation.

**Invests in Cutting-Edge Research and Development for American Prosperity and a Better Future.** The Budget provides $246 million for EPA to continue to perform research and development activities in support of core mission areas, focusing on air quality, water resources, sustainable communities, chemical safety, and human health risk assessment. These interdisciplinary research programs would apply the best available science to address current and future environmental hazards, develop new approaches, and improve the scientific foundation for making environmental protection decisions. The Agency will strengthen the alignment of its research resources to support EPA programs, regions, States, and Tribes with the goal of improving America's collective quality of life and preserving the health of the environment for future generations.

**Refocuses the Agency on Core Activities.** As part of the Administration's initiative to refocus EPA on its core mission, the President's Budget continues to eliminate funding for lower priority programs, programs that have duplicative functions with other agencies, activities that can be absorbed into other functions, and responsibilities that should be primarily for State and local governments. Examples of program eliminations include: the Climate Change Research and Partnership Programs; the Indoor Air and Radon Programs; the Marine Pollution and National Estuary Programs; the Environmental Education Program; and the Beaches Program. Total savings from eliminated EPA programs and activities would save taxpayers approximately $600 million compared to 2017 enacted levels.

# NATIONAL AERONAUTICS AND SPACE ADMINISTRATION

**Highlights:**

- The National Aeronautics and Space Administration (NASA) is responsible for leading an innovative and sustainable program of exploration with commercial and international partners to enable human expansion across the solar system and bring new knowledge and opportunities back to Earth. As it pioneers the space frontier, NASA supports growth of the Nation's economy in space, increases understanding of the universe and our place in it, works with industry to improve America's aerospace technologies, and advances American leadership.

- The Budget supports the Administration's new space exploration policy by refocusing existing NASA activities toward exploration, by redirecting funding to innovative new programs that support the new policy, and by providing additional funding to support new public-private initiatives.

- The Budget requests a total of $19.6 billion for NASA, a $500 million (2.6-percent) increase from the 2018 Budget ($61 million below NASA's 2017 funding level).

- The Budget proposes to end direct U.S. Government funding for the space station by 2025 and provides $150 million to begin a program that would encourage commercial development of capabilities that NASA can use in its place.

- The Budget refocuses and consolidates NASA's space technology development programs to support space exploration activities.

- The Budget continues strong programs in science and aeronautics, including a supersonic "X-plane," planetary defense from hazardous asteroids, and potentially a bold mission to retrieve pieces of Mars for scientific study on Earth.

**The President's 2019 Budget:**

The Budget supports an innovative and sustainable program of exploration with commercial and international partners to enable the return of humans to the Moon for long-term exploration and utilization, followed by human missions to Mars and other destinations. As it pioneers the space frontier, NASA supports growth of the Nation's space economy, increases understanding of the universe and America's place in it, and advances America's aerospace technology.

*"The directive I'm signing today will refocus America's space program on human exploration and discovery. It marks an important step in returning American astronauts to the Moon for the first time since 1972 for long-term exploration and use. This time, we will not only plant our flag and leave our footprints, we will establish a foundation for an eventual mission to Mars. And perhaps, someday, to many worlds beyond."*

President Donald J. Trump
November 11, 2017

The Budget takes concrete actions to once again launch Americans into space from American soil. The Budget partners with industry to land robotic missions on the surface of the Moon in the next few years, paving the way for a return of U.S. astronauts—this time not just to visit, but to lay the foundation for further journeys of exploration and the expansion of the U.S. economy into space. The Budget supports a sustainable space exploration program to be proud of—one that reflects American ingenuity, ambition, and leadership. Specifically, the Budget:

**Renews Focus on Human Exploration and Discovery and Expands Commercial Partnerships to Strengthen U.S. Leadership in Space.** The Budget provides $10 billion to support human space exploration and to pursue a campaign that would establish U.S. preeminence to, around, and on the Moon. This would be achieved through a renewed focus on new approaches and industrial partners, and by pursuing near-term milestones for lunar exploration, such as the commercial launch of a key power and propulsion space tug in 2022. A new lunar robotic exploration program would support innovative approaches to achieve human and science exploration goals. This new program would fund contracts for transportation services and the development of small rovers and instruments to meet lunar science and exploration needs. The Budget also supports the creation of a new Exploration Research and Technology program to enable lower-cost technology and systems needed to sustainably return humans to the Moon and beyond. In addition, the Budget fully funds the Space Launch System (SLS) rocket and Orion crew capsule as key elements of the human space exploration program. The Budget provides $3.7 billion for SLS and Orion, which would keep the programs on track for a test launch by 2020 and a first crewed launch around the Moon by 2023.

**Provides Cost Savings by Phasing out Government Programs and Replacing them with Commercial or Public-Private Operations.** The Budget proposes to end direct U.S. financial support for the International Space Station in 2025, after which NASA would rely on commercial partners for its low Earth orbit research and technology demonstration requirements. A new $150 million program would begin support for commercial partners to encourage development of capabilities that the private sector and NASA can use. The Budget also proposes a transition away from NASA's current Government-owned and operated fleet of communications satellites and associated ground stations. Instead, the Budget proposes a greater reliance on commercial communications satellite capabilities. The Budget also proposes canceling, pending an independent review, an over-budget project to upgrade the current NASA-owned system in order to make resources available for these new partnerships.

**Continues Robotic Exploration of the Solar System.** The Budget provides $2.2 billion to Planetary Science and maintains support for competed science missions and the next Mars rover, which would launch in 2020. The Budget also provides $50 million to explore possibilities for retrieving geologic samples from Mars, which has long been a high priority science goal and a keystone of future Mars exploration. A $150 million planetary defense program would help protect the Earth from potentially hazardous asteroids.

**Fully Funds an Experimental Supersonic Airplane and Increases Hypersonics Research Funding.** The Budget fully funds the Low-Boom Flight Demonstrator, an experimental supersonic (faster than the speed of sound) airplane that would make its first flight in 2021. This "X-plane" would open a new market for U.S. companies to build faster commercial airliners, creating jobs and cutting cross-country flight times in half. The Budget also increases funding for research on flight at speeds more than five times the speed of sound, commonly referred to as hypersonics. Hypersonics research is critical to understanding how crewed and robotic spacecraft can safely enter and exit the atmospheres of planets. Hypersonics also has applications for national defense.

**Supports a Focused Earth Science Program.** The Budget provides $1.8 billion for a focused, balanced Earth Science portfolio that supports the priorities of the science and applications communities. The Budget maintains the Nation's 45-year record of space-based land imagery by funding Landsat 9 and a Sustainable Land Imaging program. The Budget maintains the Administration's previous termination of five Earth Science missions—PACE, OCO-3, RBI, DSCOVR Earth-viewing instruments, and CLARREO Pathfinder—to achieve savings.

**Terminates a New Space Telescope while Increasing Support for other Astrophysics Priorities.** The Budget terminates development of the WFIRST space telescope, which was not executable within its previous budget and would have required a significant funding increase in 2019 and future years. The Budget redirects funding from this mission to competed research including smaller, principal-investigator-led astrophysics missions. These missions have a history of providing high scientific impact while training the next generation of scientists and engineers. The Budget continues to fund the $8.8 billion James Webb Space Telescope, which is expected to launch in 2019 and operate for many years to come.

**Redirects Education Funding to Higher Priorities.** The Budget continues to support the termination of the $100 million Office of Education, redirecting those funds to NASA's core mission of exploration. The Science Activation program within the Science Mission Directorate—a focused, science-driven program with clear objectives, evaluation strategies, and strong partnerships—is retained.

**Supports the Technology Demonstration of In-Space Robotic Manufacturing and Assembly.** The Budget provides $54.2 million for public-private partnerships to demonstrate new technologies used to build large structures in a space environment. Such structures could be key to supporting future exploration and commercial space activities.

> "American companies are on the cutting edge of space technology, and they're developing new rockets, spaceships, and satellites that will take us further into space, faster than ever before. Like the railroads that brought American explorers, entrepreneurs, and settlers to tame the Wild West, these groundbreaking new technologies will open untold opportunities to extend the range of American action and values into the new worlds of outer space. And by fostering much stronger partnerships between the Federal Government and the realm of industry, and bringing the full force of our national interest to bear, American leadership in space will be assured."
>
> Vice President Michael R. Pence
> October 5, 2017

# SMALL BUSINESS ADMINISTRATION

---

**Highlights:**

• The Small Business Administration (SBA) ensures that America's small business owners have the tools and resources needed to start and develop their operations, drive U.S. competitiveness, and help grow the economy. The President is committed to seeing that small businesses succeed by promoting responsible policies that produce economic growth while simultaneously reducing the regulatory and tax burdens that can impede their development.

• The Budget leverages today's strong market conditions to enable SBA to fulfill its core mission while ensuring that its operations represent the most prudent use of taxpayer dollars. The Budget introduces counter-cyclical policies in SBA's business loan guarantee programs and updates fee structures to ensure that during positive economic times, SBA is not supplanting private sector lending or creating excess risk for the Government.

• The Budget requests $834 million in new budget authority for 2019, a $53 million or 5.9-percent decrease from the 2017 enacted level. This request is offset by changes to existing fee structures across SBA's business loan guarantee programs and the elimination of unspent funds from prior years, resulting in a net request of $629 million.

---

**The President's 2019 Budget:**

America's 30 million small businesses play a critical role in job creation and retention. SBA's assistance to those firms and entrepreneurs help drive a robust U.S. economy and promote economic security. SBA achieves this through a variety of programs, from promoting access to capital and Federal contracting, to business counseling and disaster assistance. Small businesses account for more than 57 million jobs, and create two out of three net new jobs each year in the United States. As more than half of all Americans are either employed by or own a small business, SBA works to ensure that each day more Americans have the opportunity to start, scale, and succeed in businesses of their own. With this as its mission, SBA is uniquely positioned to deliver on two of the President's top priorities—job creation and economic growth. The Budget supports these priorities by assisting small business owners and entrepreneurs with securing access to capital and by providing counseling and training services, while ensuring that it does not supplant activities better provided by the private sector.

**Promotes Access to Affordable Capital for American Entrepreneurs.** The Budget supports $43 billion in business loans that would help America's small business owners access affordable capital to start or expand their businesses. Through its variety of business loan programs, SBA helps expand private lending to small business owners that cannot attain it elsewhere. These programs support financing for an array of purposes, from general business operations to fixed assets and venture capital investments in small businesses.

**U.S. Small Businesses at a Glance:**

**Economic engines.** The United States is home to 29.6 million small businesses, 99.9 percent of all U.S. businesses.

**Job creators.** Small businesses employ 57.9 million (47.8 percent of the labor force) and each year create 1.4 million net new jobs.

**Major exporters.** Small businesses represent 97.7 percent of U.S. exporters.

**Opening opportunity.** Lending to women-owned businesses by SBA totaled more than $8.5 billion in 2017, an increase of approximately $575 million from the prior year.

**Levels the Playing Field with Private Sector Small Business Lending.** SBA fills a critical void in the market when economic shocks reduce traditional lending to small businesses and when the private market is unwilling to provide capital to credit-worthy borrowers. However, during prosperous economic times such as these, the Budget proposes that SBA introduce counter-cyclical policies to its business loan guarantee programs that enables it to maintain its operations while ensuring that it is not displacing direct private lending. Through an adjustment of fees across its business loan guarantee programs, SBA would cover both its anticipated lending and operational costs, leveling the playing field among its lender community while operating at zero cost to the taxpayer.

**Targets Support for the Smallest of Small Businesses and Startups.** Through its 7(m) Direct Microloan program, SBA supports low-interest financing for non-profit intermediaries that in turn provide loans of up to $50,000 to rising entrepreneurs. In addition to the $25 million in technical assistance grant funds requested for the Microloan program, the Budget requests $4 million in subsidy resources to support $42 million in direct lending.

**Assists Businesses and Homeowners in the Direct Aftermath of Disaster.** SBA provides affordable, accessible, and immediate disaster assistance to those hardest hit when disaster strikes. The Budget supports more than $1 billion in disaster relief lending to businesses, homeowners, renters, and property owners to help American communities recover quickly in the wake of declared disasters.

**Optimizes How Support is Delivered to Business Owners and Entrepreneurs.** The Budget requests $110 million for the Small Business Development Center program, which delivers a variety of services to small businesses and prospective business owners across U.S. cities and counties. The Budget also proposes the creation of a competitive set-aside within the program that would reward those centers that most efficiently utilize their resources and provide innovative methods to help entrepreneurs.

*"Small business owners embody the American pioneering spirit and remind us that determination can turn aspiration into achievement...America's small business owners transform ideas into reality. They are a strong testament to the opportunities a market economy affords."*

President Donald J. Trump
April 28, 2017

**Opens Opportunities for Businesses in the Underserved Market.** In 2019, SBA will continue to focus on socially and economically disadvantaged communities in emerging markets. For example, SBA's 7(j) Management and Technical Assistance Program would revitalize its mission through the development and integration of new, innovative consulting solutions tailored to individual community needs and local business goals.

**Emphasizes Equal Opportunity and Representation in the Marketplace.** Through its diverse set of entrepreneurial training programs, SBA will continue reaching women, veterans, minority communities, rural business owners, and entrepreneurs in historically underutilized business zones in order to ensure that all Americans have an equal opportunity to succeed when it comes to starting, scaling, and operating a small business. These include supported investments in advising and mentoring programs such as SCORE, Women's Business Centers, and Veterans Outreach. These programs complement SBA's ongoing efforts to remove barriers that underserved populations, including women, face in accessing the capital necessary to start, grow, and expand their businesses.

> *"The mission of the SBA is to help small businesses grow, create jobs and help our economy thrive...I want to get to know small business owners and entrepreneurs across America and learn about the obstacles they face while growing a business. I also want to encourage entrepreneurs to tap into SBA resources for start-up and growth solutions."*
>
> Linda McMahon
> Administrator
> June 21, 2017

**Helps Small Businesses Gain Access to Federal Contracts and Research Opportunities.** Small business contracts represent the largest form of direct monetary support for small businesses in the Federal Government. Through its 8(a) business development and set-aside contracting programs, SBA leads Federal efforts to deliver 23 percent of contracts to small businesses. This includes set-asides of five percent for women-owned and small, disadvantaged 8(a) businesses and three percent set-asides for historically underutilized business zones and service-disabled veteran-owned small businesses. In 2019, SBA would also continue fostering high-tech innovation among small businesses by awarding highly competitive funding agreements through its Small Business Innovation Research program.

**Enables SBA to Advocate on Behalf of American Small Business Owners.** The Budget requests $9.1 million for SBA's Office of Advocacy. Through this Office, SBA is positioned to encourage and educate stakeholders and the public on policies that support the development and growth of American small businesses. The Budget accomplishes this by intervening early in Federal agencies' regulatory development processes, and serving as a liaison between them and the small business community to explain and expand on issues of concern.

**Underscores Responsibility and Transparency of SBA's Practices.** The Budget requests $21.9 million for SBA's Office of the Inspector General (OIG) to provide auditing and investigative services to support and assist SBA in achieving its mission. As with all Federal lending and contracting programs, SBA faces challenges such as improper payments and losses from defaulted loans. The OIG plays a critical role in addressing these and identifying actions to deter and detect waste, fraud, and abuse.

# Summary Tables

## Table S-1. Budget Totals [1]

(In billions of dollars and as a percent of GDP)

| | 2017 | 2018 | 2019 | 2020 | 2021 | 2022 | 2023 | 2024 | 2025 | 2026 | 2027 | 2028 | Totals 2019–2023 | Totals 2019–2028 |
|---|---|---|---|---|---|---|---|---|---|---|---|---|---|---|
| **Budget Totals in Billions of Dollars:** | | | | | | | | | | | | | | |
| Receipts | 3,316 | 3,340 | 3,422 | 3,609 | 3,838 | 4,089 | 4,386 | 4,675 | 4,946 | 5,231 | 5,506 | 5,818 | 19,344 | 45,520 |
| Outlays | 3,982 | 4,214 | 4,407 | 4,596 | 4,754 | 4,941 | 5,160 | 5,348 | 5,526 | 5,748 | 5,955 | 6,181 | 23,858 | 52,615 |
| Deficit | 665 | 873 | 984 | 987 | 916 | 852 | 774 | 672 | 579 | 517 | 450 | 363 | 4,513 | 7,095 |
| Debt held by the public | 14,665 | 15,790 | 16,872 | 17,947 | 18,950 | 19,946 | 20,809 | 21,495 | 22,137 | 22,703 | 23,194 | 23,684 | | |
| Gross domestic product (GDP) | 19,177 | 20,029 | 21,003 | 22,069 | 23,194 | 24,369 | 25,605 | 26,900 | 28,253 | 29,647 | 31,089 | 32,602 | | |
| **Budget Totals as a Percent of GDP:** | | | | | | | | | | | | | | |
| Receipts | 17.3% | 16.7% | 16.3% | 16.4% | 16.5% | 16.8% | 17.1% | 17.4% | 17.5% | 17.6% | 17.7% | 17.8% | 16.6% | 17.1% |
| Outlays | 20.8% | 21.0% | 21.0% | 20.8% | 20.5% | 20.3% | 20.2% | 19.9% | 19.6% | 19.4% | 19.2% | 19.0% | 20.5% | 20.0% |
| Deficit | 3.5% | 4.4% | 4.7% | 4.5% | 3.9% | 3.5% | 3.0% | 2.5% | 2.1% | 1.7% | 1.4% | 1.1% | 3.9% | 2.8% |
| Debt held by the public | 76.5% | 78.8% | 80.3% | 81.3% | 81.7% | 81.9% | 81.3% | 79.9% | 78.4% | 76.6% | 74.6% | 72.6% | | |

[1] Outlays and deficits are standardized to 12 monthly benefit payments, as shown on Table S–4.

## Table S–2. Effect of Budget Proposals on Projected Deficits

(Deficit increases (+) or decreases (-) in billions of dollars)

| | 2017 | 2018 | 2019 | 2020 | 2021 | 2022 | 2023 | 2024 | 2025 | 2026 | 2027 | 2028 | Totals 2019–2023 | Totals 2019–2028 |
|---|---|---|---|---|---|---|---|---|---|---|---|---|---|---|
| **Projected deficits in the pre-policy baseline** [1] | 665 | 870 | 969 | 1,049 | 1,103 | 1,115 | 1,109 | 1,123 | 1,136 | 1,242 | 1,316 | 1,378 | 5,345 | 11,540 |
| Percent of GDP | 3.5% | 4.3% | 4.6% | 4.8% | 4.8% | 4.6% | 4.4% | 4.2% | 4.1% | 4.3% | 4.3% | 4.3% | | |
| **Proposals in the 2019 Budget:** | | | | | | | | | | | | | | |
| **Changes to mandatory spending and receipts:** | | | | | | | | | | | | | | |
| Repeal and replace Obamacare | ........ | ........ | 3 | 23 | -27 | -41 | -56 | -73 | -92 | -113 | -137 | -161 | -98 | -675 |
| Support at least $1 trillion in private/public infrastructure investment | ........ | ........ | 45 | 11 | 18 | 25 | 31 | 29 | 20 | 12 | 5 | 2 | 130 | 199 |
| Provide paid parental leave | ........ | ........ | 1 | 1 | 2 | 2 | 2 | 2 | 2 | 2 | 2 | 3 | 7 | 19 |
| Reform the welfare system | ........ | ........ | -21 | -23 | -25 | -25 | -27 | -27 | -27 | -29 | -29 | -28 | -123 | -263 |
| Reform Federal student loans | ........ | ........ | -6 | -12 | -16 | -19 | -22 | -24 | -25 | -26 | -27 | -27 | -75 | -203 |
| Reduce improper payments Government-wide | ........ | ........ | -* | -1 | -2 | -3 | -6 | -6 | -12 | -22 | -40 | -59 | -11 | -151 |
| Reform disability programs | ........ | ........ | -1 | -2 | -2 | -2 | -2 | -5 | -8 | -12 | -17 | -22 | -9 | -72 |
| Reform retirement and health benefits for Federal employees | ........ | ........ | -3 | -1 | -4 | -5 | -6 | -8 | -9 | -10 | -11 | -12 | -18 | -68 |
| Limit Farm Bill subsidies and make other agricultural reforms | ........ | ........ | -1 | -4 | -5 | -6 | -6 | -7 | -7 | -7 | -7 | -7 | -23 | -58 |
| Eliminate wasteful spending in Medicare and improve drug pricing and payment policies [2] | ........ | ........ | -2 | -11 | -16 | -22 | -26 | -26 | -29 | -32 | -34 | -38 | -77 | -236 |
| Other spending reductions and program reforms [3] | ........ | 5 | -4 | -13 | -15 | -11 | -18 | -22 | -11 | -56 | -61 | -68 | -60 | -278 |
| Total, changes to mandatory spending and receipts | ........ | 5 | 10 | -30 | -92 | -108 | -135 | -166 | -197 | -292 | -355 | -419 | -356 | -1,786 |
| **Reprioritize discretionary spending:** | | | | | | | | | | | | | | |
| Eliminate the defense sequester and raise the cap on defense discretionary spending | ........ | 32 | 43 | 66 | 76 | 82 | 84 | 85 | 86 | 86 | 86 | 85 | 350 | 777 |
| Reorganize Government and apply two-penny plan to non-defense discretionary spending | ........ | -32 | -27 | -57 | -92 | -122 | -140 | -163 | -187 | -211 | -235 | -260 | -438 | -1,495 |
| Phase down the use of Overseas Contingency Operations funding | ........ | -13 | -5 | -20 | -33 | -40 | -43 | -75 | -94 | -102 | -109 | -113 | -141 | -634 |
| Provide 2018 emergency funding and align emergency and disaster funding with the ten-year average [4] | | 11 | 1 | -5 | -12 | -20 | -21 | -22 | -23 | -23 | -24 | -25 | -57 | -174 |
| Total, reprioritize discretionary spending | ........ | -2 | 11 | -16 | -62 | -100 | -120 | -176 | -218 | -251 | -283 | -313 | -287 | -1,527 |
| Debt service and indirect interest effects | ........ | * | * | * | -3 | -9 | -16 | -26 | -38 | -54 | -74 | -98 | -28 | -319 |
| **Total changes to spending and receipts in the 2019 Budget** | ........ | 4 | 21 | -46 | -157 | -217 | -272 | -368 | -453 | -597 | -713 | -830 | -671 | -3,631 |
| Effect of post-policy boost to economic growth | ........ | ........ | -5 | -16 | -30 | -46 | -63 | -82 | -104 | -128 | -153 | -185 | -160 | -813 |
| **Total deficit reduction in the 2019 Budget** [5] | ........ | 4 | 16 | -62 | -187 | -263 | -335 | -451 | -557 | -725 | -866 | -1,015 | -832 | -4,445 |
| **Resulting deficits in the 2019 Budget** | 665 | 873 | 984 | 987 | 916 | 852 | 774 | 672 | 579 | 517 | 450 | 363 | 4,513 | 7,095 |
| Percent of GDP | 3.5% | 4.4% | 4.7% | 4.5% | 3.9% | 3.5% | 3.0% | 2.5% | 2.1% | 1.7% | 1.4% | 1.1% | | |

\* $500 million or less.

[1] Includes adjustments to standardize the number of benefit payments in each year. See Table S-3 for more information on the baseline.

[2] Includes the following categories of proposals on Table S-6: Address fraud and abuse in Medicare, Eliminate wasteful spending on Government-imposed provider burdens in Medicare, Eliminate wasteful spending, Medicare drug pricing and payment improvements, Improve the Medicare appeals system, and Medicare interactions.

[3] Includes interaction between 2019 Budget proposals and the adjustment to standardize the number of benefit payments in each year.

[4] The Balanced Budget and Emergency Deficit Control Act of 1985 (BBEDCA) requires the baseline for discretionary appropriations, including disaster and emergency spending, to reflect the most recent enacted levels, extended through the budget window with adjustments for inflation. This line represents the effect of providing needed emergency funding for 2018 and then aligning emergency and disaster funding with the average of funding provided over the previous ten years, relative to the inflated spending levels in the BBEDCA baseline.

[5] Includes differences between baseline and policy estimates of the outlay effects of 2019 mandatory sequestration.

## Table S-3. Baseline by Category [1]

(In billions of dollars)

| | 2017 | 2018 | 2019 | 2020 | 2021 | 2022 | 2023 | 2024 | 2025 | 2026 | 2027 | 2028 | Totals 2019–2023 | Totals 2019–2028 |
|---|---|---|---|---|---|---|---|---|---|---|---|---|---|---|
| **Outlays:** | | | | | | | | | | | | | | |
| Discretionary programs: | | | | | | | | | | | | | | |
| Defense | 590 | 611 | 637 | 668 | 678 | 690 | 705 | 719 | 737 | 755 | 774 | 793 | 3,378 | 7,156 |
| Non-defense | 610 | 661 | 656 | 659 | 670 | 669 | 676 | 689 | 705 | 721 | 738 | 756 | 3,330 | 6,940 |
| Subtotal, discretionary programs | 1,200 | 1,271 | 1,293 | 1,327 | 1,349 | 1,359 | 1,381 | 1,408 | 1,442 | 1,476 | 1,512 | 1,549 | 6,708 | 14,096 |
| Mandatory programs: | | | | | | | | | | | | | | |
| Social Security | 939 | 987 | 1,047 | 1,109 | 1,174 | 1,245 | 1,319 | 1,398 | 1,480 | 1,566 | 1,656 | 1,752 | 5,894 | 13,745 |
| Medicare | 591 | 582 | 640 | 688 | 743 | 845 | 876 | 902 | 1,005 | 1,103 | 1,196 | 1,353 | 3,792 | 9,350 |
| Medicaid | 375 | 402 | 420 | 439 | 464 | 490 | 519 | 549 | 583 | 624 | 661 | 701 | 2,332 | 5,450 |
| Exchange subsidies (including Basic Health Care Program) | 39 | 48 | 48 | 48 | 49 | 52 | 54 | 57 | 60 | 63 | 66 | 69 | 251 | 565 |
| Other mandatory programs | 574 | 570 | 576 | 589 | 612 | 654 | 655 | 658 | 684 | 745 | 764 | 815 | 3,086 | 6,751 |
| Subtotal, mandatory programs | 2,519 | 2,588 | 2,731 | 2,873 | 3,042 | 3,286 | 3,423 | 3,564 | 3,811 | 4,100 | 4,343 | 4,689 | 15,355 | 35,861 |
| Net interest | 263 | 310 | 364 | 447 | 515 | 577 | 636 | 684 | 727 | 772 | 815 | 859 | 2,538 | 6,396 |
| Total outlays | 3,982 | 4,170 | 4,388 | 4,647 | 4,906 | 5,222 | 5,439 | 5,656 | 5,980 | 6,348 | 6,670 | 7,098 | 24,601 | 56,353 |
| **Receipts:** | | | | | | | | | | | | | | |
| Individual income taxes | 1,587 | 1,660 | 1,687 | 1,790 | 1,917 | 2,050 | 2,198 | 2,348 | 2,504 | 2,700 | 2,883 | 3,062 | 9,642 | 23,140 |
| Corporation income taxes | 297 | 218 | 225 | 265 | 273 | 314 | 374 | 417 | 435 | 417 | 406 | 414 | 1,451 | 3,539 |
| Social insurance and retirement receipts: | | | | | | | | | | | | | | |
| Social Security payroll taxes | 851 | 852 | 905 | 941 | 995 | 1,049 | 1,103 | 1,164 | 1,226 | 1,296 | 1,361 | 1,442 | 4,994 | 11,483 |
| Medicare payroll taxes | 256 | 259 | 275 | 287 | 304 | 322 | 339 | 359 | 379 | 401 | 422 | 448 | 1,528 | 3,535 |
| Unemployment insurance | 46 | 48 | 47 | 47 | 47 | 46 | 47 | 48 | 49 | 50 | 52 | 55 | 233 | 488 |
| Other retirement | 10 | 10 | 11 | 11 | 12 | 12 | 13 | 14 | 14 | 15 | 16 | 17 | 59 | 135 |
| Excise taxes | 84 | 108 | 108 | 112 | 118 | 121 | 124 | 128 | 132 | 136 | 140 | 146 | 584 | 1,265 |
| Estate and gift taxes | 23 | 25 | 17 | 18 | 19 | 21 | 23 | 24 | 26 | 28 | 29 | 31 | 98 | 236 |
| Customs duties | 35 | 40 | 44 | 47 | 48 | 50 | 51 | 52 | 53 | 55 | 56 | 58 | 240 | 515 |
| Deposits of earnings, Federal Reserve System | 81 | 72 | 55 | 49 | 52 | 59 | 67 | 73 | 77 | 82 | 86 | 91 | 282 | 691 |
| Other miscellaneous receipts | 48 | 48 | 50 | 47 | 47 | 49 | 50 | 52 | 52 | 54 | 56 | 57 | 243 | 515 |
| Total receipts | 3,316 | 3,340 | 3,424 | 3,613 | 3,833 | 4,095 | 4,389 | 4,678 | 4,948 | 5,233 | 5,508 | 5,820 | 19,354 | 45,541 |
| **Deficit** | 665 | 829 | 964 | 1,033 | 1,073 | 1,127 | 1,051 | 978 | 1,032 | 1,115 | 1,162 | 1,277 | 5,247 | 10,812 |
| Net interest | 263 | 310 | 364 | 447 | 515 | 577 | 636 | 684 | 727 | 772 | 815 | 859 | 2,538 | 6,396 |
| Primary deficit | 403 | 519 | 600 | 586 | 558 | 550 | 415 | 294 | 305 | 343 | 347 | 418 | 2,709 | 4,416 |
| On-budget deficit | 715 | 824 | 955 | 1,000 | 1,029 | 1,070 | 975 | 887 | 925 | 1,003 | 1,035 | 1,142 | 5,028 | 10,021 |
| Off-budget deficit/surplus (−) | −49 | 5 | 9 | 33 | 44 | 57 | 76 | 91 | 107 | 112 | 127 | 135 | 219 | 791 |

## Table S–3. Baseline by Category ¹—Continued

(In billions of dollars)

| | 2017 | 2018 | 2019 | 2020 | 2021 | 2022 | 2023 | 2024 | 2025 | 2026 | 2027 | 2028 | Totals 2019–2023 | Totals 2019–2028 |
|---|---|---|---|---|---|---|---|---|---|---|---|---|---|---|
| **Memorandum, totals with pre-policy economic assumptions and standardized to 12 monthly benefit payments:²** | | | | | | | | | | | | | | |
| Receipts | 3,316 | 3,340 | 3,419 | 3,597 | 3,804 | 4,051 | 4,329 | 4,600 | 4,850 | 5,115 | 5,366 | 5,650 | 19,200 | 44,781 |
| Outlays | 3,982 | 4,210 | 4,388 | 4,647 | 4,906 | 5,166 | 5,438 | 5,723 | 5,986 | 6,357 | 6,682 | 7,029 | 24,545 | 56,322 |
| Deficit | 665 | 870 | 969 | 1,049 | 1,103 | 1,115 | 1,109 | 1,123 | 1,136 | 1,242 | 1,316 | 1,378 | 5,345 | 11,540 |
| **Memorandum, budget authority for discretionary programs:** | | | | | | | | | | | | | | |
| Defense | 634 | 637 | 652 | 668 | 684 | 701 | 718 | 736 | 754 | 773 | 792 | 811 | 3,422 | 7,287 |
| Non-defense | 586 | 565 | 580 | 594 | 608 | 623 | 639 | 655 | 672 | 689 | 706 | 724 | 3,044 | 6,489 |
| Total, discretionary budget authority | 1,220 | 1,202 | 1,232 | 1,262 | 1,292 | 1,324 | 1,357 | 1,391 | 1,425 | 1,461 | 1,498 | 1,535 | 6,466 | 13,776 |

\* $500 million or less.

¹ Baseline estimates are on the basis of the economic assumptions shown in Table S–9, which incorporate the effects of the Administration's fiscal policies. Baseline totals reflecting current-law economic assumptions are shown in a memorandum bank.

² When October 1 falls on a weekend, certain mandatory benefit payments are accelerated to the previous business day, and as a result certain fiscal years can have 11 or 13 benefit payments rather than the normal 12 payments.

## Table S–4. Proposed Budget by Category
(In billions of dollars)

| | 2017 | 2018 | 2019 | 2020 | 2021 | 2022 | 2023 | 2024 | 2025 | 2026 | 2027 | 2028 | Totals 2019–2023 | Totals 2019–2028 |
|---|---|---|---|---|---|---|---|---|---|---|---|---|---|---|
| **Outlays:** | | | | | | | | | | | | | | |
| Discretionary programs: | | | | | | | | | | | | | | |
| Defense | 590 | 634 | 678 | 721 | 730 | 744 | 759 | 743 | 744 | 755 | 768 | 783 | 3,633 | 7,426 |
| Non-defense | 610 | 636 | 626 | 584 | 549 | 498 | 483 | 470 | 461 | 452 | 443 | 436 | 2,740 | 5,002 |
| Subtotal, discretionary programs | 1,200 | 1,270 | 1,304 | 1,305 | 1,280 | 1,242 | 1,243 | 1,214 | 1,205 | 1,207 | 1,211 | 1,219 | 6,373 | 12,428 |
| Mandatory programs: | | | | | | | | | | | | | | |
| Social Security | 939 | 987 | 1,046 | 1,108 | 1,173 | 1,243 | 1,317 | 1,395 | 1,476 | 1,562 | 1,652 | 1,748 | 5,887 | 13,720 |
| Medicare | 591 | 582 | 625 | 656 | 703 | 798 | 824 | 848 | 955 | 1,024 | 1,107 | 1,257 | 3,605 | 8,796 |
| Medicaid and Market-Based Health Care Grant | 375 | 400 | 412 | 483 | 480 | 495 | 512 | 528 | 546 | 564 | 579 | 597 | 2,382 | 5,196 |
| Exchange subsidies (including Basic Health Program) | 39 | 48 | 45 | 11 | ...... | ...... | ...... | ...... | ...... | ...... | ...... | ...... | 56 | 56 |
| Other mandatory programs | 574 | 577 | 567 | 575 | 590 | 626 | 621 | 617 | 636 | 664 | 662 | 680 | 2,979 | 6,238 |
| Allowance for infrastructure initiative | ...... | ...... | 45 | 11 | 18 | 25 | 31 | 29 | 19 | 11 | 4 | 1 | 129 | 193 |
| Subtotal, mandatory programs | 2,519 | 2,593 | 2,739 | 2,845 | 2,964 | 3,187 | 3,303 | 3,416 | 3,632 | 3,825 | 4,004 | 4,283 | 15,038 | 34,199 |
| Net interest | 263 | 310 | 363 | 447 | 510 | 568 | 619 | 658 | 688 | 717 | 740 | 761 | 2,507 | 6,070 |
| Total outlays | 3,982 | 4,173 | 4,407 | 4,596 | 4,754 | 4,996 | 5,165 | 5,288 | 5,526 | 5,748 | 5,955 | 6,263 | 23,918 | 52,697 |
| **Receipts:** | | | | | | | | | | | | | | |
| Individual income taxes | 1,587 | 1,660 | 1,688 | 1,791 | 1,919 | 2,053 | 2,202 | 2,353 | 2,511 | 2,707 | 2,890 | 3,070 | 9,652 | 23,182 |
| Corporation income taxes | 297 | 218 | 225 | 265 | 273 | 314 | 374 | 417 | 435 | 417 | 406 | 413 | 1,451 | 3,539 |
| Social insurance and retirement receipts: | | | | | | | | | | | | | | |
| Social Security payroll taxes | 851 | 852 | 905 | 941 | 994 | 1,049 | 1,103 | 1,164 | 1,226 | 1,296 | 1,361 | 1,442 | 4,992 | 11,481 |
| Medicare payroll taxes | 256 | 259 | 275 | 287 | 304 | 322 | 339 | 359 | 379 | 401 | 422 | 448 | 1,528 | 3,536 |
| Unemployment insurance | 46 | 48 | 47 | 47 | 48 | 49 | 50 | 50 | 52 | 53 | 55 | 59 | 241 | 510 |
| Other retirement | 10 | 10 | 11 | 13 | 16 | 19 | 21 | 23 | 24 | 25 | 26 | 26 | 80 | 204 |
| Excise taxes | 84 | 108 | 108 | 112 | 119 | 106 | 109 | 111 | 114 | 117 | 121 | 125 | 555 | 1,144 |
| Estate and gift taxes | 23 | 25 | 17 | 18 | 19 | 21 | 23 | 24 | 26 | 28 | 29 | 31 | 98 | 236 |
| Customs duties | 35 | 40 | 44 | 47 | 48 | 50 | 51 | 52 | 53 | 54 | 56 | 58 | 239 | 511 |
| Deposits of earnings, Federal Reserve System | 81 | 72 | 55 | 49 | 53 | 60 | 68 | 73 | 78 | 83 | 87 | 92 | 285 | 698 |
| Other miscellaneous receipts | 48 | 48 | 51 | 47 | 47 | 49 | 50 | 52 | 53 | 54 | 56 | 58 | 244 | 516 |
| Allowance for Obamacare repeal and replacement | ...... | ...... | –3 | –9 | –3 | –3 | –3 | –3 | –3 | –3 | –4 | –4 | –20 | –38 |
| Total receipts | 3,316 | 3,340 | 3,422 | 3,609 | 3,838 | 4,089 | 4,386 | 4,675 | 4,946 | 5,231 | 5,506 | 5,818 | 19,344 | 45,520 |
| **Deficit** | 665 | 833 | 984 | 987 | 916 | 908 | 778 | 612 | 579 | 517 | 450 | 445 | 4,574 | 7,177 |
| Net interest | 263 | 310 | 363 | 447 | 510 | 568 | 619 | 658 | 688 | 717 | 740 | 761 | 2,507 | 6,070 |
| Primary deficit/surplus (–) | 403 | 522 | 621 | 540 | 406 | 340 | 160 | –46 | –109 | –199 | –291 | –316 | 2,067 | 1,107 |
| On-budget deficit | 715 | 828 | 977 | 956 | 875 | 853 | 706 | 525 | 477 | 410 | 328 | 315 | 4,367 | 6,423 |
| Off-budget deficit/surplus (–) | –49 | 5 | 7 | 31 | 41 | 54 | 72 | 87 | 102 | 107 | 122 | 130 | 206 | 754 |

## Table S–4.  Proposed Budget by Category—Continued

(In billions of dollars)

| | 2017 | 2018 | 2019 | 2020 | 2021 | 2022 | 2023 | 2024 | 2025 | 2026 | 2027 | 2028 | Totals 2019–2023 | Totals 2019–2028 |
|---|---|---|---|---|---|---|---|---|---|---|---|---|---|---|
| **Memorandum, totals standardized to 12 monthly benefit payments:** [1] | | | | | | | | | | | | | | |
| Receipts | 3,316 | 3,340 | 3,422 | 3,609 | 3,838 | 4,089 | 4,386 | 4,675 | 4,946 | 5,231 | 5,506 | 5,818 | 19,344 | 45,520 |
| Outlays | 3,982 | 4,214 | 4,407 | 4,596 | 4,754 | 4,941 | 5,160 | 5,348 | 5,526 | 5,748 | 5,955 | 6,181 | 23,858 | 52,615 |
| Deficit | 665 | 873 | 984 | 987 | 916 | 852 | 774 | 672 | 579 | 517 | 450 | 363 | 4,513 | 7,095 |
| **Memorandum, budget authority for discretionary programs:** | | | | | | | | | | | | | | |
| Defense | 634 | 675 | 716 | 733 | 743 | 760 | 778 | 737 | 752 | 768 | 784 | 800 | 3,729 | 7,570 |
| Non-defense | 586 | 545 | 483 | 469 | 455 | 434 | 425 | 415 | 408 | 400 | 392 | 385 | 2,267 | 4,266 |
| Total, discretionary budget authority | 1,220 | 1,220 | 1,199 | 1,202 | 1,198 | 1,194 | 1,203 | 1,152 | 1,160 | 1,168 | 1,176 | 1,185 | 5,996 | 11,836 |
| **Memorandum, repeal & replace Obamacare—Medicaid and other outlays for health care coverage:** | | | | | | | | | | | | | | |
| Medicaid | 375 | 400 | 412 | 363 | 357 | 370 | 383 | 397 | 411 | 426 | 438 | 453 | 1,885 | 4,011 |
| Exchange Subsidies (including Basic Health Program) | 39 | 48 | 45 | 11 | ......... | ......... | ......... | ......... | ......... | ......... | ......... | ......... | 56 | 56 |
| Market-Based Health Care Grant | ......... | ......... | ......... | 120 | 123 | 126 | 128 | 131 | 134 | 138 | 141 | 144 | 497 | 1,185 |
| Total, outlays | 414 | 448 | 457 | 494 | 480 | 495 | 512 | 528 | 546 | 564 | 579 | 597 | 2,438 | 5,251 |

[1] When October 1 falls on a weekend, certain mandatory benefit payments are accelerated to the previous business day, and as a result certain fiscal years can have 11 or 13 benefit payments rather than the normal 12 payments.

## Table S–5.  Proposed Budget by Category as a Percent of GDP

(As a percent of GDP)

| | 2017 | 2018 | 2019 | 2020 | 2021 | 2022 | 2023 | 2024 | 2025 | 2026 | 2027 | 2028 | Averages 2019–2023 | Averages 2019–2028 |
|---|---|---|---|---|---|---|---|---|---|---|---|---|---|---|
| **Outlays:** | | | | | | | | | | | | | | |
| Discretionary programs: | | | | | | | | | | | | | | |
| Defense | 3.1 | 3.2 | 3.2 | 3.3 | 3.1 | 3.1 | 3.0 | 2.8 | 2.6 | 2.5 | 2.5 | 2.4 | 3.1 | 2.8 |
| Non-defense | 3.2 | 3.2 | 3.0 | 2.6 | 2.4 | 2.0 | 1.9 | 1.7 | 1.6 | 1.5 | 1.4 | 1.3 | 2.4 | 2.0 |
| Subtotal, discretionary programs | 6.3 | 6.3 | 6.2 | 5.9 | 5.5 | 5.1 | 4.9 | 4.5 | 4.3 | 4.1 | 3.9 | 3.7 | 5.5 | 4.8 |
| Mandatory programs: | | | | | | | | | | | | | | |
| Social Security | 4.9 | 4.9 | 5.0 | 5.0 | 5.1 | 5.1 | 5.1 | 5.2 | 5.2 | 5.3 | 5.3 | 5.4 | 5.1 | 5.2 |
| Medicare | 3.1 | 2.9 | 3.0 | 3.0 | 3.0 | 3.3 | 3.2 | 3.2 | 3.4 | 3.5 | 3.6 | 3.9 | 3.1 | 3.3 |
| Medicaid and Market-Based Health Care Grant | 2.0 | 2.0 | 2.0 | 2.2 | 2.1 | 2.0 | 2.0 | 2.0 | 1.9 | 1.9 | 1.9 | 1.8 | 2.1 | 2.0 |
| Exchange subsidies (including Basic Health Program) | 0.2 | 0.2 | 0.2 | 0.1 | ......... | ......... | ......... | ......... | ......... | ......... | ......... | ......... | 0.1 | * |
| Other mandatory programs | 3.0 | 2.9 | 2.7 | 2.6 | 2.5 | 2.6 | 2.4 | 2.3 | 2.2 | 2.2 | 2.1 | 2.1 | 2.6 | 2.4 |
| Allowance for infrastructure initiative | ......... | ......... | 0.2 | 0.1 | 0.1 | 0.1 | 0.1 | 0.1 | 0.1 | * | * | * | 0.1 | 0.1 |
| Subtotal, mandatory programs | 13.1 | 12.9 | 13.0 | 12.9 | 12.8 | 13.1 | 12.9 | 12.7 | 12.9 | 12.9 | 12.9 | 13.1 | 12.9 | 12.9 |
| Net interest | 1.4 | 1.5 | 1.7 | 2.0 | 2.2 | 2.3 | 2.4 | 2.4 | 2.4 | 2.4 | 2.4 | 2.3 | 2.1 | 2.3 |
| Total outlays | 20.8 | 20.8 | 21.0 | 20.8 | 20.5 | 20.5 | 20.2 | 19.7 | 19.6 | 19.4 | 19.2 | 19.2 | 20.6 | 20.0 |
| **Receipts:** | | | | | | | | | | | | | | |
| Individual income taxes | 8.3 | 8.3 | 8.0 | 8.1 | 8.3 | 8.4 | 8.6 | 8.7 | 8.9 | 9.1 | 9.3 | 9.4 | 8.3 | 8.7 |
| Corporation income taxes | 1.5 | 1.1 | 1.1 | 1.2 | 1.2 | 1.3 | 1.5 | 1.5 | 1.5 | 1.4 | 1.3 | 1.3 | 1.2 | 1.3 |
| Social insurance and retirement receipts: | | | | | | | | | | | | | | |
| Social Security payroll taxes | 4.4 | 4.3 | 4.3 | 4.3 | 4.3 | 4.3 | 4.3 | 4.3 | 4.3 | 4.4 | 4.4 | 4.4 | 4.3 | 4.3 |
| Medicare payroll taxes | 1.3 | 1.3 | 1.3 | 1.3 | 1.3 | 1.3 | 1.3 | 1.3 | 1.3 | 1.4 | 1.4 | 1.4 | 1.3 | 1.3 |
| Unemployment insurance | 0.2 | 0.2 | 0.2 | 0.2 | 0.2 | 0.2 | 0.2 | 0.2 | 0.2 | 0.2 | 0.2 | 0.2 | 0.2 | 0.2 |
| Other retirement | * | 0.1 | 0.1 | 0.1 | 0.1 | 0.1 | 0.1 | 0.1 | 0.1 | 0.1 | 0.1 | 0.1 | 0.1 | 0.1 |
| Excise taxes | 0.4 | 0.5 | 0.5 | 0.5 | 0.5 | 0.4 | 0.4 | 0.4 | 0.4 | 0.4 | 0.4 | 0.4 | 0.5 | 0.4 |
| Estate and gift taxes | 0.1 | 0.1 | 0.1 | 0.1 | 0.1 | 0.1 | 0.1 | 0.1 | 0.1 | 0.1 | 0.1 | 0.1 | 0.1 | 0.1 |
| Customs duties | 0.2 | 0.2 | 0.2 | 0.2 | 0.2 | 0.2 | 0.2 | 0.2 | 0.2 | 0.2 | 0.2 | 0.2 | 0.2 | 0.2 |
| Deposits of earnings, Federal Reserve System | 0.4 | 0.4 | 0.3 | 0.2 | 0.2 | 0.3 | 0.3 | 0.3 | 0.3 | 0.3 | 0.3 | 0.3 | 0.2 | 0.3 |
| Other miscellaneous receipts | 0.2 | 0.2 | 0.2 | 0.2 | 0.2 | 0.2 | 0.2 | 0.2 | 0.2 | 0.2 | 0.2 | 0.2 | 0.2 | 0.2 |
| Allowance for Obamacare repeal and replacement | ......... | ......... | * | * | * | * | * | * | * | * | * | * | * | * |
| Total receipts | 17.3 | 16.7 | 16.3 | 16.4 | 16.5 | 16.8 | 17.1 | 17.4 | 17.5 | 17.6 | 17.7 | 17.8 | 16.6 | 17.1 |
| **Deficit** | **3.5** | **4.2** | **4.7** | **4.5** | **3.9** | **3.7** | **3.0** | **2.3** | **2.1** | **1.7** | **1.4** | **1.4** | **4.0** | **2.9** |
| Net interest | 1.4 | 1.5 | 1.7 | 2.0 | 2.2 | 2.3 | 2.4 | 2.4 | 2.4 | 2.4 | 2.4 | 2.3 | 2.1 | 2.3 |
| Primary deficit/surplus (–) | 2.1 | 2.6 | 3.0 | 2.4 | 1.7 | 1.4 | 0.6 | -0.2 | -0.4 | -0.7 | -0.9 | -1.0 | 1.8 | 0.6 |
| On-budget deficit | 3.7 | 4.1 | 4.7 | 4.3 | 3.8 | 3.5 | 2.8 | 2.0 | 1.7 | 1.4 | 1.1 | 1.0 | 3.8 | 2.6 |
| Off-budget deficit/surplus (–) | -0.3 | * | * | 0.1 | 0.2 | 0.2 | 0.3 | 0.3 | 0.4 | 0.4 | 0.4 | 0.4 | 0.2 | 0.3 |

## Table S–5.  Proposed Budget by Category as a Percent of GDP—Continued

(As a percent of GDP)

| | 2017 | 2018 | 2019 | 2020 | 2021 | 2022 | 2023 | 2024 | 2025 | 2026 | 2027 | 2028 | Averages 2019–2023 | Averages 2019–2028 |
|---|---|---|---|---|---|---|---|---|---|---|---|---|---|---|
| **Memorandum, totals standardized to 12 monthly benefit payments:** | | | | | | | | | | | | | | |
| Receipts | 17.3 | 16.7 | 16.3 | 16.4 | 16.5 | 16.8 | 17.1 | 17.4 | 17.5 | 17.6 | 17.7 | 17.8 | 16.6 | 17.1 |
| Outlays | 20.8 | 21.0 | 21.0 | 20.8 | 20.5 | 20.3 | 20.2 | 19.9 | 19.6 | 19.4 | 19.2 | 19.0 | 20.5 | 20.0 |
| Deficit | 3.5 | 4.4 | 4.7 | 4.5 | 3.9 | 3.5 | 3.0 | 2.5 | 2.1 | 1.7 | 1.4 | 1.1 | 3.9 | 2.8 |
| **Memorandum, budget authority for discretionary programs:** | | | | | | | | | | | | | | |
| Defense | 3.3 | 3.4 | 3.4 | 3.3 | 3.2 | 3.1 | 3.0 | 2.7 | 2.7 | 2.6 | 2.5 | 2.5 | 3.2 | 2.9 |
| Non-defense | 3.1 | 2.7 | 2.3 | 2.1 | 2.0 | 1.8 | 1.7 | 1.5 | 1.4 | 1.3 | 1.3 | 1.2 | 2.0 | 1.7 |
| Total, discretionary budget authority | 6.4 | 6.1 | 5.7 | 5.4 | 5.2 | 4.9 | 4.7 | 4.3 | 4.1 | 3.9 | 3.8 | 3.6 | 5.2 | 4.6 |
| **Memorandum, repeal & replace Obamacare—Medicaid and other outlays for health care coverage:** | | | | | | | | | | | | | | |
| Medicaid | 2.0 | 2.0 | 2.0 | 1.6 | 1.5 | 1.5 | 1.5 | 1.5 | 1.5 | 1.4 | 1.4 | 1.4 | 1.6 | 1.5 |
| Exchange Subsidies (including Basic Health Program) | 0.2 | 0.2 | 0.2 | 0.1 | ..... | ..... | ..... | ..... | ..... | ..... | ..... | ..... | 0.1 | * |
| Market-Based Health Care Grant | ..... | ..... | ..... | 0.5 | 0.5 | 0.5 | 0.5 | 0.5 | 0.5 | 0.5 | 0.5 | 0.4 | 0.4 | 0.4 |
| Total, outlays | 2.2 | 2.2 | 2.2 | 2.2 | 2.1 | 2.0 | 2.0 | 2.0 | 1.9 | 1.9 | 1.9 | 1.8 | 2.1 | 2.0 |

*0.05 percent of GDP or less.

## Table S–6. Mandatory and Receipt Proposals

(Deficit increases (+) or decreases (−) in millions of dollars)

| | 2018 | 2019 | 2020 | 2021 | 2022 | 2023 | 2024 | 2025 | 2026 | 2027 | 2028 | Totals 2019–2023 | Totals 2019–2028 |
|---|---|---|---|---|---|---|---|---|---|---|---|---|---|
| **Agriculture:** | | | | | | | | | | | | | |
| *Farm Bill savings:* | | | | | | | | | | | | | |
| Limit eligibility for agricultural commodity payments to $500,000 Adjusted Gross Income (AGI) | ........ | –114 | –89 | –142 | –135 | –124 | –120 | –111 | –102 | –98 | –90 | –604 | –1,125 |
| Limit Crop Insurance eligibility to $500,000 AGI | ........ | ........ | –56 | –58 | –67 | –71 | –77 | –84 | –92 | –102 | –117 | –252 | –724 |
| Limit Crop Insurance premium subsidies | ........ | ........ | –2,231 | –2,258 | –2,482 | –2,502 | –2,540 | –2,556 | –2,587 | –2,606 | –2,609 | –9,473 | –22,371 |
| Streamline conservation programs | ........ | –136 | –189 | –483 | –876 | –1,291 | –1,689 | –2,017 | –2,121 | –2,120 | –2,120 | –2,975 | –13,042 |
| Eliminate lower priority Farm Bill programs | ........ | –54 | –112 | –94 | –98 | –100 | –100 | –100 | –100 | –100 | –100 | –458 | –958 |
| Cap Crop Insurance companies' underwriting gains | ........ | ........ | ........ | ........ | –413 | –420 | –423 | –426 | –430 | –437 | –439 | –833 | –2,988 |
| Eliminate Food for Progress food aid program | ........ | –166 | –166 | –166 | –166 | –166 | –166 | –166 | –166 | –166 | –166 | –830 | –1,660 |
| Eliminate farm payment limit loopholes | ........ | –149 | –143 | –141 | –137 | –135 | –132 | –130 | –128 | –127 | –126 | –705 | –1,348 |
| Eliminate Livestock Forage Program | ........ | –416 | –421 | –434 | –444 | –451 | –456 | –460 | –462 | –468 | –471 | –2,166 | –4,483 |
| Total, Farm Bill savings | ........ | –1,035 | –3,407 | –3,776 | –4,818 | –5,260 | –5,703 | –6,050 | –6,188 | –6,224 | –6,238 | –18,296 | –48,699 |
| Establish Food Safety and Inspection Service (FSIS) user fee | ........ | ........ | –660 | –660 | –660 | –660 | –660 | –660 | –660 | –660 | –660 | –2,640 | –5,940 |
| Establish Animal and Plant Health Inspection Service (APHIS) user fee | ........ | –23 | –23 | –23 | –23 | –23 | –23 | –23 | –23 | –23 | –23 | –115 | –230 |
| Establish Packers and Stockyards Program user fee | ........ | –23 | –23 | –23 | –23 | –23 | –23 | –23 | –23 | –23 | –23 | –115 | –230 |
| Establish Agricultural Marketing Service (AMS) user fee | ........ | –20 | –20 | –20 | –20 | –20 | –20 | –20 | –20 | –20 | –20 | –100 | –200 |
| Eliminate interest payments to electric and telecommunications utilities | ........ | –129 | –127 | –130 | –130 | –128 | –129 | –129 | –129 | –129 | –129 | –644 | –1,289 |
| Eliminate the Rural Economic Development Program | ........ | ........ | –158 | –160 | ........ | ........ | ........ | ........ | ........ | ........ | ........ | –318 | –318 |
| Outyear mandatory effects of discretionary changes to the Conservation Stewardship Program | ........ | ........ | –27 | –135 | –180 | –180 | –180 | –180 | –180 | –180 | –180 | –522 | –1,422 |
| Total, Agriculture | ........ | –1,230 | –4,445 | –4,927 | –5,854 | –6,294 | –6,738 | –7,085 | –7,223 | –7,259 | –7,273 | –22,750 | –58,328 |
| **Education:** | | | | | | | | | | | | | |
| Create single income-driven student loan repayment plan [1] | ........ | –2,429 | –6,006 | –9,365 | –11,883 | –13,885 | –15,458 | –16,317 | –17,228 | –17,695 | –18,099 | –43,568 | –128,365 |
| Eliminate subsidized student loans | ........ | –1,500 | –2,580 | –2,886 | –2,973 | –2,992 | –3,008 | –3,050 | –3,096 | –3,216 | –3,254 | –12,931 | –28,555 |
| Eliminate Public Service Loan Forgiveness | ........ | –1,720 | –2,979 | –3,873 | –4,411 | –4,851 | –5,303 | –5,511 | –5,597 | –5,758 | –5,859 | –17,834 | –45,862 |
| Eliminate account maintenance fee payments to guaranty agencies | ........ | –656 | ........ | ........ | ........ | ........ | ........ | ........ | ........ | ........ | ........ | –656 | –656 |
| Move Iraq-Afghanistan Service Grants into the Pell Grant program | ........ | ........ | ........ | ........ | ........ | –1 | –1 | –1 | –1 | –1 | –1 | –1 | –6 |
| Expand Pell Grants to short-term programs | ........ | 7 | 27 | 34 | 40 | 46 | 48 | 49 | 49 | 50 | 51 | 154 | 401 |

## Table S-6. Mandatory and Receipt Proposals—Continued

(Deficit increases (+) or decreases (−) in millions of dollars)

| | 2018 | 2019 | 2020 | 2021 | 2022 | 2023 | 2024 | 2025 | 2026 | 2027 | 2028 | Totals 2019–2023 | Totals 2019–2028 |
|---|---|---|---|---|---|---|---|---|---|---|---|---|---|
| Reallocate mandatory Pell funding to support short-term programs | ...... | −7 | −27 | −34 | −40 | −46 | −48 | −49 | −49 | −50 | −51 | −154 | −401 |
| Total, Education | ...... | −6,305 | −11,565 | −16,124 | −19,267 | −21,729 | −23,770 | −24,879 | −25,922 | −26,670 | −27,213 | −74,990 | −203,444 |
| **Energy:** | | | | | | | | | | | | | |
| Repeal borrowing authority for Western Area Power Administration (WAPA) | ...... | −450 | −875 | −75 | 575 | 275 | 110 | ...... | ...... | ...... | ...... | −550 | −640 |
| Divest WAPA transmission assets | ...... | ...... | −580 | ...... | ...... | ...... | ...... | ...... | ...... | ...... | ...... | −580 | −580 |
| Divest Southwestern Power Administration transmission assets | ...... | ...... | −15 | ...... | ...... | ...... | ...... | ...... | ...... | ...... | ...... | −15 | −15 |
| Divest Bonneville Power Administration transmission assets | ...... | ...... | −1,733 | −488 | −483 | −493 | −452 | −386 | −386 | −386 | −386 | −3,197 | −5,193 |
| Reform the laws governing how Power Marketing Administrations establish power rates | ...... | −162 | −169 | −173 | −182 | −188 | −192 | −199 | −206 | −211 | −217 | −874 | −1,899 |
| Restart Nuclear Waste Fund Fee in 2021 | ...... | ...... | ...... | −359 | −359 | −364 | −367 | −364 | −360 | −360 | −360 | −1,082 | −2,893 |
| Total, Energy | ...... | −612 | −3,372 | −1,095 | −449 | −770 | −901 | −999 | −1,002 | −1,007 | −1,013 | −6,298 | −11,220 |
| **Health and Human Services (HHS):** | | | | | | | | | | | | | |
| Create child welfare flexible funding option | ...... | ...... | ...... | 7 | 8 | 8 | 8 | 21 | 22 | 18 | 18 | 23 | 110 |
| Reform the title IV-E adoption assistance savings provision | ...... | ...... | ...... | ...... | ...... | ...... | ...... | ...... | ...... | ...... | ...... | ...... | ...... |
| Provide tribal access to the Federal Parent Locator Service | ...... | ...... | ...... | ...... | ...... | ...... | ...... | ...... | ...... | ...... | ...... | ...... | ...... |
| Reauthorize the Promoting Safe and Stable Families program (title IV-B) | ...... | ...... | ...... | ...... | ...... | ...... | ...... | ...... | ...... | ...... | ...... | ...... | ...... |
| Expand the Regional Partnership Grants program | ...... | 13 | 35 | 40 | 40 | 40 | 27 | 5 | ...... | ...... | ...... | 168 | 200 |
| Maintain Federal funding for key child care programs | ...... | 499 | 499 | 499 | 499 | 499 | 499 | 499 | 499 | 499 | 499 | 2,495 | 4,990 |
| Reauthorize and modify Abstinence Education and the Personal Responsibility Education Program | ...... | 4 | 52 | 66 | 15 | 2 | 3 | 8 | ...... | ...... | ...... | 139 | 150 |
| Reauthorize Health Profession Opportunity Grants | ...... | 3 | 45 | 18 | 13 | 4 | 2 | ...... | ...... | ...... | ...... | 83 | 85 |
| Drug pricing and payment improvements: | | | | | | | | | | | | | |
| Improve 340B program integrity | ...... | ...... | ...... | ...... | ...... | ...... | ...... | ...... | ...... | ...... | ...... | ...... | ...... |
| Medicare: | | | | | | | | | | | | | |
| Authorize the HHS Secretary to leverage Medicare Part D plans' negotiating power for certain drugs covered under Part B[2] | ...... | ...... | ...... | ...... | ...... | ...... | ...... | ...... | ...... | ...... | ...... | ...... | ...... |
| Permanently authorize a successful pilot on retroactive Medicare Part D coverage for low-income beneficiaries | ...... | ...... | −20 | −30 | −30 | −30 | −30 | −40 | −40 | −40 | −40 | −110 | −300 |

## Table S–6.　Mandatory and Receipt Proposals—Continued

(Deficit increases (+) or decreases (–) in millions of dollars)

| | 2018 | 2019 | 2020 | 2021 | 2022 | 2023 | 2024 | 2025 | 2026 | 2027 | 2028 | Totals 2019–2023 | Totals 2019–2028 |
|---|---|---|---|---|---|---|---|---|---|---|---|---|---|
| Increase Medicare Part D plan formulary flexibility | ........ | –280 | –404 | –444 | –487 | –530 | –576 | –618 | –669 | –725 | –784 | –2,145 | –5,517 |
| Eliminate cost-sharing on generic drugs for low-income beneficiaries | ........ | –30 | –40 | –40 | –20 | –20 | –10 | –20 | –10 | –10 | –10 | –150 | –210 |
| Require Medicare Part D plans to apply a substantial portion of rebates at the point of sale | ........ | 1,785 | 2,727 | 3,139 | 3,533 | 3,930 | 4,351 | 4,801 | 5,356 | 5,983 | 6,555 | 15,114 | 42,160 |
| Exclude manufacturer discounts from the calculation of beneficiary out-of-pocket costs in the Medicare Part D coverage gap | ........ | –1,490 | –2,370 | –3,360 | –4,800 | –5,300 | –4,740 | –5,360 | –5,840 | –6,330 | –7,430 | –17,320 | –47,020 |
| Establish a beneficiary out-of-pocket maximum in the Medicare Part D catastrophic phase | ........ | 377 | 541 | 592 | 648 | 706 | 767 | 825 | 892 | 966 | 1,045 | 2,864 | 7,359 |
| Address abusive drug pricing by manufacturers by establishing an inflation limit for reimbursement of Medicare Part B drugs [2] | ........ | ........ | ........ | ........ | ........ | ........ | ........ | ........ | ........ | ........ | ........ | ........ | ........ |
| Improve manufacturers' reporting of average sales prices to set accurate payment rates [2] | ........ | ........ | ........ | ........ | ........ | ........ | ........ | ........ | ........ | ........ | ........ | ........ | ........ |
| Modify payment for drugs hospitals purchase through the 340B discount program and require a minimum level of charity care for hospitals to receive a payment adjustment related to uncompensated care [2] | ........ | ........ | ........ | ........ | ........ | ........ | ........ | ........ | ........ | ........ | ........ | ........ | ........ |
| Reduce Wholesale Acquisition Cost (WAC)-based payments [2] | ........ | ........ | ........ | ........ | ........ | ........ | ........ | ........ | ........ | ........ | ........ | ........ | ........ |
| Reform exclusivity for first generics to spur greater competition and access | ........ | –118 | –130 | –142 | –169 | –169 | –165 | –194 | –209 | –225 | –267 | –728 | –1,788 |
| Total, Medicare | ........ | 244 | 304 | –285 | –1,325 | –1,413 | –403 | –606 | –520 | –381 | –931 | –2,475 | –5,316 |
| Medicaid: | | | | | | | | | | | | | |
| Test allowing State Medicaid programs to negotiate prices directly with drug manufacturers and set formulary for coverage | ........ | ........ | –5 | –10 | –10 | –10 | –10 | –10 | –10 | –10 | –10 | –35 | –85 |
| Clarify definitions under the Medicaid Drug Rebate Program to prevent inappropriately low manufacturer rebates | ........ | –26 | –26 | –26 | –26 | –31 | –31 | –37 | –37 | –37 | –42 | –135 | –319 |
| Total, Medicaid | ........ | –26 | –31 | –36 | –36 | –41 | –41 | –47 | –47 | –47 | –52 | –170 | –404 |
| Total, drug pricing and payment improvements | ........ | 218 | 273 | –321 | –1,361 | –1,454 | –444 | –653 | –567 | –428 | –983 | –2,645 | –5,720 |

## Table S-6. Mandatory and Receipt Proposals—Continued

(Deficit increases (+) or decreases (–) in millions of dollars)

| | 2018 | 2019 | 2020 | 2021 | 2022 | 2023 | 2024 | 2025 | 2026 | 2027 | 2028 | Totals 2019-2023 | Totals 2019-2028 |
|---|---|---|---|---|---|---|---|---|---|---|---|---|---|
| **Address opioids:** | | | | | | | | | | | | | |
| Prevent abusive prescribing by establishing HHS reciprocity with the Drug Enforcement Administration to terminate provider prescribing authority | ....... | ....... | ....... | ....... | ....... | ....... | ....... | ....... | ....... | ....... | ....... | ....... | ....... |
| Require plan participation in a program to prevent prescription drug abuse in Medicare Part D | ....... | –10 | –10 | –10 | –10 | –10 | –10 | –10 | –10 | –10 | –10 | –50 | –100 |
| Provide comprehensive coverage of substance abuse treatment in Medicare[2] | ....... | ....... | ....... | ....... | ....... | ....... | ....... | ....... | ....... | ....... | ....... | ....... | ....... |
| Track high prescribers and utilizers of prescription drugs in Medicaid[2] | ....... | ....... | ....... | ....... | ....... | ....... | ....... | ....... | ....... | ....... | ....... | ....... | ....... |
| Require coverage of all medication assisted treatment options in Medicaid | ....... | 35 | 25 | –20 | –75 | –110 | –130 | –135 | –145 | –150 | –160 | –145 | –865 |
| *Provide $5 billion over five years to address the opioid crisis (non-add)[3]* | ....... | *500* | *800* | *950* | *1,000* | *1,000* | *500* | *200* | *50* | ....... | ....... | *4,250* | *5,000* |
| Total, address opioids | ....... | 25 | 15 | –30 | –85 | –120 | –140 | –145 | –155 | –160 | –170 | –195 | –965 |
| **Eliminate wasteful Federal spending:** | | | | | | | | | | | | | |
| Consolidate graduate medical education payments | ....... | –370 | –1,200 | –2,090 | –3,070 | –4,120 | –5,230 | –6,270 | –7,360 | –8,580 | –9,800 | –10,850 | –48,090 |
| Reduce Medicare coverage of bad debts | ....... | –400 | –1,330 | –2,820 | –3,760 | –4,090 | –4,350 | –4,620 | –4,910 | –5,220 | –5,530 | –12,400 | –37,030 |
| Modify payments to hospitals for uncompensated care | ....... | ....... | –4,100 | –5,180 | –6,000 | –6,870 | –7,690 | –8,540 | –9,420 | –10,370 | –11,370 | –22,150 | –69,540 |
| Address excessive payment for post-acute care providers by establishing a unified payment system based on patients' clinical needs rather than the site of care | ....... | –780 | –1,960 | –3,420 | –5,820 | –8,640 | –9,650 | –10,830 | –11,800 | –12,850 | –14,440 | –20,620 | –80,190 |
| Pay all hospital-owned physician offices located off-campus at the physician office rate | ....... | –1,240 | –2,260 | –2,510 | –2,810 | –3,140 | –3,490 | –3,860 | –4,280 | –4,750 | –5,640 | –11,960 | –33,980 |
| Address excessive hospital payments by reducing payment when a patient is quickly discharged to hospice | ....... | –70 | –100 | –110 | –110 | –120 | –130 | –140 | –150 | –160 | –170 | –510 | –1,260 |
| Expand basis for beneficiary assignment for Accountable Care Organizations (ACOs) | ....... | ....... | ....... | –10 | –10 | –20 | –20 | –20 | –20 | –20 | –20 | –40 | –140 |
| Allow ACOs to cover the cost of primary care visits to encourage use of the ACO's providers | ....... | ....... | –10 | –10 | –10 | –10 | –10 | ....... | ....... | ....... | –10 | –40 | –60 |
| Expand the ability of Medicare Advantage organizations to pay for services delivered via telehealth | ....... | ....... | ....... | ....... | ....... | ....... | ....... | ....... | ....... | ....... | ....... | ....... | ....... |

## Table S–6. Mandatory and Receipt Proposals—Continued

(Deficit increases (+) or decreases (−) in millions of dollars)

| | 2018 | 2019 | 2020 | 2021 | 2022 | 2023 | 2024 | 2025 | 2026 | 2027 | 2028 | Totals 2019–2023 | Totals 2019–2028 |
|---|---|---|---|---|---|---|---|---|---|---|---|---|---|
| Require prior authorization when physicians order certain services excessively relative to their peers [2] | | | | | | | | | | | | | |
| Reform and expand durable medical equipment competitive bidding | | | −330 | −600 | −630 | −690 | −740 | −780 | −840 | −910 | −960 | −2,250 | −6,480 |
| Reform physician self-referral law to better support and align with alternative payment models and to address overutilization [2] | | | | | | | | | | | | | |
| Allow for Federal/State coordinated review of dual eligible Special Needs Plan marketing materials | | | | | | | | | | | | | |
| Improve appeals notifications for dually eligible individuals in Integrated Health Plans | | | | | | | | | | | | | |
| Clarify the Part D special enrollment period for dually eligible beneficiaries | | −38 | −53 | −57 | −62 | −67 | −72 | −77 | −83 | −89 | −95 | −277 | −693 |
| Cancel funding from the Medicare Improvement Fund (MIF) | | | | | −193 | | | | | | | −193 | −193 |
| Give Medicare beneficiaries with high deductible health plans the option to make tax deductible contributions to Health Savings Accounts and Medical Savings Accounts [4] | | | | 610 | 1,081 | 1,305 | 1,513 | 1,619 | 1,704 | 1,786 | 1,847 | 2,996 | 11,465 |
| Total, eliminate wasteful Federal spending | −2,898 | −11,343 | −16,197 | −21,394 | −26,462 | −29,869 | −33,518 | −37,159 | −41,163 | −46,188 | | −78,294 | −266,191 |
| Eliminate wasteful spending on Government-imposed provider burdens in Medicare: | | | | | | | | | | | | | |
| Repeal the Independent Payment Advisory Board (IPAB) | | | | | | | | | | | | | |
| Improve and tailor the way Medicare educates beneficiaries about the program | | | | | | 1,579 | 3,449 | 4,591 | 5,366 | 6,288 | 8,209 | 1,579 | 29,482 |
| Eliminate the reporting burden and arbitrary requirements for use of electronic health records | | | | | | | | | | | | | |
| Eliminate arbitrary thresholds and other burdens to encourage participation in advanced Alternative Payment Models [2] | | | | | | | | | | | | | |
| Simplify and eliminate reporting burdens for clinicians participating in the Merit-based Incentive Payment System [2] | | | | | | | | | | | | | |
| Tailor the frequency of skilled nursing facility surveys to more efficiently use resources and alleviate burden for top-performing nursing homes | | | | | | | | | | | | | |

## Table S-6. Mandatory and Receipt Proposals—Continued

(Deficit increases (+) or decreases (–) in millions of dollars)

| | 2018 | 2019 | 2020 | 2021 | 2022 | 2023 | 2024 | 2025 | 2026 | 2027 | 2028 | Totals 2019–2023 | Totals 2019–2028 |
|---|---|---|---|---|---|---|---|---|---|---|---|---|---|
| Eliminate the unnecessary requirement of a face-to-face provider visit for durable medical equipment | ........ | ........ | ........ | ........ | ........ | ........ | ........ | ........ | ........ | ........ | ........ | ........ | ........ |
| Total, eliminate wasteful spending on Government-imposed provider burdens in Medicare | ........ | ........ | ........ | ........ | ........ | 1,579 | 3,449 | 4,591 | 5,366 | 6,288 | 8,209 | 1,579 | 29,482 |
| Address fraud and abuse in Medicare: | | | | | | | | | | | | | |
| Suspend coverage and payment for questionable Part D prescriptions and incomplete clinical information | ........ | –30 | –30 | –40 | –40 | –50 | –40 | –40 | –50 | –50 | –50 | –190 | –420 |
| Prevent abuse of Medicare coverage when another source has primary responsibility for prescription drug coverage | ........ | –10 | –30 | –30 | –30 | –40 | –40 | –50 | –50 | –60 | –70 | –140 | –410 |
| Expand prior authorization to additional Medicare fee-for-service items at high risk of fraud, waste, and abuse [2] | ........ | ........ | ........ | ........ | ........ | ........ | ........ | ........ | ........ | ........ | ........ | ........ | ........ |
| Prevent fraud by enforcing reporting of enrollment changes through civil monetary penalties for providers and suppliers who fail to update enrollment records | ........ | –2 | –2 | –3 | –3 | –3 | –3 | –4 | –4 | –4 | –4 | –13 | –32 |
| Allow revocation and denial of provider enrollment based on affiliation with a sanctioned entity | ........ | ........ | ........ | –6 | –6 | –6 | –6 | –6 | –6 | –6 | –11 | –18 | –53 |
| Require clearinghouses and billing agents acting on behalf of Medicare providers and suppliers to enroll in the program | ........ | ........ | ........ | ........ | ........ | ........ | ........ | ........ | ........ | ........ | ........ | ........ | ........ |
| Ensure providers that violate Medicare's safety requirements and have harmed patients cannot quickly re-enter the program | ........ | ........ | ........ | ........ | ........ | ........ | ........ | ........ | ........ | ........ | ........ | ........ | ........ |
| Assess a penalty on physicians and practitioners who order services or supplies without proper documentation | ........ | ........ | ........ | ........ | ........ | ........ | ........ | ........ | ........ | ........ | ........ | ........ | ........ |
| Clarify authority for the Healthcare Fraud Prevention Partnership | ........ | ........ | ........ | ........ | ........ | ........ | ........ | ........ | ........ | ........ | ........ | ........ | ........ |
| Alter the Open Payments reporting and publication cycle | ........ | ........ | ........ | ........ | ........ | ........ | ........ | ........ | ........ | ........ | ........ | ........ | ........ |
| Publish the National Provider Identifier for covered recipients in the Open Payments Program | ........ | ........ | ........ | ........ | ........ | ........ | ........ | ........ | ........ | ........ | ........ | ........ | ........ |
| Improve the safety and quality of care by requiring accreditation organizations to publicly report Medicare survey and certification reports | ........ | ........ | ........ | ........ | ........ | ........ | ........ | ........ | ........ | ........ | ........ | ........ | ........ |
| Total, address fraud and abuse in Medicare | ........ | –42 | –62 | –79 | –79 | –99 | –89 | –100 | –110 | –120 | –135 | –361 | –915 |

## Table S–6. Mandatory and Receipt Proposals—Continued

(Deficit increases (+) or decreases (–) in millions of dollars)

| | 2018 | 2019 | 2020 | 2021 | 2022 | 2023 | 2024 | 2025 | 2026 | 2027 | 2028 | Totals 2019–2023 | Totals 2019–2028 |
|---|---|---|---|---|---|---|---|---|---|---|---|---|---|
| **Medicare appeals:** | | | | | | | | | | | | | |
| Improve the Medicare appeals system [5] ... | ...... | 112 | 112 | 112 | 112 | 112 | 112 | 112 | 112 | 112 | 112 | 560 | 1,120 |
| **Strengthen Medicaid operations and increase State flexibility:** | | | | | | | | | | | | | |
| Allow States to apply asset test to modified adjusted gross income standard populations ... | ...... | –50 | –100 | –190 | –200 | –220 | –230 | –240 | –260 | –270 | –290 | –760 | –2,050 |
| Reduce maximum allowable home equity for Medicaid eligibility ... | ...... | ...... | ...... | ...... | ...... | ...... | ...... | ...... | ...... | ...... | ...... | ...... | ...... |
| Require documentation of satisfactory immigration status before receipt of Medicaid benefits ... | ...... | –170 | –180 | –190 | –200 | –210 | –220 | –230 | –250 | –260 | –280 | –950 | –2,190 |
| Increase limit on Medicaid copayments for non-emergency use of emergency department ... | ...... | –60 | –110 | –110 | –120 | –130 | –140 | –140 | –150 | –160 | –170 | –530 | –1,290 |
| Define lottery winnings and other lump-sum payments as income for purpose of Medicaid eligibility ... | ...... | –3 | –3 | –4 | –5 | –5 | –5 | –6 | –6 | –6 | –7 | –20 | –50 |
| Increase flexibility in the duration of section 1915(b) managed care waivers ... | ...... | ...... | ...... | ...... | ...... | ...... | ...... | ...... | ...... | ...... | ...... | ...... | ...... |
| Provide a pathway to make permanent established Medicaid managed care waivers ... | ...... | ...... | ...... | ...... | ...... | ...... | ...... | ...... | ...... | ...... | ...... | ...... | ...... |
| Total, strengthen Medicaid operations and increase State flexibility ... | ...... | –283 | –393 | –494 | –525 | –565 | –595 | –616 | –666 | –696 | –747 | –2,260 | –5,580 |
| **Address wasteful spending, fraud and abuse in Medicaid:** | | | | | | | | | | | | | |
| Continue Medicaid Disproportionate Share Hospital (DSH) allotment reductions ... | ...... | ...... | ...... | ...... | ...... | ...... | ...... | ...... | –6,510 | –6,490 | –6,470 | ...... | –19,470 |
| Consolidate provider enrollment screening for Medicare, Medicaid, and Children's Health Insurance Program (CHIP) ... | ...... | ...... | ...... | ...... | ...... | ...... | ...... | ...... | ...... | ...... | ...... | ...... | ...... |
| Implement pre-payment controls to prevent inappropriate personal care services payments [2] ... | ...... | ...... | ...... | ...... | ...... | ...... | ...... | ...... | ...... | ...... | ...... | ...... | ...... |
| Streamline the Medicaid terminations process ... | ...... | ...... | ...... | ...... | ...... | ...... | ...... | ...... | ...... | ...... | ...... | ...... | ...... |
| Expand Medicaid Fraud Control Unit review to additional care settings [2] ... | ...... | ...... | ...... | ...... | ...... | ...... | ...... | ...... | ...... | ...... | ...... | ...... | ...... |
| Prohibit Medicaid payments to public providers in excess of costs [2] ... | ...... | ...... | ...... | ...... | ...... | ...... | ...... | ...... | ...... | ...... | ...... | ...... | ...... |
| Total, address wasteful spending, fraud and abuse in Medicaid ... | ...... | ...... | ...... | ...... | ...... | ...... | ...... | ...... | –6,510 | –6,490 | –6,470 | ...... | –19,470 |

## Table S-6.  Mandatory and Receipt Proposals—Continued

(Deficit increases (+) or decreases (–) in millions of dollars)

| | | | | | | | | | | | | Totals | |
|---|---|---|---|---|---|---|---|---|---|---|---|---|---|
| | 2018 | 2019 | 2020 | 2021 | 2022 | 2023 | 2024 | 2025 | 2026 | 2027 | 2028 | 2019–2023 | 2019–2028 |
| **Children's Health Insurance Program (CHIP):** | | | | | | | | | | | | | |
| Extend CHIP through 2019 with reforms [4] | 2,620 | –560 | 2,565 | 510 | ...... | ...... | ...... | ...... | ...... | ...... | ...... | 2,515 | 2,515 |
| **Other health:** [6] | | | | | | | | | | | | | |
| Reform medical liability [4,7] | ...... | –178 | –712 | –1,862 | –3,253 | –4,552 | –6,098 | –7,783 | –8,614 | –9,122 | –9,945 | –10,557 | –52,119 |
| Reduce the grace period for Exchange premiums [4] | ...... | –975 | –325 | ...... | ...... | ...... | ...... | ...... | ...... | ...... | ...... | –1,300 | –1,300 |
| Permit federally-facilitated Exchange States to conduct Qualified Health Plan certification | ...... | ...... | ...... | ...... | ...... | ...... | ...... | ...... | ...... | ...... | ...... | ...... | ...... |
| Prohibit governmental discrimination against health care providers that refuse to cover abortion | ...... | ...... | ...... | ...... | ...... | ...... | ...... | ...... | ...... | ...... | ...... | ...... | ...... |
| Fully fund the Risk Corridors program [4] | 812 | ...... | ...... | ...... | ...... | ...... | ...... | ...... | ...... | ...... | ...... | ...... | ...... |
| Provide CMS Program Management implementation funding | ...... | 12 | 150 | 38 | ...... | ...... | ...... | ...... | ...... | ...... | ...... | 200 | 200 |
| Extend Medicare Enrollment Assistance Programs through 2019 | 38 | 38 | ...... | ...... | ...... | ...... | ...... | ...... | ...... | ...... | ...... | 38 | 38 |
| Total, other health | 850 | –1,103 | –887 | –1,824 | –3,253 | –4,552 | –6,098 | –7,783 | –8,614 | –9,122 | –9,945 | –11,619 | –53,181 |
| **Public health:** | | | | | | | | | | | | | |
| Extend Health Centers through 2019 | 1,372 | 3,235 | 1,939 | 68 | 36 | ...... | ...... | ...... | ...... | ...... | ...... | 5,278 | 5,278 |
| Extend the National Health Service Corps through 2019 | 54 | 210 | 217 | 54 | 14 | 6 | ...... | ...... | ...... | ...... | ...... | 501 | 501 |
| Extend Teaching Health Centers Graduate Medical Education through 2019 | 30 | 60 | ...... | ...... | ...... | ...... | ...... | ...... | ...... | ...... | ...... | 60 | 60 |
| Extend Family to Family Health Information Centers through 2019 | 1 | 4 | 4 | 1 | ...... | ...... | ...... | ...... | ...... | ...... | ...... | 9 | 9 |
| Extend the Maternal, Infant, and Early Childhood Home Visiting Program through 2019 | 16 | 120 | 320 | 264 | 64 | 16 | ...... | ...... | ...... | ...... | ...... | 784 | 784 |
| Extend the Special Diabetes Program for the National Institutes of Health and Indian Health Service (IHS) through 2019 | 84 | 203 | 103 | 69 | 19 | 5 | 3 | 1 | ...... | ...... | ...... | 399 | 403 |
| Provide tax exemption for IHS Health Professions scholarship and loan repayment programs in return for obligatory service requirement [4] | ...... | 5 | 12 | 13 | 14 | 14 | 14 | 14 | 15 | 17 | 19 | 58 | 137 |
| Total, public health | 1,557 | 3,837 | 2,595 | 469 | 147 | 41 | 17 | 15 | 15 | 17 | 19 | 7,089 | 7,172 |
| **Interactions:** | | | | | | | | | | | | | |
| Medicare Interactions | ...... | 190 | 381 | 471 | 538 | 613 | 665 | 708 | 760 | 807 | 863 | 2,193 | 5,996 |
| Medicaid Interactions | ...... | ...... | 146 | 237 | 352 | 462 | 552 | 633 | 723 | 818 | 933 | 1,197 | 4,856 |
| Total, Interactions | ...... | 190 | 527 | 708 | 890 | 1,075 | 1,217 | 1,341 | 1,483 | 1,625 | 1,796 | 3,390 | 10,852 |
| Total, Health and Human Services | 5,027 | 15 | –5,967 | –16,516 | –24,973 | –29,892 | –31,901 | –36,223 | –46,284 | –49,620 | –53,985 | –77,333 | –295,346 |

## Table S-6. Mandatory and Receipt Proposals—Continued

(Deficit increases (+) or decreases (−) in millions of dollars)

| | 2018 | 2019 | 2020 | 2021 | 2022 | 2023 | 2024 | 2025 | 2026 | 2027 | 2028 | Totals 2019-2023 | Totals 2019-2028 |
|---|---|---|---|---|---|---|---|---|---|---|---|---|---|
| **Homeland Security:** | | | | | | | | | | | | | |
| Extend expiring Customs and Border Protection (CBP) fees | ........ | ........ | ........ | ........ | ........ | ........ | ........ | ........ | -3,406 | -4,556 | -4,796 | ........ | -12,758 |
| Increase customs user fees | ........ | -113 | -126 | -137 | -148 | -162 | -176 | -191 | -206 | -223 | -214 | -686 | -1,696 |
| Increase immigration user fees | ........ | ........ | ........ | ........ | ........ | ........ | ........ | ........ | ........ | ........ | ........ | ........ | ........ |
| Establish Electronic Visa Update System user fee [4] | ........ | ........ | ........ | ........ | ........ | ........ | ........ | ........ | ........ | ........ | ........ | ........ | ........ |
| Authorize mandatory outlays for U.S. Coast Guard Continuation Pay | ........ | 5 | 6 | 7 | 9 | 9 | 10 | 10 | 10 | 10 | 10 | 36 | 86 |
| Eliminate BrandUSA; make revenue available to CBP | ........ | 60 | 66 | ........ | ........ | ........ | ........ | ........ | ........ | ........ | ........ | 126 | 126 |
| Make full Electronic System for Travel Authorization (ESTA) receipts available to CBP [4] | ........ | ........ | ........ | ........ | ........ | ........ | ........ | ........ | ........ | ........ | ........ | ........ | ........ |
| Expand authority of the Aviation Security Capital Fund | ........ | ........ | ........ | ........ | ........ | ........ | ........ | ........ | ........ | ........ | ........ | ........ | ........ |
| Establish an immigration services surcharge [4] | ........ | -453 | -465 | -479 | -493 | -507 | -522 | -538 | -553 | -569 | -587 | -2,397 | -5,166 |
| Increase worksite enforcement penalties [4] | ........ | -13 | -14 | -15 | -15 | -15 | -15 | -15 | -15 | -15 | -15 | -72 | -147 |
| Establish National Flood Insurance Program affordability assistance [8] | ........ | 2 | -2 | -11 | 26 | 39 | 50 | 64 | 80 | 91 | 95 | 54 | 434 |
| Reauthorize the Oil Spill Liability Trust Fund excise tax [4,9] | ........ | -354 | -466 | -473 | -480 | -489 | -494 | -500 | -507 | -511 | -511 | -2,262 | -4,785 |
| Total, Homeland Security | ........ | -866 | -1,001 | -1,108 | -1,101 | -1,125 | -1,147 | -1,170 | -4,597 | -5,773 | -6,018 | -5,201 | -23,906 |
| **Interior:** | | | | | | | | | | | | | |
| Cancel Southern Nevada Public Land Management Act (SNPLMA) balances | ........ | -83 | -69 | -78 | ........ | ........ | ........ | ........ | ........ | ........ | ........ | -230 | -230 |
| Repeal enhanced geothermal payments to counties | ........ | -4 | -4 | -4 | -4 | -4 | -4 | -4 | -4 | -4 | -4 | -20 | -40 |
| Reauthorize the Federal Land Transaction Facilitation Act (FLTFA) | ........ | -5 | -6 | -9 | -12 | -3 | ........ | ........ | ........ | ........ | ........ | -35 | -35 |
| Permanently reauthorize the Federal Lands Recreation Enhancement Act (FLREA) | ........ | ........ | ........ | ........ | ........ | ........ | ........ | ........ | ........ | ........ | ........ | ........ | ........ |
| Establish a Public Lands Infrastructure Fund | ........ | 152 | 420 | 614 | 766 | 764 | 766 | 781 | 810 | 842 | 878 | 2,716 | 6,793 |
| Total, Interior | ........ | 60 | 341 | 523 | 750 | 757 | 762 | 777 | 806 | 838 | 874 | 2,431 | 6,488 |
| **Labor:** | | | | | | | | | | | | | |
| Establish a paid parental leave program: | | | | | | | | | | | | | |
| Provide paid parental leave benefits [4,9,10] | ........ | 700 | 1,000 | 1,767 | 1,678 | 1,942 | 2,174 | 2,228 | 2,351 | 2,464 | 2,568 | 7,087 | 18,872 |
| Establish an Unemployment Insurance (UI) solvency standard [4,9] | ........ | ........ | ........ | -633 | -1,615 | -2,230 | -919 | -1,613 | -927 | -1,267 | -1,907 | -4,478 | -11,111 |
| Improve UI program integrity [4,9] | ........ | -83 | -188 | -211 | -211 | -174 | -195 | -181 | -229 | -194 | -216 | -867 | -1,882 |
| Provide for Reemployment Services and Eligibility Assessments [4,9] | ........ | ........ | -73 | -465 | -440 | -417 | -445 | -413 | -346 | -413 | -277 | -1,395 | -3,289 |
| Total, establish a paid parental leave program | ........ | 617 | 739 | 458 | -588 | -879 | 615 | 21 | 849 | 590 | 168 | 347 | 2,590 |

## Table S-6. Mandatory and Receipt Proposals—Continued

(Deficit increases (+) or decreases (–) in millions of dollars)

| | 2018 | 2019 | 2020 | 2021 | 2022 | 2023 | 2024 | 2025 | 2026 | 2027 | 2028 | Totals 2019-2023 | Totals 2019-2028 |
|---|---|---|---|---|---|---|---|---|---|---|---|---|---|
| Improve Pension Benefit Guaranty Corporation (PBGC) solvency | 32 | 74 | -1,470 | -1,564 | -1,663 | -1,760 | -1,810 | 1,428 | -5,128 | -1,901 | -1,936 | -6,383 | -15,730 |
| Expand Foreign Labor Certification fees | | | | | | | | | | | | | |
| Reform the Federal Employees' Compensation Act (FECA) | | -62 | -7 | -5 | -5 | -5 | -6 | -6 | -8 | -8 | -5 | -84 | -117 |
| Reform the Trade Adjustment Assistance program | | -98 | -211 | -318 | -281 | -260 | -158 | -77 | -81 | -112 | -148 | -1,168 | -1,744 |
| Adjust the HIRE Vets Medallion Program | | 1 | 3 | 4 | 4 | 4 | 4 | 4 | 4 | 4 | 4 | 16 | 36 |
| Total, Labor | 32 | 532 | -946 | -1,425 | -2,533 | -2,900 | -1,355 | 1,370 | -4,364 | -1,427 | -1,917 | -7,272 | -14,965 |
| **Transportation:** | | | | | | | | | | | | | |
| *Air Traffic Control:* | | | | | | | | | | | | | |
| Reform Air Traffic Control [4] | | | | | 15,495 | 16,241 | 17,027 | 17,870 | 18,674 | 19,497 | 20,536 | 31,736 | 125,340 |
| Outlay savings from discretionary cap adjustment | | | | | -8,681 | -9,453 | -9,829 | -10,060 | -10,173 | -10,173 | -10,173 | -18,134 | -68,542 |
| Reform Essential Air Service [4] | | | | | 61 | 1 | 2 | 2 | 1 | 2 | 2 | 62 | 71 |
| Total, Transportation | | | | | 6,875 | 6,789 | 7,200 | 7,812 | 8,502 | 9,326 | 10,365 | 13,664 | 56,869 |
| **Treasury:** | | | | | | | | | | | | | |
| Provide authority for Bureau of Engraving and Printing to construct new facility [4] | | -12 | | -3 | 89 | -360 | -53 | 20 | -3 | -222 | -3 | -318 | -579 |
| Increase and extend guarantee fee charged by Government-sponsored enterprises | | -212 | -967 | -1,699 | -2,350 | -3,475 | -4,258 | -4,034 | -3,398 | -2,858 | -2,401 | -8,703 | -25,652 |
| Subject Financial Research Fund to appropriations with reforms to the Financial Stability Oversight Council and Office of Financial Research [4,9] | | | 33 | -13 | -18 | -18 | -18 | -18 | -18 | -18 | -18 | -17 | -107 |
| Increase delinquent Federal non-tax debt collections | | -32 | -32 | -32 | -32 | -32 | -32 | -32 | -32 | -32 | -32 | -160 | -320 |
| Increase and streamline recovery of unclaimed assets | | -8 | -8 | -8 | -8 | -8 | -8 | -8 | -8 | -8 | -8 | -40 | -80 |
| Implement tax enforcement program integrity cap adjustment [4] | | -152 | -787 | -1,825 | -3,033 | -4,330 | -5,554 | -6,416 | -6,931 | -7,270 | -7,505 | -10,127 | -43,803 |
| *Discretionary outlays from tax enforcement program integrity cap adjustment (non-add)* | | 320 | 693 | 1,040 | 1,386 | 1,737 | 1,850 | 1,865 | 1,875 | 1,885 | 1,893 | 5,176 | 14,544 |
| Increase oversight of paid tax return preparers [4] | | -22 | -31 | -36 | -39 | -43 | -47 | -52 | -57 | -63 | -67 | -171 | -457 |
| Provide more flexible authority for the Internal Revenue Service to address correctable errors [4] | | -42 | -63 | -65 | -66 | -69 | -70 | -73 | -75 | -76 | -79 | -305 | -678 |
| Total, Treasury | | -481 | -1,887 | -3,681 | -5,457 | -8,335 | -10,040 | -10,613 | -10,522 | -10,547 | -10,113 | -19,841 | -71,676 |
| **Veterans Affairs (VA):** | | | | | | | | | | | | | |
| Provide for a smooth transition to the new Veterans Community Care program | | 236 | 479 | 479 | 361 | 215 | 95 | | | | | 1,770 | 1,865 |

## Table S–6. Mandatory and Receipt Proposals—Continued

(Deficit increases (+) or decreases (−) in millions of dollars)

| | 2018 | 2019 | 2020 | 2021 | 2022 | 2023 | 2024 | 2025 | 2026 | 2027 | 2028 | Totals 2019–2023 | Totals 2019–2028 |
|---|---|---|---|---|---|---|---|---|---|---|---|---|---|
| Cap Post–9/11 GI Bill flight training programs at public schools | ...... | –43 | –45 | –46 | –47 | –49 | –51 | –53 | –55 | –57 | –59 | –230 | –505 |
| Extension of home loan fees | ...... | ...... | ...... | ...... | ...... | ...... | ...... | ...... | ...... | ...... | –356 | ...... | –356 |
| Enhance burial benefits for veterans | ...... | 2 | 2 | ...... | 2 | 2 | 2 | 2 | 3 | 3 | 3 | 10 | 23 |
| Reinstate COLA round-down | ...... | –34 | –92 | –148 | –207 | –268 | –281 | –296 | –311 | –323 | –336 | –749 | –2,296 |
| Standardize and enhance VA Compensation and Pension benefit programs | ...... | –78 | –80 | –83 | –85 | –88 | –90 | –93 | –95 | –98 | –397 | –414 | –1,187 |
| Standardize, extend, and improve veteran Specially Adapted Housing programs | ...... | 4 | 4 | 5 | 4 | 5 | ...... | ...... | ...... | 1 | 1 | 22 | 24 |
| Standardize and improve veteran vocational rehabilitation and education benefit programs | ...... | 72 | –20 | –22 | –25 | –26 | –33 | –35 | –37 | –39 | –41 | –21 | –206 |
| Extend authority for securitization of vendee loans | ...... | 89 | 19 | 52 | 3 | 50 | 3 | 55 | 4 | 58 | ...... | 213 | 333 |
| Extend housing assistance for homeless veterans and include permanent housing options | ...... | 29 | | | | | | | | | | 29 | 29 |
| Total, Veterans Affairs | ...... | 277 | 267 | 239 | 6 | –159 | –355 | –420 | –491 | –455 | –1,185 | 630 | –2,276 |
| Corps of Engineers: | | | | | | | | | | | | | |
| Divest the Washington Aqueduct | ...... | ...... | ...... | –120 | ...... | ...... | ...... | ...... | ...... | ...... | ...... | –120 | –120 |
| Reform inland waterways financing [4] | ...... | –178 | –178 | –178 | –178 | –178 | –178 | –178 | –178 | –178 | –178 | –890 | –1,780 |
| Reduce the Harbor Maintenance Tax [4,9] | ...... | 265 | 281 | 292 | 299 | 307 | 314 | 323 | 333 | 345 | 359 | 1,444 | 3,118 |
| Total, Corps of Engineers | ...... | 87 | 103 | –6 | 121 | 129 | 136 | 145 | 155 | 167 | 181 | 434 | 1,218 |
| Environmental Protection Agency: | | | | | | | | | | | | | |
| Expand use of pesticide licensing fees | ...... | 5 | 4 | 4 | 4 | 4 | 3 | 2 | 1 | 1 | 1 | 21 | 29 |
| International Assistance Programs: | | | | | | | | | | | | | |
| Transfer funds from Overseas Private Investment Corporation to Development Finance Institution | ...... | ...... | ...... | ...... | ...... | ...... | ...... | ...... | ...... | ...... | ...... | ...... | ...... |
| Office of Personnel Management (OPM): | | | | | | | | | | | | | |
| Federal Employees Health Benefits (FEHB) Program: | | | | | | | | | | | | | |
| Provide OPM authority to incorporate provisions of the Anti-Kickback Act to the FEHB Program | ...... | ...... | ...... | ...... | ...... | ...... | ...... | ...... | ...... | ...... | ...... | ...... | ...... |
| Modify the Government contribution to FEHB premiums | ...... | ...... | ...... | –192 | –301 | –321 | –342 | –363 | –387 | –412 | –439 | –814 | –2,757 |
| Modify existing statute on indemnity benefit plans in FEHB | ...... | ...... | ...... | ...... | ...... | ...... | ...... | ...... | ...... | ...... | ...... | ...... | ...... |
| Provide tax preemption for Federal Employees Dental/Vision Program | ...... | ...... | ...... | ...... | ...... | ...... | ...... | ...... | ...... | ...... | ...... | ...... | ...... |
| Total, Federal Employees Health Benefits (FEHB) Program | ...... | ...... | ...... | –192 | –301 | –321 | –342 | –363 | –387 | –412 | –439 | –814 | –2,757 |

## Table S-6. Mandatory and Receipt Proposals—Continued

(Deficit increases (+) or decreases (−) in millions of dollars)

| | 2018 | 2019 | 2020 | 2021 | 2022 | 2023 | 2024 | 2025 | 2026 | 2027 | 2028 | Totals 2019–2023 | Totals 2019–2028 |
|---|---|---|---|---|---|---|---|---|---|---|---|---|---|
| **Reform retirement benefits for Federal employees:** | | | | | | | | | | | | | |
| Increase employee contributions to 50% of cost, phased in at 1% per year [4] | ...... | ...... | −2,267 | −4,602 | −6,442 | −8,068 | −9,441 | −9,456 | −9,470 | −9,480 | −9,479 | −21,379 | −68,705 |
| Eliminate Federal Employee Retirement System COLA; reduce Civil Service Retirement System COLA by 0.5% | ...... | −1,119 | −1,783 | −2,524 | −3,350 | −4,247 | −5,213 | −6,250 | −7,357 | −8,539 | −9,798 | −13,023 | −50,180 |
| Eliminate the Special Retirement Supplement | ...... | −497 | −867 | −1,274 | −1,596 | −1,818 | −2,028 | −2,290 | −2,540 | −2,762 | −3,003 | −6,052 | −18,675 |
| Change retirement calculation from high–3 years to high–5 years | ...... | −277 | −339 | −405 | −476 | −549 | −623 | −698 | −778 | −860 | −944 | −2,046 | −5,949 |
| Reduce the G-fund interest rate | ...... | −694 | −382 | −1,142 | −671 | −798 | −877 | −957 | −1,052 | −1,132 | −1,216 | −3,687 | −8,921 |
| Loss of mandatory offsetting receipts from retirement proposals | ...... | ...... | 11,580 | 14,047 | 16,094 | 17,919 | 19,486 | 19,692 | 19,898 | 20,098 | 20,283 | 59,640 | 159,097 |
| Discretionary effect of retirement proposals | ...... | ...... | −6,461 | −7,482 | −8,026 | −8,544 | −8,919 | −8,619 | −8,324 | −8,034 | −7,743 | −30,513 | −72,152 |
| Total, reform retirement benefits for Federal employees | ...... | −2,587 | −519 | −3,382 | −4,467 | −6,105 | −7,615 | −8,578 | −9,623 | −10,709 | −11,900 | −17,060 | −65,485 |
| Total, Office of Personnel Management | ...... | −2,587 | −519 | −3,574 | −4,768 | −6,426 | −7,957 | −8,941 | −10,010 | −11,121 | −12,339 | −17,874 | −68,242 |
| **Other Independent Agencies:** | | | | | | | | | | | | | |
| **Federal Communications Commission:** | | | | | | | | | | | | | |
| Enact Spectrum License User Fee | ...... | −50 | −150 | −300 | −450 | −500 | −500 | −500 | −500 | −500 | −500 | −1,450 | −3,950 |
| Conduct spectrum auctions below 6 gigahertz | ...... | ...... | −300 | −300 | ...... | ...... | ...... | ...... | ...... | ...... | −6,000 | −600 | −6,600 |
| Total, Federal Communications Commission | ...... | −50 | −450 | −600 | −450 | −500 | −500 | −500 | −500 | −500 | −6,500 | −2,050 | −10,550 |
| Restructure the Consumer Financial Protection Bureau | ...... | −147 | −610 | −656 | −672 | −687 | −704 | −720 | −737 | −755 | −773 | −2,772 | −6,461 |
| Eliminate the Securities and Exchange Commission Reserve Fund | ...... | ...... | −17 | −41 | −50 | −50 | −50 | −50 | −50 | −50 | −50 | −158 | −408 |
| Allow District of Columbia Courts to retain bar exam and application fees [11] | ...... | ...... | ...... | ...... | ...... | ...... | ...... | ...... | ...... | ...... | ...... | ...... | ...... |
| Reform the Postal Service | ...... | −4,592 | −4,586 | −4,530 | −4,501 | −4,453 | −4,438 | −4,436 | −4,392 | −4,308 | −4,254 | −22,662 | −44,490 |
| Divest Tennessee Valley Authority (TVA) transmission assets | ...... | 241 | −3,760 | −19 | −19 | −19 | −19 | −19 | −19 | −19 | −19 | −3,576 | −3,671 |
| Mandatory effects of agency eliminations | ...... | ...... | ...... | ...... | −1 | ...... | ...... | ...... | ...... | ...... | ...... | −1 | −1 |
| Total, Other Independent Agencies | ...... | −4,548 | −9,423 | −5,846 | −5,693 | −5,709 | −5,711 | −5,725 | −5,698 | −5,632 | −11,596 | −31,219 | −65,581 |
| **Cross-cutting reforms:** | | | | | | | | | | | | | |
| **Repeal and replace Obamacare:** | | | | | | | | | | | | | |
| Proposal modeled after the Graham-Cassidy-Heller-Johnson bill: [4] | | | | | | | | | | | | | |
| Medicaid reforms | ...... | −2,885 | −67,165 | −92,350 | −98,060 | −104,475 | −112,350 | −126,155 | −140,800 | −159,945 | −179,385 | −364,935 | −1,083,570 |
| Market-Based Health Care Grant program | ...... | ...... | 146,000 | 146,000 | 157,000 | 168,000 | 179,000 | 190,000 | 190,000 | 210,000 | 220,000 | 617,000 | 1,606,000 |

## Table S–6. Mandatory and Receipt Proposals—Continued

(Deficit increases (+) or decreases (−) in millions of dollars)

| | 2018 | 2019 | 2020 | 2021 | 2022 | 2023 | 2024 | 2025 | 2026 | 2027 | 2028 | Totals 2019–2023 | Totals 2019–2028 |
|---|---|---|---|---|---|---|---|---|---|---|---|---|---|
| Other⁴ | ...... | 15,142 | −4,991 | −41,217 | −48,946 | −50,891 | −53,815 | −57,221 | −60,387 | −63,435 | −66,091 | −130,903 | −431,852 |
| Total, proposal modeled after the Graham-Cassidy-Heller-Johnson bill | ...... | 12,257 | 73,844 | 12,433 | 9,994 | 12,634 | 12,835 | 6,624 | −11,187 | −13,380 | −25,476 | 121,162 | 90,578 |
| Additional deficit reduction: | | | | | | | | | | | | | |
| Medicaid reforms | | ...... | −4,500 | −11,410 | −19,920 | −28,630 | −37,635 | −42,640 | −48,145 | −53,845 | −58,940 | −64,460 | −305,665 |
| Market-Based Health Care Grant program | | | −26,000 | −23,240 | −31,417 | −39,528 | −47,573 | −55,550 | −52,458 | −69,295 | −76,058 | −120,185 | −421,119 |
| State implementation | | 1,000 | 750 | 250 | | | | | | | | 2,000 | 2,000 |
| Other | | −10,000 | −21,000 | −5,000 | | −750 | −750 | −750 | −750 | −750 | −750 | −36,750 | −40,500 |
| Total, additional deficit reduction | | −9,000 | −50,750 | −39,400 | −51,337 | −68,908 | −85,958 | −98,940 | −101,353 | −123,890 | −135,748 | −219,395 | −765,284 |
| Total, repeal and replace Obamacare | | 3,257 | 23,094 | −26,967 | −41,343 | −56,274 | −73,123 | −92,316 | −112,540 | −137,270 | −161,224 | −98,233 | −674,706 |
| Reform welfare programs: | | | | | | | | | | | | | |
| Reform the Supplemental Nutrition Assistance Program | | −17,169 | −18,521 | −20,451 | −20,468 | −21,615 | −22,213 | −22,353 | −23,686 | −23,893 | −23,157 | −98,224 | −213,526 |
| Reduce Temporary Assistance for Needy Families (TANF) block grant | | −1,155 | −1,435 | −1,514 | −1,552 | −1,584 | −1,600 | −1,600 | −1,600 | −1,600 | −1,600 | −7,240 | −15,240 |
| Strengthen TANF | | ...... | ...... | ...... | ...... | ...... | ...... | ...... | ...... | ...... | ...... | ...... | ...... |
| Eliminate the TANF Contingency Fund | | −545 | −608 | −608 | −608 | −608 | −608 | −608 | −608 | −608 | −608 | −2,977 | −6,017 |
| Get noncustodial parents to work | | 4 | 5 | 7 | 8 | 10 | 9 | 11 | 13 | 14 | 15 | 34 | 96 |
| Strengthen Child Support enforcement and establishment | | −22 | −42 | −57 | −68 | −76 | −80 | −82 | −82 | −83 | −94 | −265 | −686 |
| Establish a Child Support technology fund | | 63 | −12 | −20 | −28 | −37 | −110 | −120 | −131 | −194 | −205 | −34 | −794 |
| Eliminate Social Services Block Grant (SSBG) | | −1,411 | −1,649 | −1,700 | −1,700 | −1,700 | −1,700 | −1,700 | −1,700 | −1,700 | −1,700 | −8,160 | −16,660 |
| Shift SSBG expenditures to Foster Care and Permanency | | 18 | 21 | 22 | 22 | 22 | 23 | 23 | 23 | 23 | 23 | 105 | 220 |
| Require Social Security Number (SSN) for Child Tax Credit & Earned Income Tax Credit | | −1,186 | −1,218 | −1,164 | −1,086 | −1,104 | −1,009 | −921 | −903 | −790 | −702 | −5,758 | −10,083 |
| Promote Welfare to Work Projects | | | | | | | | | | | | | |
| Total, reform welfare programs | | −21,403 | −23,459 | −25,485 | −25,480 | −26,692 | −27,288 | −27,350 | −28,674 | −28,831 | −28,028 | −122,519 | −262,690 |
| Reform disability programs and test new approaches: | | | | | | | | | | | | | |
| Improve SSI youth transition to work | | −5 | −28 | 6 | 46 | 21 | −6 | −35 | −59 | −80 | −108 | 40 | −248 |
| Simplify administration of the SSI program | | ...... | −347 | −86 | −68 | −50 | −29 | −18 | −6 | 6 | 19 | −551 | −579 |
| Test new approaches to increase labor force participation | | 100 | 100 | 100 | 100 | 100 | −2,384 | −5,070 | −9,171 | −13,610 | −18,632 | 500 | −48,367 |
| Reduce 12 month retroactive Disability Insurance (DI) benefits to six months | | −362 | −669 | −846 | −992 | −1,057 | −1,126 | −1,198 | −1,268 | −1,337 | −1,401 | −3,926 | −10,256 |

## Table S-6. Mandatory and Receipt Proposals—Continued

(Deficit increases (+) or decreases (−) in millions of dollars)

| | 2018 | 2019 | 2020 | 2021 | 2022 | 2023 | 2024 | 2025 | 2026 | 2027 | 2028 | Totals 2019–2023 | Totals 2019–2028 |
|---|---|---|---|---|---|---|---|---|---|---|---|---|---|
| Create sliding scale for multi-recipient Supplemental Security Income (SSI) families | ........ | −588 | −618 | −636 | −693 | −661 | −631 | −702 | −720 | −738 | −814 | −3,196 | −6,801 |
| Offset overlapping unemployment and disability payments [4,9] | ........ | ........ | −81 | −209 | −255 | −281 | −296 | −311 | −325 | −343 | −356 | −826 | −2,457 |
| Reinstate the reconsideration review application stage in 10 States | ........ | ........ | −76 | −295 | −424 | −362 | −354 | −420 | −469 | −519 | −579 | −1,066 | −3,407 |
| Eliminate Workers Compensation (WC) Reverse Offsets | ........ | 91 | ........ | −22 | −22 | −23 | −25 | −26 | −28 | −30 | −31 | −67 | −207 |
| Change the representative fee and approval process | ........ | ........ | 3 | 16 | 29 | 43 | 41 | 45 | 44 | 44 | 45 | 91 | 310 |
| Eliminate the requirement for representative payees to provide an annual accounting report | ........ | ........ | ........ | ........ | ........ | ........ | ........ | ........ | ........ | ........ | ........ | ........ | ........ |
| Administrative Law Judge (ALJ) reforms | ........ | ........ | ........ | ........ | ........ | ........ | ........ | ........ | ........ | ........ | ........ | ........ | ........ |
| Total, reform disability programs and test new approaches | ........ | −764 | −1,716 | −1,972 | −2,279 | −2,270 | −4,810 | −7,735 | −12,002 | −16,607 | −21,857 | −9,001 | −72,012 |
| Reduce improper payments: | | | | | | | | | | | | | |
| Reduce improper payments Government-wide | ........ | ........ | −719 | −1,482 | −2,383 | −4,288 | −4,549 | −9,652 | −20,480 | −38,024 | −57,633 | −8,872 | −139,210 |
| Provide additional debt collection authority for civil monetary penalties (CMPs) and assessments | ........ | ........ | ........ | ........ | ........ | ........ | ........ | ........ | ........ | ........ | ........ | ........ | ........ |
| Allow Government-wide use of CBP entry/exit data to prevent improper payments | ........ | ........ | ........ | −1 | −5 | −13 | −19 | −25 | −34 | −39 | −47 | −19 | −183 |
| Authorize Social Security Administration (SSA) to use all collection tools to recover funds in certain scenarios | ........ | −1 | −2 | −2 | −4 | −4 | −5 | −6 | −7 | −7 | −7 | −13 | −45 |
| Hold fraud facilitators liable for overpayments | ........ | ........ | ........ | ........ | −1 | −1 | −1 | −1 | −1 | ........ | −1 | −2 | −6 |
| Increase overpayment collection threshold for Old Age, Survivors, and Disability Insurance | ........ | −11 | −72 | −91 | −102 | −124 | −148 | −167 | −219 | −233 | −231 | −400 | −1,398 |
| Exclude SSA debts from discharge in bankruptcy | ........ | −7 | −15 | −21 | −25 | −30 | −32 | −34 | −35 | −37 | −39 | −98 | −275 |
| Allow SSA to use commercial database to verify real property | ........ | −26 | −40 | −50 | −61 | −62 | −62 | −70 | −73 | −77 | −83 | −239 | −604 |
| Improve collection of pension information from States and localities | ........ | 18 | 28 | 24 | −441 | −1,058 | −1,505 | −1,618 | −1,534 | −1,442 | −1,332 | −1,429 | −8,860 |
| Total, reduce improper payments | ........ | −27 | −820 | −1,623 | −3,022 | −5,580 | −6,321 | −11,573 | −22,383 | −39,859 | −59,373 | −11,072 | −150,581 |
| Infrastructure initiative: | | | | | | | | | | | | | |
| Encourage increased State, local, and private infrastructure by awarding competitive incentive grants | ........ | 1,000 | 5,000 | 11,000 | 17,500 | 21,750 | 19,500 | 13,250 | 7,250 | 3,000 | 750 | 56,250 | 100,000 |

## Table S–6. Mandatory and Receipt Proposals—Continued

(Deficit increases (+) or decreases (−) in millions of dollars)

| | 2018 | 2019 | 2020 | 2021 | 2022 | 2023 | 2024 | 2025 | 2026 | 2027 | 2028 | Totals 2019–2023 | Totals 2019–2028 |
|---|---|---|---|---|---|---|---|---|---|---|---|---|---|
| Address the need for investment in rural infrastructure | ...... | 41,350 | 3,407 | 2,851 | 1,058 | 399 | 300 | 245 | 200 | 145 | 45 | 49,065 | 50,000 |
| Support bold, innovative, and transformative projects | ...... | 15 | 140 | 770 | 2,475 | 4,327 | 5,135 | 3,972 | 2,220 | 784 | 202 | 7,727 | 20,040 |
| Expand existing Federal infrastructure credit programs | ...... | 311 | 933 | 1,556 | 2,178 | 2,800 | 2,489 | 1,867 | 1,244 | 622 | ...... | 7,778 | 14,000 |
| Establish a Federal Capital Revolving Fund [12] | ...... | 1,867 | 1,733 | 1,600 | 1,467 | 1,333 | 1,200 | -53 | -57 | -61 | -65 | 8,000 | 8,964 |
| Expand flexibility and broaden eligibility for Private Activity Bonds [4] | ...... | 31 | 138 | 296 | 457 | 616 | 753 | 839 | 893 | 945 | 992 | 1,538 | 5,960 |
| Total, infrastructure initiative | ...... | 44,574 | 11,351 | 18,073 | 25,135 | 31,225 | 29,377 | 20,120 | 11,750 | 5,435 | 1,924 | 130,358 | 198,964 |
| Authorize additional Afghan Special Immigrant Visas | ...... | 22 | 25 | 26 | 23 | 22 | 23 | 20 | 18 | 18 | 19 | 118 | 216 |
| Eliminate allocations to the Housing Trust Fund and Capital Magnet Fund [4] | ...... | -263 | -158 | -227 | -296 | -357 | -385 | -399 | -419 | -426 | -433 | -1,301 | -3,363 |
| Extend Joint Committee mandatory sequestration | ...... | ...... | ...... | ...... | ...... | ...... | ...... | 8,342 | -21,297 | -28,570 | -31,298 | ...... | -72,823 |
| Lease Shared Secondary Licenses | ...... | -50 | -55 | -55 | -60 | -65 | -70 | -70 | -80 | -80 | -85 | -285 | -670 |
| Improve clarity in worker classification and information reporting requirements [4] | 100 | 100 | -100 | ...... | ...... | ...... | ...... | ...... | ...... | -100 | -105 | ...... | -205 |
| Total, cross-cutting reforms | 100 | 25,446 | 8,162 | -38,230 | -47,322 | -59,991 | -82,597 | -110,961 | -185,627 | -246,290 | -300,460 | -111,935 | -1,037,870 |
| **Total, mandatory and receipt proposals** | **5,159** | **9,793** | **-30,248** | **-91,766** | **-109,661** | **-135,651** | **-164,371** | **-196,910** | **-292,276** | **-355,469** | **-421,691** | **-357,533** | **-1,788,250** |

Note: For receipt effects, positive figures indicate lower receipts. For outlay effects, positive figures indicate higher outlays. For net costs, positive figures indicate higher deficits.

[1] The single income-driven repayment plan proposal has sizable interactive effects with the proposals to eliminate subsidized loans and Public Service Loan Forgiveness. These effects, $19.2 billion over 10 years, are included in the single income-driven repayment plan subtotal.

[2] Estimates were not available at the time of Budget publication.

[3] This funding is included within the estimates of the proposal to repeal and replace Obamacare.

[4] The estimates for this proposal include effects on receipts. The receipt effects included in the totals above are as follows:

| | 2018 | 2019 | 2020 | 2021 | 2022 | 2023 | 2024 | 2025 | 2026 | 2027 | 2028 | Totals 2019–2023 | Totals 2019–2028 |
|---|---|---|---|---|---|---|---|---|---|---|---|---|---|
| Give Medicare beneficiaries with high deductible health plans the option to make tax deductible contributions to Health Savings Accounts and Medical Savings Accounts | ...... | ...... | ...... | 610 | 1,071 | 1,285 | 1,493 | 1,599 | 1,674 | 1,746 | 1,807 | 2,966 | 11,285 |
| Extend Children's Health Insurance Program through 2019 with reforms | ...... | -388 | -58 | ...... | ...... | ...... | ...... | ...... | ...... | ...... | ...... | -446 | -446 |
| Reform medical liability | ...... | -24 | -222 | -548 | -987 | -1,476 | -2,067 | -2,687 | -3,079 | -3,290 | -3,475 | -3,257 | -17,855 |
| Reduce the grace period for Exchange premiums | ...... | -164 | -55 | ...... | ...... | ...... | ...... | ...... | ...... | ...... | ...... | -219 | -219 |
| Provide tax exemption for IHS Health Professions scholarship and loan repayment programs in return for obligatory service requirement | ...... | 5 | 12 | 13 | 14 | 14 | 14 | 14 | 15 | 17 | 19 | 58 | 137 |

## Table S–6.  Mandatory and Receipt Proposals—Continued

(Deficit increases (+) or decreases (–) in millions of dollars)

| | 2018 | 2019 | 2020 | 2021 | 2022 | 2023 | 2024 | 2025 | 2026 | 2027 | 2028 | Totals 2019–2023 | Totals 2019–2028 |
|---|---|---|---|---|---|---|---|---|---|---|---|---|---|
| Establish Electronic Visa Update System user fee | ...... | –25 | –28 | –31 | –34 | –38 | –42 | –46 | –52 | –57 | –64 | –156 | –417 |
| Make full Electronic System for Travel Authorization (ESTA) receipts available to CBP | ...... | ...... | ...... | –171 | –177 | –183 | –189 | –196 | –202 | –209 | –216 | –531 | –1,543 |
| Establish an immigration services surcharge | ...... | –453 | –465 | –479 | –493 | –507 | –522 | –538 | –553 | –569 | –587 | –2,397 | –5,166 |
| Increase worksite enforcement penalties | ...... | –13 | –14 | –15 | –15 | –15 | –15 | –15 | –15 | –15 | –15 | –72 | –147 |
| Reauthorize the Oil Spill Liability Trust Fund excise tax | ...... | –354 | –466 | –473 | –480 | –489 | –494 | –500 | –507 | –511 | –511 | –2,262 | –4,785 |
| Provide paid parental leave benefits | ...... | ...... | ...... | ...... | –962 | –971 | –1,001 | –1,194 | –1,300 | –1,401 | –1,495 | –1,933 | –8,324 |
| Establish an Unemployment Insurance (UI) solvency standard | ...... | ...... | ...... | –633 | –1,615 | –2,230 | –919 | –1,613 | –927 | –1,267 | –1,907 | –4,478 | –11,111 |
| Improve UI program integrity | ...... | ...... | 1 | 9 | 21 | 72 | 66 | 98 | 69 | 127 | 105 | 103 | 568 |
| Provide for Reemployment Services and Eligibility Assessments | ...... | ...... | 3 | 14 | 69 | 125 | 128 | 199 | 307 | 287 | 469 | 211 | 1,601 |
| Reform Air Traffic Control | ...... | ...... | ...... | ...... | 15,495 | 16,241 | 17,027 | 17,870 | 18,674 | 19,497 | 20,536 | 31,736 | 125,340 |
| Reform Essential Air Service | ...... | ...... | ...... | ...... | 152 | 156 | 160 | 164 | 168 | 172 | 177 | 308 | 1,149 |
| Provide authority for Bureau of Engraving and Printing to construct new facility | ...... | –12 | –32 | –3 | 89 | –360 | –53 | 20 | –3 | –222 | –3 | –318 | –579 |
| Subject Financial Research Fund to appropriations with reforms to the Financial Stability Oversight Council and Office of Financial Research | ...... | –1 | 50 | 50 | 50 | 50 | 50 | 50 | 50 | 50 | 50 | 199 | 449 |
| Implement tax enforcement program integrity cap adjustment | ...... | –152 | –787 | –1,825 | –3,033 | –4,330 | –5,554 | –6,416 | –6,931 | –7,270 | –7,505 | –10,127 | –43,803 |
| Increase oversight of paid tax return preparers | ...... | –17 | –18 | –21 | –23 | –25 | –28 | –31 | –34 | –38 | –41 | –104 | –276 |
| Provide more flexible authority for the Internal Revenue Service to address correctable errors | ...... | –7 | –11 | –12 | –12 | –13 | –13 | –14 | –15 | –15 | –16 | –55 | –128 |
| Reform inland waterways financing | ...... | –178 | –178 | –178 | –178 | –178 | –178 | –178 | –178 | –178 | –178 | –890 | –1,780 |
| Reduce the Harbor Maintenance Tax | ...... | 265 | 281 | 292 | 299 | 307 | 314 | 323 | 333 | 345 | 359 | 1,444 | 3,118 |
| Increase employee contributions to 50% of cost, phased in at 1% per year | ...... | ...... | –2,267 | –4,602 | –6,442 | –8,068 | –9,441 | –9,456 | –9,470 | –9,480 | –9,479 | –21,379 | –68,705 |
| Proposal modeled after the Graham-Cassidy-Heller-Johnson bill | ...... | 3,452 | 8,617 | 2,503 | 2,829 | 2,883 | 2,959 | 3,192 | 3,473 | 3,676 | 4,092 | 20,284 | 37,676 |
| Offset overlapping unemployment and disability payments | ...... | ...... | ...... | 3 | 6 | 7 | 14 | 18 | 25 | 29 | 31 | 16 | 133 |
| Expand flexibility and broaden eligibility for Private Activity Bonds | ...... | 31 | 138 | 296 | 457 | 616 | 753 | 839 | 893 | 945 | 992 | 1,538 | 5,960 |
| Eliminate allocations to the Housing Trust Fund and Capital Magnet Fund | ...... | –62 | –74 | –73 | –78 | –82 | –84 | –85 | –87 | –89 | –90 | –369 | –804 |
| Improve clarity in worker classification and information reporting requirements | 100 | 100 | –100 | ...... | ...... | ...... | ...... | ...... | ...... | –100 | –105 | ...... | –205 |
| Total receipt effects of mandatory proposals | 100 | 2,003 | 4,327 | –5,274 | 6,023 | 2,791 | 2,378 | 1,417 | 2,328 | 2,180 | 2,950 | 9,870 | 21,123 |

## Table S–6. Mandatory and Receipt Proposals—Continued

(Deficit increases (+) or decreases (–) in millions of dollars)

[5] The 2019 Budget requests $127 million in mandatory resources to support Medicare appeals adjudication at the Office of Medicare Hearings and Appeals and the Departmental Appeals Board. While the total mandatory request is $127 million annually, the cost to the Government is $112 million annually, which reflects Medicare Part A and Part B contributions, net of premiums.

[6] In addition to the proposals listed, the Budget requests mandatory appropriations for the Risk Corridors program and for Cost Sharing Reduction payments. These proposals have no deficit effect.

[7] In addition to effects within HHS, the estimates for the proposal include effects within OPM and Treasury.

[8] While this proposal increases Government outlays in the form of means-tested assistance to low-income policyholders, the National Flood Insurance Program is also accelerating premium increases on other policyholders that currently do not pay full-risk premiums.

[9] Net of income offsets.

[10] The paid parental leave proposal consists of $27,196 million in benefit and program administration costs over the 2019–2028 period, offset by $8,324 million in savings associated with increased State revenues.

[11] The proposal would allow the District of Columbia (DC) Courts to retain a portion of the bar examination and application fees it currently deposits into the DC Crime Victim's Compensation Fund. Retained fees are estimated at $360,000 annually beginning in 2019.

[12] The Federal Capital Revolving Fund is capitalized with $10 billion in mandatory funds in 2019. Agency repayments to the fund are reflected as offsetting collections, which reduce the total outlays estimated from the fund over the 10 year window. However, the initial $10 billion in capitalization funding is fully expended by 2023.

## Table S–7.   Proposed Discretionary Caps for 2019 Budget

(Net budget authority in billions of dollars)

| | 2018 | 2019 | 2020 | 2021 | 2022 | 2023 | 2024 | 2025 | 2026 | 2027 | 2028 | Totals, 2019–2028 |
|---|---|---|---|---|---|---|---|---|---|---|---|---|
| **Current Law Base Caps:[1]** | | | | | | | | | | | | |
| Defense | 549 | 562 | 576 | 590 | 605 | 620 | 636 | 652 | 669 | 686 | 703 | 6,300 |
| Non-Defense | 516 | 530 | 543 | 556 | 570 | 584 | 599 | 614 | 630 | 646 | 662 | 5,935 |
| **Total, Base Current Law Caps** | **1,065** | **1,092** | **1,119** | **1,146** | **1,175** | **1,205** | **1,235** | **1,267** | **1,299** | **1,332** | **1,366** | **12,236** |
| *Proposed Base Cap Changes:[2]* | | | | | | | | | | | | |
| *Defense* | *+54* | *+65* | *+84* | *+87* | *+89* | *+92* | *+91* | *+90* | *+89* | *+88* | *+87* | *+861* |
| *Non-Defense* | *–54* | *–65* | *–87* | *–109* | *–132* | *–155* | *–179* | *–202* | *–226* | *–250* | *–274* | *–1,680* |
| *Total, Base Cap Changes* | *+\** | *–\** | *–3* | *–22* | *–43* | *–64* | *–88* | *–113* | *–137* | *–162* | *–188* | *–820* |
| **Proposed Base Caps:** | | | | | | | | | | | | |
| Defense | 603 | 627 | 660 | 677 | 694 | 712 | 727 | 742 | 758 | 774 | 790 | 7,161 |
| Non-Defense | 462 | 465 | 456 | 447 | 438 | 429 | 420 | 412 | 404 | 396 | 388 | 4,255 |
| **Total, Proposed Base Caps** | **1,065** | **1,092** | **1,116** | **1,124** | **1,132** | **1,141** | **1,147** | **1,154** | **1,162** | **1,170** | **1,178** | **11,416** |
| *Additional Non-Defense (NDD) Cap Reductions for Budget Proposals:[3]* | | | | | | | | | | | | |
| Air Traffic Control Reform | | | | | –10 | –10 | –10 | –10 | –10 | –10 | –10 | –71 |
| Federal Employee Retirement Cost Share Reduction | | | –6 | –7 | –8 | –9 | –9 | –9 | –8 | –8 | –8 | –72 |
| *Total, Proposed NDD Cap Reductions* | | | *–6* | *–7* | *–18* | *–19* | *–19* | *–19* | *–18* | *–18* | *–18* | *–143* |
| **Proposed Base Caps with Additional NDD Adjustments:** | | | | | | | | | | | | |
| Defense | 603 | 627 | 660 | 677 | 694 | 712 | 727 | 742 | 758 | 774 | 790 | 7,161 |
| Non-Defense | 462 | 465 | 450 | 440 | 420 | 410 | 401 | 393 | 386 | 378 | 370 | 4,112 |
| **Total, Proposed Base Caps with Adjustments** | **1,065** | **1,092** | **1,110** | **1,117** | **1,114** | **1,122** | **1,128** | **1,135** | **1,144** | **1,152** | **1,160** | **11,273** |
| **Cap Adjustments:[4]** | | | | | | | | | | | | |
| Overseas Contingency Operations | 78 | 101 | 81 | 70 | 68 | 68 | 12 | 12 | 12 | 12 | 12 | 447 |
| *Defense[5]* | *66* | *89* | *73* | *66* | *66* | *66* | *10* | *10* | *10* | *10* | *10* | *409* |
| *Non-Defense[6]* | *12* | *12* | *8* | *4* | *2* | *2* | *2* | *2* | *2* | *2* | *2* | *38* |
| Emergency Requirements | 68 | | | | | | | | | | | |
| Program Integrity[7] | 2 | 2 | 3 | 3 | 3 | 4 | 4 | 4 | 4 | 4 | 4 | 35 |
| Disaster Relief[8] | 7 | 7 | 7 | 7 | 7 | 7 | 7 | 7 | 7 | 7 | 7 | 67 |
| Wildfire Suppression[7] | | 2 | 2 | 2 | 2 | 2 | 2 | 2 | 2 | 2 | 2 | 15 |
| **Total, Cap Adjustments** | **154** | **111** | **92** | **81** | **80** | **79** | **24** | **24** | **24** | **24** | **24** | **564** |
| **Total, Proposed Discretionary Caps:** | | | | | | | | | | | | |
| Defense | 675 | 716 | 733 | 743 | 760 | 778 | 737 | 752 | 768 | 784 | 800 | 7,570 |
| Non-Defense | 544 | 487 | 468 | 455 | 433 | 424 | 415 | 407 | 400 | 392 | 385 | 4,266 |
| **Total, Proposed Discretionary Caps** | **1,219** | **1,203** | **1,201** | **1,197** | **1,193** | **1,202** | **1,152** | **1,159** | **1,168** | **1,176** | **1,185** | **11,837** |

## Table S–7. Proposed Discretionary Caps for 2019 Budget—Continued

(Net budget authority in billions of dollars)

| | 2018 | 2019 | 2020 | 2021 | 2022 | 2023 | 2024 | 2025 | 2026 | 2027 | 2028 | Totals, 2019–2028 |
|---|---|---|---|---|---|---|---|---|---|---|---|---|
| *Memorandum - Appropriations Counted Outside of Discretionary Caps:* | | | | | | | | | | | | |
| 21st Century CURES Appropriations[9] | 1 | 1 | 1 | * | 1 | 1 | * | * | * | ...... | ...... | 4 |
| Non-BBEDCA Emergency Funding[10] | ...... | -5 | ...... | ...... | ...... | ...... | ...... | ...... | ...... | ...... | ...... | -5 |

\* $500 million or less.

[1] The caps presented here are equal to the levels estimated for 2018 through 2021 in the Balanced Budget and Emergency Deficit Control Act of 1985 (BBEDCA) with separate categories of funding for "defense" (or Function 050) and "non-defense" programs and include OMB estimates of Joint Committee enforcement (also known as "sequestration"). For 2022 through 2028, the caps are assumed to grow at current services growth rates.

[2] The Administration's proposed changes to the caps build off the proposals in the 2018 Budget that was transmitted on May 23, 2017: proposed increases to the existing defense caps for 2018 and 2019 are offset with decreases to the non-defense caps. After 2019, the 2019 Budget proposes defense caps through 2028 that resource the Administration's National Security and National Defense Strategies. Non-defense caps reflect an annual two percent (or "2-penny") decrease each year.

[3] These cap reductions are for reforms in the Budget that would shift the Federal Aviation Administration's air traffic control function to an independent, non-governmental organization beginning in 2022 and reduce Federal agency costs through changes to current civilian employee retirement plans.

[4] The funding amounts below are existing or proposed cap adjustments that are designated pursuant to Section 251(b)(2) of BBEDCA.

[5] The outyear OCO amounts for defense for 2020 through 2023 are consistent with the National Security and National Defense Strategies, while amounts from 2024 through 2028 reflect notional placeholders consistent with a potential transition of certain OCO costs into the base budget while continuing to fund contingency operations. The placeholder amounts for 2024 through 2028 do not reflect specific decisions or assumptions about OCO funding in any particular year.

[6] The outyear OCO amounts for non-defense in the 2019 Budget reflect notional placeholders consistent with a potential transition of certain OCO costs into the base budget. The placeholder amounts do not reflect specific decisions or assumptions about OCO funding in any particular year.

[7] The Budget proposes new cap adjustments related to program integrity in the Internal Revenue Service and wildfire suppression in the Departments of Agriculture and the Interior. For more information on these proposals see the Budget Process chapter of the *Analytical Perspectives* volume of the Budget.

[8] "Disaster Relief" appropriations are amounts designated as such by the Congress provided they are for activities carried out pursuant to a Presidential disaster declaration under the Robert T. Stafford Disaster Relief and Emergency Assistance Act. These amounts are held to a funding ceiling that is determined one year at a time according to a statutory formula. The Administration proposes to change this formula to address the declining ceiling for Disaster Relief appropriations, as discussed in the Budget Process chapter of the *Analytical Perspectives* volume of the Budget. OMB currently estimates the 2019 ceiling to be $7.4 billion under current law. The Administration is requesting $6.7 billion for Disaster Relief in 2019, but does not explicitly request disaster-designated appropriations in any year after the budget year. A placeholder set at the budget year request level is included in each of the outyears.

[9] The 21st Century CURES Act permitted funds to be appropriated each year and not counted towards the discretionary caps so long as the appropriations were specifically provided for the authorized purposes. These amounts are displayed outside of the discretionary cap totals for this reason and the levels included through the budget window reflect authorized levels.

[10] The 2019 Budget includes permanent cancellations of balances of emergency funding in the Departments of Energy and Housing and Urban Development that are not designated pursuant to BBEDCA. These cancellations are not being re-designated as emergency, therefore no savings are being achieved under the caps nor will the caps be adjusted for these cancellations.

# Table S–8. 2019 Discretionary Overview by Major Agency

(Net budget authority in billions of dollars)

| | 2017 Enacted[1] | 2018 Estimate[2] | 2019 Request | 2019 Request less 2017 Enacted | |
| --- | --- | --- | --- | --- | --- |
| | | | | Dollar | Percent |
| **Base Discretionary Funding:** | | | | | |
| **Cabinet Departments:** | | | | | |
| Agriculture[3] | 22.7 | 22.5 | 19.0 | –3.7 | –16.4% |
| Commerce | 9.3 | 9.3 | 9.9 | +0.6 | +6.1% |
| Defense[2] | 523.2 | 574.5 | 597.1 | +73.9 | +14.1% |
| Education | 66.9 | 67.8 | 59.9 | –7.1 | –10.5% |
| Energy | 30.2 | 30.0 | 29.2 | –1.0 | –3.4% |
| *National Nuclear Security Administration* | *12.8* | *12.8* | *15.1* | *+2.2* | *+17.5%* |
| *Other Energy* | *17.3* | *17.2* | *14.1* | *–3.3* | *–18.9%* |
| Health and Human Services[4] | 87.1 | 86.3 | 69.5 | –17.6 | –20.3% |
| Homeland Security (DHS)[2] | 42.4 | 44.1 | 46.0 | +3.6 | +8.6% |
| Housing and Urban Development (HUD): | | | | | |
| *HUD gross total (excluding receipts)* | *48.0* | *47.7* | *39.2* | *–8.8* | *–18.3%* |
| *HUD receipts* | *–14.0* | *–10.3* | *–10.0* | *+3.9* | *–28.2%* |
| Interior | 13.5 | 13.4 | 11.2 | –2.3 | –16.8% |
| Justice | 28.4 | 28.1 | 28.0 | –0.4 | –1.3% |
| Labor | 12.0 | 12.0 | 9.4 | –2.6 | –21.4% |
| State and Other International Programs[3] | 38.7 | 38.1 | 28.3 | –10.4 | –26.9% |
| Transportation | 19.3 | 19.2 | 15.6 | –3.7 | –19.2% |
| Treasury | 12.7 | 12.6 | 12.3 | –0.4 | –3.0% |
| Veterans Affairs | 74.4 | 77.3 | 83.1 | +8.7 | +11.7% |
| **Major Agencies:** | | | | | |
| Corps of Engineers | 6.2 | 6.0 | 4.8 | –1.4 | –22.2% |
| Environmental Protection Agency | 8.2 | 8.0 | 5.4 | –2.8 | –33.7% |
| General Services Administration | –1.2 | –0.9 | 0.6 | +1.8 | N/A |
| National Aeronautics & Space Administration | 19.7 | 19.5 | 19.6 | –0.1 | –0.3% |
| National Science Foundation | 7.5 | 7.4 | 5.3 | –2.2 | –29.5% |
| Small Business Administration | 0.8 | 0.8 | 0.6 | –0.2 | –24.5% |
| Social Security Administration[4] | 9.3 | 9.3 | 8.8 | –0.5 | –4.9% |
| Other Agencies | 20.8 | 20.6 | 18.0 | –2.8 | –13.5% |
| Changes in mandatory programs | .......... | –20.1 | –18.6 | .......... | N/A |
| Adjustment for 2018 Budget Policy[2] | .......... | –58.2 | .......... | .......... | N/A |
| **Subtotal, Base Discretionary Funding** | **1,085.9** | **1,065.0** | **1,092.0** | **+6.1** | **+0.6%** |
| **Cap Adjustment Funding:** | | | | | |
| **Overseas Contingency Operations:** | | | | | |
| Defense[2] | 82.8 | 65.8 | 89.0 | +6.2 | +7.5% |
| Homeland Security | 0.2 | 0.2 | .......... | –0.2 | –100.0% |

## Table S–8.   2019 Discretionary Overview by Major Agency—Continued

(Net budget authority in billions of dollars)

| | 2017 Enacted[1] | 2018 Estimate[2] | 2019 Request | 2019 Request less 2017 Enacted Dollar | Percent |
|---|---|---|---|---|---|
| State and Other International Programs | 20.8 | 20.8 | 12.0 | –8.8 | –42.2% |
| Adjustment for 2018 Budget Policy[2] | | –8.9 | | ...... | N/A |
| Subtotal, Overseas Contingency Operations | 103.7 | 77.8 | 101.0 | –2.7 | –2.6% |
| Emergency Requirements: | | | | | |
| Agriculture and Interior | 0.6 | 0.2 | ...... | –0.6 | –100.0% |
| Defense | ...... | 4.7 | ...... | ...... | N/A |
| Homeland Security | 7.4 | 18.7 | ...... | –7.4 | –100.0% |
| Housing and Urban Development | 8.2 | ...... | ...... | –8.2 | –100.0% |
| Transportation | 1.5 | ...... | ...... | –1.5 | –100.0% |
| Corps of Engineers | 1.0 | ...... | ...... | –1.0 | –100.0% |
| National Aeronautics & Space Administration | 0.2 | ...... | ...... | –0.2 | –100.0% |
| Small Business Administration | 0.5 | ...... | ...... | –0.5 | –100.0% |
| Subtotal, Emergency Requirements | 19.4 | 23.6 | ...... | –19.4 | –100.0% |
| Emergency Hurricane Request:[5] | | | | | |
| Allowance for Defense Hurricane Request | ...... | 1.2 | ...... | ...... | N/A |
| Allowance for Non-Defense Hurricane Request | ...... | 42.8 | ...... | ...... | N/A |
| Subtotal, Emergency Request | ...... | 44.0 | ...... | ...... | N/A |
| Program Integrity: | | | | | |
| Health and Human Services | 0.4 | 0.4 | 0.5 | +0.0 | +9.7% |
| Treasury[6] | ...... | ...... | 0.4 | +0.4 | N/A |
| Social Security Administration | 1.5 | 1.5 | 1.4 | –0.1 | –8.8% |
| Subtotal, Program Integrity | 2.0 | 1.9 | 2.2 | +0.3 | +13.6% |
| Disaster Relief:[7] | | | | | |
| Homeland Security | 6.7 | 6.7 | 6.7 | –0.1 | –0.9% |
| Housing and Urban Development | 1.4 | ...... | ...... | –1.4 | –100.0% |
| Subtotal, Disaster Relief | 8.1 | 6.7 | 6.7 | –1.5 | –18.2% |
| Wildfire Suppression Operations[6] | ...... | ...... | 1.5 | +1.5 | N/A |
| **Subtotal, Cap Adjustment Funding** | **133.2** | **154.0** | **111.4** | **–21.8** | **–16.4%** |
| **Total, Discretionary Budget Authority Under the Caps** | **1,219.1** | **1,219.0** | **1,203.4** | **–15.7** | **–1.3%** |
| *Memorandum - Appropriations Counted Outside of Discretionary Caps:* | | | | | |
| *21st Century CURES Appropriations:[8]* | | | | | |
| *Health and Human Services* | *0.9* | *0.9* | *0.8* | *–0.1* | *–10.4%* |
| *Non-BBEDCA Emergency Appropriations:[9]* | | | | | |
| *Energy* | ...... | ...... | *–4.7* | *–4.7* | *N/A* |
| *Housing and Urban Development* | ...... | ...... | *–** | *–** | *N/A* |

# Table S–8.   2019 Discretionary Overview by Major Agency—Continued

(Net budget authority in billions of dollars)

\* $50 million or less.

[1] 2017 Enacted reflects the actual amounts, and include many changes that occur after appropriations are enacted that are part of budget execution such as transfers, reestimates, and the rebasing as mandatory any changes in mandatory programs enacted in appropriations bills.

[2] At the time the 2019 Budget was prepared, 2018 appropriations remained incomplete and the 2018 column reflects at the account level enacted full-year and annualized continuing appropriations provided under the Continuing Appropriations Act, 2018 (Division D of Public Law 115–56, as amended by Division A of Public Laws 115–90 and 115–96). The 2018 levels are further adjusted through policy allowances to illustratively reflect the base and Overseas Contingency Operations totals proposed in the Administration's amended 2018 Budget request. These allowances appear within the Department of Defense, the Department of Homeland Security, and Government-wide.

[3] Funding for Food for Peace Title II Grants is included in the State and Other International Programs total. Although the funds are appropriated to the Department of Agriculture, the funds are administered by the U.S. Agency for International Development.

[4] Funding from the Hospital Insurance and Supplementary Medical Insurance trust funds for administrative expenses incurred by the Social Security Administration that support the Medicare program are included in the Health and Human Services total and not in the Social Security Administration total.

[5] The emergency hurricane request represents the Administration's pending proposal for additional Hurricane relief and recovery funding that was transmitted to the Congress on November 17, 2017.

[6] The Budget proposes new cap adjustments related to program integrity in the Internal Revenue Service and wildfire suppression in the Departments of Agriculture and the Interior. For more information on these proposals see the Budget Process chapter of the *Analytical Perspectives* volume of the Budget.

[7] "Disaster Relief" appropriations are amounts designated as such by the Congress provided they are for activities carried out pursuant to a Presidential disaster declaration under the Robert T. Stafford Disaster Relief and Emergency Assistance Act. These amounts are held to a funding ceiling that is determined one year at a time according to a statutory formula. The Administration proposes to change this formula to address the declining ceiling for Disaster Relief appropriations, as discussed in the Budget Process chapter of the *Analytical Perspectives* volume of the Budget. OMB currently estimates the 2019 ceiling to be $7.4 billion under current law. The Administration is requesting $6.7 billion for Disaster Relief in 2019.

[8] The 21st Century CURES Act permitted funds to be appropriated each year for certain activities and not counted toward the discretionary caps so long as the appropriations were specifically provided for the authorized purposes. These amounts are displayed outside of the discretionary caps totals for this reason.

[9] The 2019 Budget includes permanent cancellations of balances of emergency funding in the Departments of Energy and Housing and Urban Development that are not designated pursuant to BBEDCA. These cancellations are not being re-designated as emergency, therefore no savings are being achieved under the caps nor will the caps be adjusted for these cancellations.

## Table S-9. Economic Assumptions[1]

(Calendar years)

| | Actual | | | | | Projections | | | | | | | |
|---|---|---|---|---|---|---|---|---|---|---|---|---|---|
| | 2016 | 2017 | 2018 | 2019 | 2020 | 2021 | 2022 | 2023 | 2024 | 2025 | 2026 | 2027 | 2028 |
| **Gross Domestic Product (GDP):** | | | | | | | | | | | | | |
| Nominal level, billions of dollars | 18,624 | 19,372 | 20,262 | 21,263 | 22,345 | 23,482 | 24,672 | 25,923 | 27,235 | 28,598 | 30,001 | 31,461 | 32,991 |
| Percent change, nominal GDP, year/year | 2.8 | 4.0 | 4.6 | 4.9 | 5.1 | 5.1 | 5.1 | 5.1 | 5.1 | 5.0 | 4.9 | 4.9 | 4.9 |
| Real GDP, percent change, year/year | 1.5 | 2.2 | 3.0 | 3.2 | 3.1 | 3.0 | 3.0 | 3.0 | 3.0 | 2.9 | 2.8 | 2.8 | 2.8 |
| Real GDP, percent change, Q4/Q4 | 1.8 | 2.5 | 3.1 | 3.2 | 3.1 | 3.0 | 3.0 | 3.0 | 3.0 | 2.9 | 2.8 | 2.8 | 2.8 |
| GDP chained price index, percent change, year/year | 1.3 | 1.7 | 1.6 | 1.7 | 1.9 | 2.0 | 2.0 | 2.0 | 2.0 | 2.0 | 2.0 | 2.0 | 2.0 |
| **Consumer Price Index,[2] percent change, year/year** | 1.3 | 2.1 | 2.1 | 2.0 | 2.2 | 2.3 | 2.3 | 2.3 | 2.3 | 2.3 | 2.3 | 2.3 | 2.3 |
| **Interest rates, percent:[3]** | | | | | | | | | | | | | |
| 91-day Treasury bills[4] | 0.3 | 0.9 | 1.5 | 2.3 | 2.9 | 3.0 | 3.0 | 2.9 | 2.9 | 2.9 | 2.9 | 2.9 | 2.9 |
| 10-year Treasury notes | 1.8 | 2.3 | 2.6 | 3.1 | 3.4 | 3.6 | 3.7 | 3.7 | 3.6 | 3.6 | 3.6 | 3.6 | 3.6 |
| **Unemployment rate, civilian, percent[3]** | 4.9 | 4.4 | 3.9 | 3.7 | 3.8 | 3.9 | 4.0 | 4.2 | 4.3 | 4.5 | 4.7 | 4.8 | 4.8 |

Note: A more detailed table of economic assumptions appears in Chapter 2, "Economic Assumptions and Interactions with the Budget," in the *Analytical Perspectives* volume of the Budget.

[1] Based on information available as of mid-November 2017.
[2] Seasonally adjusted CPI for all urban consumers.
[3] Annual average.
[4] Average rate, secondary market (bank discount basis).

## Table S–10. Federal Government Financing and Debt

(Dollar amounts in billions)

| | Actual 2017 | Estimate 2018 | 2019 | 2020 | 2021 | 2022 | 2023 | 2024 | 2025 | 2026 | 2027 | 2028 |
|---|---|---|---|---|---|---|---|---|---|---|---|---|
| **Financing:** | | | | | | | | | | | | |
| *Unified budget deficit:* | | | | | | | | | | | | |
| Primary deficit/surplus (–) | 403 | 522 | 621 | 540 | 406 | 340 | 160 | –46 | –109 | –199 | –291 | –316 |
| Net interest | 263 | 310 | 363 | 447 | 510 | 568 | 619 | 658 | 688 | 717 | 740 | 761 |
| Unified budget deficit | 665 | 833 | 984 | 987 | 916 | 908 | 778 | 612 | 579 | 517 | 450 | 445 |
| As a percent of GDP | 3.5% | 4.2% | 4.7% | 4.5% | 3.9% | 3.7% | 3.0% | 2.3% | 2.1% | 1.7% | 1.4% | 1.4% |
| *Other transactions affecting borrowing from the public:* | | | | | | | | | | | | |
| *Changes in financial assets and liabilities:[1]* | | | | | | | | | | | | |
| Change in Treasury operating cash balance | –194 | 191 | ...... | ...... | ...... | ...... | ...... | ...... | ...... | ...... | ...... | ...... |
| *Net disbursements of credit financing accounts:* | | | | | | | | | | | | |
| Direct loan and Troubled Asset Relief Program (TARP) equity purchase accounts | 54 | 101 | 94 | 87 | 87 | 90 | 87 | 80 | 69 | 59 | 50 | 46 |
| Guaranteed loan accounts | –14 | 1 | 5 | 3 | 2 | –* | –2 | –4 | –5 | –9 | –8 | –1 |
| Net purchases of non-Federal securities by the National Railroad Retirement Investment Trust (NRRIT) | 1 | –1 | –1 | –1 | –1 | –1 | –1 | –1 | –1 | –1 | –* | –* |
| Net change in other financial assets and liabilities[2] | –15 | ...... | ...... | ...... | ...... | ...... | ...... | ...... | ...... | ...... | ...... | ...... |
| Subtotal, changes in financial assets and liabilities | –167 | 292 | 98 | 89 | 88 | 88 | 84 | 75 | 63 | 49 | 41 | 45 |
| Seigniorage on coins | –* | –* | –* | –* | –* | –* | –* | –* | –* | –* | –* | –* |
| Total, other transactions affecting borrowing from the public | –168 | 292 | 98 | 88 | 88 | 88 | 84 | 75 | 62 | 49 | 41 | 45 |
| Total, requirement to borrow from the public (equals change in debt held by the public) | 498 | 1,124 | 1,082 | 1,075 | 1,004 | 996 | 862 | 687 | 642 | 566 | 491 | 490 |
| **Changes in Debt Subject to Statutory Limitation:** | | | | | | | | | | | | |
| Change in debt held by the public | 498 | 1,124 | 1,082 | 1,075 | 1,004 | 996 | 862 | 687 | 642 | 566 | 491 | 490 |
| Change in debt held by Government accounts | 168 | 148 | 143 | 123 | 116 | 65 | 89 | 119 | 56 | 53 | –55 | –138 |
| Change in other factors | 4 | 1 | 2 | 3 | 2 | 2 | 2 | 2 | 1 | 1 | 2 | 2 |
| Total, change in debt subject to statutory limitation | 670 | 1,274 | 1,227 | 1,201 | 1,121 | 1,063 | 953 | 808 | 699 | 620 | 438 | 353 |
| **Debt Subject to Statutory Limitation, End of Year:** | | | | | | | | | | | | |
| Debt issued by Treasury | 20,180 | 21,452 | 22,678 | 23,877 | 24,997 | 26,059 | 27,011 | 27,818 | 28,517 | 29,137 | 29,574 | 29,926 |
| Adjustment for discount, premium, and coverage[3] | 29 | 30 | 32 | 33 | 35 | 36 | 37 | 38 | 38 | 38 | 39 | 40 |
| Total, debt subject to statutory limitation[4] | 20,209 | 21,483 | 22,709 | 23,910 | 25,032 | 26,094 | 27,048 | 27,856 | 28,555 | 29,175 | 29,613 | 29,966 |
| **Debt Outstanding, End of Year:** | | | | | | | | | | | | |
| *Gross Federal debt:[5]* | | | | | | | | | | | | |
| Debt issued by Treasury | 20,180 | 21,452 | 22,678 | 23,877 | 24,997 | 26,059 | 27,011 | 27,818 | 28,517 | 29,137 | 29,574 | 29,926 |
| Debt issued by other agencies | 26 | 26 | 25 | 24 | 23 | 22 | 21 | 20 | 19 | 18 | 17 | 16 |
| Total, gross Federal debt | 20,206 | 21,478 | 22,703 | 23,901 | 25,020 | 26,081 | 27,032 | 27,838 | 28,536 | 29,155 | 29,591 | 29,942 |
| As a percent of GDP | 105.4% | 107.2% | 108.1% | 108.3% | 107.9% | 107.0% | 105.6% | 103.5% | 101.0% | 98.3% | 95.2% | 91.8% |

## Table S–10. Federal Government Financing and Debt—Continued

(Dollar amounts in billions)

| | Actual 2017 | Estimate 2018 | 2019 | 2020 | 2021 | 2022 | 2023 | 2024 | 2025 | 2026 | 2027 | 2028 |
|---|---|---|---|---|---|---|---|---|---|---|---|---|
| **Held by:** | | | | | | | | | | | | |
| Debt held by Government accounts | 5,540 | 5,689 | 5,831 | 5,954 | 6,070 | 6,135 | 6,223 | 6,343 | 6,399 | 6,452 | 6,397 | 6,258 |
| Debt held by the public[6] | 14,665 | 15,790 | 16,872 | 17,947 | 18,950 | 19,946 | 20,809 | 21,495 | 22,137 | 22,703 | 23,194 | 23,684 |
| As a percent of GDP | 76.5% | 78.8% | 80.3% | 81.3% | 81.7% | 81.9% | 81.3% | 79.9% | 78.4% | 76.6% | 74.6% | 72.6% |
| **Debt Held by the Public Net of Financial Assets:** | | | | | | | | | | | | |
| Debt held by the public | 14,665 | 15,790 | 16,872 | 17,947 | 18,950 | 19,946 | 20,809 | 21,495 | 22,137 | 22,703 | 23,194 | 23,684 |
| Less financial assets net of liabilities: | | | | | | | | | | | | |
| Treasury operating cash balance | 159 | 350 | 350 | 350 | 350 | 350 | 350 | 350 | 350 | 350 | 350 | 350 |
| Credit financing account balances: | | | | | | | | | | | | |
| Direct loan and TARP equity purchase accounts | 1,281 | 1,382 | 1,476 | 1,563 | 1,650 | 1,740 | 1,827 | 1,906 | 1,975 | 2,034 | 2,084 | 2,130 |
| Guaranteed loan accounts | 14 | 15 | 20 | 23 | 25 | 25 | 23 | 19 | 14 | 4 | –4 | –4 |
| Government-sponsored enterprise preferred stock | 93 | 95 | 95 | 95 | 95 | 95 | 95 | 95 | 95 | 95 | 95 | 95 |
| Non-Federal securities held by NRRIT | 25 | 25 | 24 | 23 | 22 | 21 | 20 | 19 | 18 | 18 | 18 | 17 |
| Other assets net of liabilities | –58 | –58 | –58 | –58 | –58 | –58 | –58 | –58 | –58 | –58 | –58 | –58 |
| Total, financial assets net of liabilities | 1,515 | 1,809 | 1,906 | 1,995 | 2,083 | 2,172 | 2,256 | 2,331 | 2,394 | 2,443 | 2,485 | 2,530 |
| Debt held by the public net of financial assets | 13,151 | 13,981 | 14,965 | 15,952 | 16,867 | 17,775 | 18,553 | 19,164 | 19,743 | 20,260 | 20,709 | 21,154 |
| As a percent of GDP | 68.6% | 69.8% | 71.3% | 72.3% | 72.7% | 72.9% | 72.5% | 71.2% | 69.9% | 68.3% | 66.6% | 64.9% |

\* $500 million or less.

[1] A decrease in the Treasury operating cash balance (which is an asset) is a means of financing a deficit and therefore has a negative sign. An increase in checks outstanding (which is a liability) is also a means of financing a deficit and therefore also has a negative sign.

[2] Includes checks outstanding, accrued interest payable on Treasury debt, uninvested deposit fund balances, allocations of special drawing rights, and other liability accounts; and, as an offset, cash and monetary assets (other than the Treasury operating cash balance), other asset accounts, and profit on sale of gold.

[3] Consists mainly of debt issued by the Federal Financing Bank (which is not subject to limit), the unamortized discount (less premium) on public issues of Treasury notes and bonds (other than zero-coupon bonds), and the unrealized discount on Government account series securities.

[4] The statutory debt limit is approximately $20,456 billion, as increased after December 8, 2017.

[5] Treasury securities held by the public and zero-coupon bonds held by Government accounts are almost all measured at sales price plus amortized discount or less amortized premium. Agency debt securities are almost all measured at face value. Treasury securities in the Government account series are otherwise measured at face value less unrealized discount (if any).

[6] At the end of 2017, the Federal Reserve Banks held $2,465.4 billion of Federal securities and the rest of the public held $12,200.0 billion. Debt held by the Federal Reserve Banks is not estimated for future years.

# OMB CONTRIBUTORS TO THE 2019 BUDGET

The following personnel contributed to the preparation of this publication. Hundreds, perhaps thousands, of others throughout the Government also deserve credit for their valuable contributions.

## A

Andrew Abrams
Chandana L. Achanta
Brenda Aguilar
Natalie Ahinakwa
Shagufta Ahmed
Steve Aitken
Jason Alleman
Victoria Allred
Lois E. Altoft
Vishal Amin
Jessica C. Anderson
Jessica A. Andreasen
Analisa Archer
David Armitage
Benton Arnett
Anna R. Arroyo
Emily Schultz Askew
Lisa L. August
Renee Austin
Kristin B. Aveille

## B

Michelle B. Bacon
Jessie W. Bailey
Ally P. Bain
Coalter Baker
Paul W. Baker
Christian Bale
Carol A. Bales
Pratik S. Banjade
Avital Bar-Shalom
Amy C. Barker
Patti A. Barnett
John L. Barone
Jody M. Barringer
Jennifer Wagner Bell
Anna M. Bellantoni
Nathaniel Benjamin
Joseph J. Berger
Elizabeth A. Bernhard
Antonia K. Bernhardt

Emily R. Bilbao
Bradley Bishop
Samuel J. Black
Robert B. Blair
Mathew C. Blum
James Boden
Cassie L. Boles
Melissa B. Bomberger
William J. Boyd
Mollie Bradlee
Sean W. T. Branchaw
Michael Branson
Alex M. Brant
Joseph F. Breighner
Julie A. Brewer
Andrea M. Brian
Erik G. Brine
Candice M. Bronack
Dustin S. Brown
Sheila Bruce
Michael T. Brunetto
Pearl Buenvenida
Tom D. Bullers
Scott H. Burgess
Ben Burnett
John D. Burnim
Jordan C. Burris
Meghan K. Burris
John C. Burton
Nicholas S. Burton
Mark Bussow
Dylan W. Byrd

## C

Steve E. Cahill
Anthony Campau
Amy Canfield
Ryan N. Canfield
Eric Cardoza
Matthew B. Carney
Kerrie Carr
William S. S. Carroll

Scott D. Carson
Sean C. Casey
Mary I. Cassell
James Chase
Nida Chaudhary
Michael Chelen
Anita Chellaraj
Gezime Christian
Michael Clark
Jasmine A. Clemons
Sarah A. Cline
Angela Colamaria
William P. Cole
Victoria W. Collin
Debra M. Collins
Kelly T. Colyar
Jose A. Conde
Alyson M. Conley
David Connolly
Matthew Conway
Matthew T. Cornelius
Drew W. Cramer
Catherine E. Crato
Joseph A. Croce
Tyler Overstreet
   Cromer
Rose Crow
Juliana Crump
Craig Crutchfield
David M. Cruz-
   Glaudemans
Lily Cuk
Pennee Cumberlander
C. Tyler Curtis
William Curtis
Charles R. Cutshall
Ashley Czin
John (CZ) Czwartacki

## D

Nadir Dalal
D. Michael Daly

Rody Damis
Neil B. Danberg
Charlie Dankert
Kristy L. Daphnis
Alexander J. Daumit
Joanne Chow
   Davenport
Kenneth L. Davis
Margaret B. Davis-
   Christian
Chad J. Day
Brandon F. DeBruhl
Tasha M. Demps
Paul J. Denaro
Laura Dennehy
Catherine A. Derbes
John H. Dick
Amie Didlo
Julie Allen Dingley
Angela M. Donatelli
Paul S. Donohue
Vladik Dorjets
Tobias A. Dorsey
Anjelica B. Dortch
Emma Doyle
Lisa Cash Driskill
James R. Dubois Jr.
Carolyn R. Dula-
   Wilson

## E

Matthew C. Eanes
Jacqueline A. Easley
Jeanette Edwards
Anthony J. Eleftherion
Tonya L. Ellison-Mays
Michelle Enger
Diana F. Epstein
Neal R. Erickson
Edward V. Etzkorn
Patrick Evans

Lexi Marten
Brendán A. Martin
Rochelle Martinez
Nicholas T. Matich IV
Shelly McAllister
Alexander J.
  McClelland
Jeremy P. McCrary
Connor G. McCrone
Jennifer McDannell
Anthony W. McDonald
Cheryl McDonald
Christine A. McDonald
Katrina A. McDonald
Renford A. McDonald
Kevin E. McGinnis
Kevin J. McKernin
Charlie E. McKiver
Moutray McLaren
Mey McLean
Megan B. McPhaden
William J. Mea
Melissa R. Medeiros
Inna L. Melamed
Patrick J. Mellon
Barbara A. Menard
Flavio Menasce
Jose A. Mendez
P. Thaddeus
  Messenger
Todd Messer
William L. Metzger
Daniel J. Michelson-
  Horowitz
Julie L. Miller
Kimberly Miller
Susan M. Minson
Mia Mitchell
Rehana I. Mohammed
Emily A. Mok
Kirsten J. Moncada
Claire Monteiro
Joseph Montoni
Caroline Moore
Zachary Morgan
Kelly Morrison
William Morrison
Joshua A. Moses
Robin McLaughry
  Mullins
Mick Mulvaney
Christian G. Music
Hayley W. Myers
Kimberley L Myers

**N**

Jennifer M. Nading
Jeptha E. Nafziger
Larry J. Nagl
Anna M. Naimark
Barry Napear
Robert Nassif
Kimberly P. Nelson
Melissa K. Neuman
Joanie F. Newhart
Kimberly Armstrong
  Newman
Anthony (Tony)
  Nguyen
Teresa O. Nguyen
Brian A. Nichols
Tim H. Nusraty
Frederick Nutt
Joseph B. Nye

**O**

Erin O'Brien
Matthew J. O'Kane
Brendan J. O'Meara
Jared Ostermiller

**P**

Benjamin J. Page
Heather C. Pajak
Rosario Palmieri
Mark R. Paoletta
John C. Pasquantino
Jagir Patel
Neal A. Patel
Brian Paxton
Terri B. Payne
Liuyi Pei
Falisa L. Peoples-Tittle
Michael A. Perz
David B. Peterson
Andrea M. Petro
Alexandra Petrucci
Stacey Que-Chi Pham
Carolyn R. Phelps
Karen A. Pica
Kailey Pickitt
Barbara Pike
Brian K. Pipa
Joseph Pipan
Adrian L. Plater
Mark J. Pomponio

Ruxandra Pond
Julianne Poston
Nancy Potok
Victoria Premaza
Celestine Pressley
Larrimer S. Prestosa
Jamie M. Price
Daniel Proctor
Rob Purdy
Joye E. Purser
Rob Pyron

**R**

Lucas R. Radzinschi
Latonda Glass Raft
Moshiur Rahman
Neomi Rao
Maria S. Raphael
Aaron D. Ray
Alex Reed
Meagan E. Reed
Mark A. Reger
Rudolph G. Regner
Paul B. Rehmus
Thomas M. Reilly
Bryant D. Renaud
Keri A. Rice
Shannon A. Richter
Kyle S. Riggs
Emma K. Roach
Amanda Robbins
Beth Higa Roberts
Kelly M. Roberts
Taylor C. Roberts
Donovan Robinson
Marshall J. Rodgers
Meredith B. Romley
Eric Rosenfield
Jefferson Rosman
David J. Rowe
Mario D. Roy
Jacqueline Rudas
Erika H. Ryan

**S**

Fouad P. Saad
Andrea Sabaliauskas
John Asa Saldivar
Alvand A. Salehi
Cesar Xicotencatl
  Sanchez
Mark S. Sandy

Joel J. Savary
Jeff Schlagenhauf
Daniel K. Schory
Nancy E. Schwartz
Mariarosaria
  Sciannameo
Jasmeet K. Seehra
Kimberly Segura
Robert B. Seidner
Catherine L. Seif
Andrew Self
Megan Shade
Shahid N. Shah
Shabnam
  Sharbatoghlie
Amy K. Sharp
Dianne Shaughnessy
Paul Shawcross
David Shorkrai
Gary F. Shortencarrier
Letticia Sierra
Sara R. Sills
Daniel Liam Singer
Robert Sivinski
Benjamin J. Skidmore
Jonathan Slemrod
Jack Smalligan
Curtina O. Smith
Somer Smith
Stannis M. Smith
Rachel B. Snyderman
Erica Socker
Silvana Solano
Roderic A. Solomon
Jenina Soto
Amanda R.K. Sousane
Rebecca L. Spavins
Raquel A. Spencer
Valeria Spinner
Sarah Whittle Spooner
Travis C. Stalcup
Scott R. Stambaugh
Nora Stein
Beth A. Stephenson
Lamar R. Stewart
Ryan E. Stoffers
Gary R. Stofko
Terry W. Stratton
Thomas J. Suarez
Kathy L. Suber
Iven T. Sugai
Alec J. Sugarman
Joseph Lee Suh
Kevin J. Sullivan

Jessica L. Sun
Yasaman S. Sutton
Christina Swoope
Katherine M. Sydor

**T**

Jamie R. Taber
John Tambornino
Naomi S. Taransky
Max Tassano
Joseph Tawney
Myra L. Taylor
Thierry-Martino M.
   Tchenko
Jay Teitelbaum
Emma K. Tessier
Rich Theroux
Amanda L. Thomas
Payton A. Thomas
Will Thomas
Philip Tizzani
Thomas Tobasko
Gia Tonic
Gil M. Tran
Donald L. Tuck
Austin Turner

**U**

Nicholas J. Ufier
Shraddha A.
   Upadhyaya
Darrell J. Upshaw
Taylor J. Urbanski
Euler V. Uy

**V**

Matthew J. Vaeth
Cynthia Vallina
Sarita Vanka
Areletha L. Venson
Alexandra Ventura
Russ Vought

**W**

James A. Wade
Brett Waite
Christopher Walsh
Heather V. Walsh
Kan Wang
Tim Wang
Peter Warren

Gary Waxman
Bess M. Weaver
Margaret Weichert
Jeffrey A. Weinberg
David Weisshaar
Nathan C. Wells
Philip R. Wenger
Max W. West
Steve Wetzel
Arnette C. White
Ashley M. White
Catherine E. White
Kim S. White
RaeShawn White
Sherron R. White
Chad S. Whiteman
Katie Whitman
Brian Widuch
Debra (Debbie) L.
   Williams
Michael B. Williams
Rebecca A. Williams
Jamie S. Wilson
Paul A. Winters
Julia B. Wise
Julie Wise
Minzy Won

Raymond J.M. Wong
Jacob Wood
Charles E.
   Worthington
Sophia M. Wright
William Wu
Bert Wyman

**X**

Mohao Xi

**Y**

Melany N. Yeung
David Y. Yi
Elliot Y. Yoon

**Z**

Eliana M. Zavala
Jen Q. Zhu
Erica H. Zielewski
Kathryn Zook